D1321267

Heraldry

IN NATIONAL TRUST HOUSES

Heraldry IN NATIONAL TRUST HOUSES

Thomas Woodcock
John Martin Robinson

THE NATIONAL TRUST

First published in Great Britain in 2000 by
National Trust Enterprises Ltd
36 Queen Anne's Gate, London SW1H 9AS

http://bookshelf.nationaltrust.org.uk

Cataloguing in Publication Data is available from the British Library

ISBN 0 7078 0277 6

Line drawings by Robert Parsons

Picture research by the National Trust Photographic Library, Helen George and Helen Fewster

Designed by the Newton Engert Partnership

Production by Bob Towell

Phototypset in Sabon by SPAN Graphics Limited, Crawley, West Sussex

Printed and bound in China
Phoenix Offset

HALF TITLE: *A marquetry panel at Beningbrough Hall in Yorkshire inlaid with the impaled arms of John Bourchier and his wife, Mary Bellwood, within a circlet on which are their initials, the date 1716 and two renderings of the Bourchier knot badge.*

FRONTISPIECE: *The Library fireplace at Oxburgh Hall, Norfolk, with, from left to right, the arms of Boyle, Jerningham quartering Stafford, Bedingfeld, Paston and Howard with the Yorkist falcon and fetterlock badge on the tiles and firedogs referring to the family's allegiance.*

ACKNOWLEDGEMENTS

The authors would like to thank the following:
The Chapter of the College of Arms for permission to reproduce illustrations from the College Library; Miss Emma Bayntun-Coward; Mrs Elizabeth Cail; Mr C. E. A. Cheesman, Rouge Dragon Pursuivant; Mr D. H. B. Chesshyre LVO, Clarenceux King of Arms; Mr Oliver Garnett; Mr Jeffrey Haworth; Mr Simon Jervis; Mr Robert Parsons for the line drawings of the arms; Mr Henry Paston-Bedingfeld, York Herald; Mr Simon and the Hon. Mrs Rendall; Mrs C. G. W. Roads MVO, Lyon Clerk; Mr Ian Scott; Mrs Clare Throckmorton-MacLaren; Mr Philip Way for photography; Mr David White, Rouge Croix Pursuivant; Mr Robert Yorke, Archivist, College of Arms, and Miss Samantha Wyndham. Finally they would like to thank the Hon. Janet Grant for her outstanding contribution, and also the Publishers.

Contents

Whalley
Garstange
Hoore

Origins and Uses of Heraldry

Heraldry is the systematic hereditary use of an arrangement of charges or devices on a shield, which is the essential part of a coat of arms, though other forms of display have always played their part. It is probable that devices originally appeared on lance flags, pennants and seals before being transferred to the shield in the twelfth century. The additional elements of the full heraldic achievement – supporters on either side of the shield, the crest on the helmet above it and the mottoes, badges and coronets of rank – were developed later. The purpose of heraldry has always been, at least in part, show and pageantry, and it has long had the practical function of distinguishing, differencing and illustrating persons, families and communities.

This is particularly obvious in National Trust houses where the arms of the different families who owned and built them illustrate their rise in the world through marriage, warfare or the law – the principal avenues to noble status in medieval England – or service to the Crown, especially under the Tudors and Stuarts. With the growth of a more sophisticated economy, rich merchants, bankers and industrialists were, as in Venice or Florence, able to nourish the pool of nobility. The development of Parliament, a permanent civil service, standing army and navy and a far-flung colonial administration in the eighteenth and nineteenth centuries provided an official class, of which the most successful members also established landed dynasties.

There has been much debate about the origins and basic uses of heraldry, but the subject remains obscure. The old theory is that there were strong military associations and its purpose was to identify knights in battle by their distinctive arms on their shields. This would not, however, have been the most practical means of identification on the battlefield, as the shield would have been easily obscured and difficult to read in the chaos. In addition, many of the charges in early heraldry are very similar – for instance, a fifth of all thirteenth-century English arms contain the lion, which would not have made them very recognisable in the mêlée of hand-to-hand combat.

Knights jousting wearing coats and with horse trappings of their arms from the Military Roll of c.1446 [B.L. Add.Ms. 45133 folio 22v]. In the top row a knight named Dallingridge fights one named Whalley. In 1405 Sir John Dallingridge of Bodiam Castle challenged Ralph Green to single combat to decide which of them was entitled to the arms Argent a Cross engrailed Gules. *In the second row a knight named Hoore wears a coat of arms on which the arms of Hoare of Stourhead are based.*

Heraldry was certainly connected with medieval warfare, and the rapid adoption of arms throughout Europe in the twelfth century was partly a product of the Crusades in which knights from different countries fought together against the Infidel in the Holy Land. But it seems likely that it was more a matter of individual vanity and display by the knightly class than a practical necessity, and was popularised by the tournament – a stylised form of mock combat – rather than by real warfare.

The tournament is believed to have originated in France in the mid-eleventh century and rapidly developed as a form of regular training in the handling of weapons on horseback, and as a spectator sport. It was highly organised and hedged around with its own rules and pageantry, the participants being identified by the colours and symbols of their arms, just like the scarves and colours of a modern football team. Young knights travelled around Europe fighting in tournaments for money prizes, and this helped to spread and unify the conventions of heraldry. The heralds themselves probably originated as the umpires at tournaments and came to be the experts on coats of arms.They were permanent members of the Royal Household, as well as some noble households, from the thirteenth century onwards. Later in the Middle Ages the bearing of arms was an essential qualification for taking part in a tournament, and heraldry therefore became a distinctive badge of the knightly class. Arms were a mark of noble status and were granted by the Holy Roman Emperor and European kings as a corollary to ennoblement.

From the twelfth century there was some equation between nobility and armorial bearings which has suggested an alternative, if tentative, theory for the origins of heraldry. In its earliest stages, heraldry was largely confined to the Frankish families of north-western Europe – French, Flemings and Normans. Several of the ruling families of this area were descended in the female line from Charlemagne and perpetuated some of the administrative organisation, ceremonial and – possibly – some of the symbolic devices of his court which included badges of identification displayed on seals and banners. The Normans, who were Viking in origin, had a remarkable ability to adopt the existing culture wherever they settled and they took on many of the trappings of their Frankish neighbours, such as the use of symbolic banners. The lance flags shown in the Bayeux tapestry carry various devices including crosses and red balls (torteaux). It is not known if these were hereditary, but one of them seems to carry three buckles, and three buckles (or formalets) were the arms later used by the Malet family, one of whom, William Malet, seigneur of Graville, is in the accepted list of those who are known to have been present at Hastings with William the Conqueror.

There is evidence of charges which became hereditary being used on both sides of the Channel, by different members of a family whose common ancestor lived in the eleventh century, before the general adoption of heraldry. For example, a group of families related to Geoffrey de Mandeville, Earl of Essex (d.1144), including the Sackvilles of Knole in Kent, all bore a quarterly coat. The origins of such families are so close to the Norman Conquest that it would seem likely that the use of heraldic devices began with the Frankish custom of lance flags before being transferred to shields to become true heraldry. Whatever the origins, it is clear that what in the late eleventh century had been the inheritance of a small group of interrelated families in north-west Europe, spread rapidly through the upper ranks of society in the twelfth century. The widespread adoption of colourful devices and symbols in this period was an aspect of the twelfth-century renaissance, alongside the development of Gothic architecture, the growth of learning and the establishment of universities.

Initially most arms were self-assumed but the proliferation of armorial devices led to a growing measure of royal control as formal grants recorded from the Middle Ages show. A celebrated early example of a formal grant is that to Geoffrey Plantagenet in

1127 when Henry I hung a shield painted with gold lions around Geoffrey's neck as part of the ceremony of knighting. This is also the earliest documented example of heraldry on a shield. In England the High Court of Chivalry came to be the ultimate heraldic authority, deciding disputes over arms such as the famous Scrope *v* Grosvenor case in 1385–90 over which family had the right to bear the arms *Azure a Bend Or*.

In the fifteenth century the Crown moved against self-assumed arms that did not date from 'time immemorial' – 1189 in English Common Law but 1066 in the High Court of Chivalry. Henry V instituted the office of Garter King of Arms in 1415 declaring him, *ex officio*, the principal Officer of Arms. In 1484 Richard III constituted the heralds into a corporation, the College of Arms – an official registry for English and Welsh arms. The authority to grant new arms to eminent men and to police the bearing of arms was delegated to the Kings of Arms in their Letters Patent of appointment from the Crown. This was further developed under the Tudors who devised the system of heraldic Visitations in 1530, whereby heralds, deputising for the provincial Kings of Arms, toured different counties at regular intervals checking that all those who displayed arms could prove their right to bear them. The records of these Visitations, which continued until 1689, are kept at the College of Arms in London. The arms of medieval knightly families figure prominently, and displays in stained glass and on tombs are meticulously recorded. As the later Plantagenet Kings recognised social change and authorised the Kings of Arms to make new grants to eminent men, the system that originally related to medieval knights prospered and developed from the Middle Ages onwards.

Henry VIII further adapted heraldry both to mark social status and to recognise social mobility. The system developed then has continued to the present day: those who have had a significant public career or made a fortune through commerce have acquired a grant of arms and invested in landed property, creating a dynasty. National Trust houses provide many excellent examples of successful social mobility in England over five centuries. While some families were descended from medieval knights, and many from prosperous lawyers, others rose from humbler beginnings: the Cravens of Ashdown came of yeoman stock, the Drydens of Canons Ashby are descended from a school master, the Eltons of Clevedon from a market gardener, the Watts of Speke from a coach driver and the Winns of Nostell from Elizabeth I's draper.

Over the centuries, heraldry has tended to become more elaborate, partly the result of a need to 'difference' or personalise arms, so that no two shields are the same. The earliest shields of arms were essentially simple. Many knights adopted unadorned stripes or crosses which may have had their origins in the bands of leather or metal used to strengthen wooden shields, and offered an obvious surface for painting a basic pattern. For instance, chevrons may have originated in battens on the shield which evolved into a V-shape due to the shield's pointed convex surface. Some knights adopted specific objects such as crescents, suns, wheatsheafs, lions and eagles which may have been influenced by the Carolingian symbols of Flemish counts. Others chose punning or 'canting' arms. An important factor is the use of common charges by groups of families linked by blood or feudal tenure. There is evidence that the second tier of the feudal structure in Westmorland, for example, took arms which were variations on those of their overlord, the Vipont family of Appleby Castle, whose arms comprised black annulets (or rings) on a gold ground, and variants were borne by local families. A Vipont heiress married a Cromwell in *c.*1300, and their arms can be seen at Tattershall Castle.

As time passed, designs became increasingly complex – because of the need to difference individual coats of arms – with the introduction of fabulous and chimerical creatures, and patterns which moved far away from the simple vigorous geometry of the early days. A development originating in Spain in the late thirteenth century was the incorporation of quarterings of arms inherited via heraldic heiresses, creating ever more complex patterns. Many shields of early sixteenth-century origin were very complicated, with chevrons and chiefs covered with different charges. Eventually, arms came to include pictorial scenes, sometimes referred to as 'landscape heraldry'. This was particularly the case in the arms of the generals, admirals and governors who built up the British Empire in the eighteenth century. This sort of pictorial elaboration in heraldry, however, came to be seen as degenerate, and in the nineteenth century, as an aspect of the general Gothic Revival, there was a reaction against such 'bad' heraldry and a move towards the reinstatement of simple charges. This taste for 'real' heraldry has continued to govern most of the design of arms in the twentieth century.

The acquisition of a coat of arms was one of the signs that a family had 'arrived'. It was obvious, therefore, that heraldry would be used to decorate the country seat of such a family. From early times heraldry came to be associated with architecture, both churches and secular buildings, as an attractive form of permanent decoration. Different conventions developed at different times, and National Trust houses provide a comprehensive cross-section of heraldic display: from the spectacular fifteenth-century Gothic fireplaces with Lord Cromwell's arms at Tattershall Castle, or that with the Fastolfe arms now at Blickling, through the schemes of Tudor stained glass at Ightham Mote, Montacute, Coughton Court and Baddesley Clinton. The more restrained forms of display associated with classical architecture can be seen in the pediments at Wimpole Hall; antiquarian revival schemes at Charlecote and Oxburgh; Victorian heraldry at Knightshayes and Gawthorpe; and even grand twentieth-century displays exist at Anglesey Abbey and Castle Drogo.

The purely decorative use of heraldry can be traced back to the thirteenth century to the time of Henry III. He had a passion for heraldry and was greatly impressed by the decoration at a banquet given for him in Paris by Louis IX of France in 1254 when the walls of the Great Hall had been hung with painted wooden shields bearing the arms of the great noble families of France, as though for a tournament. On his return to London, Henry developed this idea, placing permanent carved stone shields of his own arms and those of his royal connections and those of the great English barons in the spandrels of the aisle arcades at Westminster Abbey. When coloured, these shields must have made a grand display, and it was soon widely copied. At Worcester Cathedral, an even earlier example of decorative heraldry can be seen in the Lady Chapel, where the walls were painted with shields in 1230, and even before his visit to France, Henry had used coats of arms to adorn metalwork and tiles. As early as 1237, for

Sixteenth-century heraldic glass in the window of the Great Hall at Baddesley Clinton showing, from left to right: Ferrers impaling Poynings, Clifford, Verdon, Ufford, Lovaine and Segrave.

instance, he commissioned a silver platter ornamented with the royal arms as a present for the Queen. In 1240 he ordered his arms to be painted on the window shutters of his Great Chamber at the Tower of London, and in 1266 extended the practice to all the doors and shutters of the New Hall and Chamber at Winchester Castle. The Great Hall at Rochester Castle and the Chapel at Havering in Essex were embellished with heraldic glass at about the same time and in 1268 Henry instructed the Keeper of the Works at Westminster to send to the Palace of Havering twenty glass windows decorated with forty shields of arms for the Queen's Chamber. At Westminster Abbey, the floor tiles of the Chapter House had been decorated with heraldry in *c.*1253.

The Sovereign's example was soon widely emulated by the barons and great ecclesiastics, which accounts for the rapid spread of heraldic decoration in the thirteenth century. It was also an aspect of the growth of courtly romanticism at that time, and a manifestation of the more secular trends of the age – heraldry taking some of the place hitherto occupied by religious symbolism. Within a short time coats of arms became the standard form of embellishment on the tombs of both the laity and the clergy, at first modestly and then with increasing elaboration and decorative fancy. For instance, in Gloucester Cathedral the early thirteenth-century figure of the Crusader Robert Curthose, Duke of Normandy (d.1134) shows him wearing a coat of arms on a tomb decorated with ten shields.

Heraldry not only decorated tombs, but it also became a feature at funerals. From the thirteenth century, the burials of the great were grandiose heraldic spectacles, with the lying-in-state, the funeral procession and not least the catafalque itself all used to display the crests, coronets, arms, supporters, badges and motto of the deceased. The heralds usually attended and recorded the funerals of the nobility, but this practice gradually fell into desuetude in the course of the eighteenth century and today the heralds only take part in the Sovereign's funeral, that of the Earl Marshal, or state funerals like Sir Winston Churchill's, when they carried shields of the deceased's arms and his banner in the procession in St Paul's Cathedral. Late but well-recorded examples of heraldic funerals are those of Sir Robert Dryden at Canons Ashby in 1708, where the funeral accoutrements still hang in the church which is now the property of the National Trust, or Viscount Tyrconnel's funeral at Belton in 1754. The custom of displaying a hatchment with the arms of the deceased over the front door of his house continued well into the nineteenth century, and many hatchments survive in National Trust houses and in the adjoining parish churches, as at Dyrham or Coughton, where they were usually deposited after a year.

The word hatchment is a corruption of achievement (achievement of arms), and

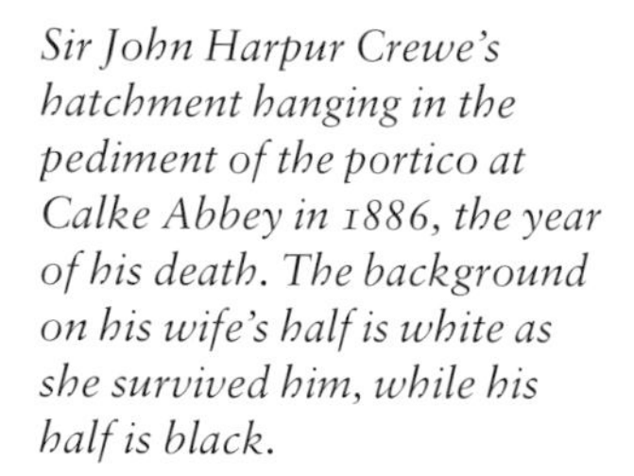

Sir John Harpur Crewe's hatchment hanging in the pediment of the portico at Calke Abbey in 1886, the year of his death. The background on his wife's half is white as she survived him, while his half is black.

Needlework at Hardwick showing Cavendish with a cadency mark of a crescent impaling an occasionally used variation of Talbot Azure a Lion rampant in a plain bordure Or *for Henry Cavendish, who married Grace Talbot in 1567. His father was a younger son, hence the crescent.*

dates back to the sixteenth century, being used, for instance, by Shakespeare. The depiction of arms on a hatchment follows a particular format. They are painted on square wooden boards or canvas, and hung diamond-wise with black frames. Where the deceased was married, his arms are shown impaled with those of his wife. If she outlived him, only the half behind the deceased's arms is painted black, and the background of his widow painted white. If the wife is divorced, her arms no longer appear.

Heraldic decoration was not confined to the architecture of churches, palaces, houses and tombs. Heraldry soon found its way into illuminated manuscripts, where medallions of arms took their place alongside religious, naturalistic and grotesque decorations in the coloured borders and initial letters. Manuscripts with heraldic illumination are preserved in several National Trust libraries, notably at Blickling.

Heraldry made its mark on needlework too. Much has disappeared, but it is likely that secular decorative hangings and tapestries were often enlivened with coats of arms, and church vestments certainly were: bishops and abbots, for instance, enjoyed the right to display their own arms on the orphreys of their copes or at the bottom of the cross on the back of their chasubles. The Syon Cope in the Victoria and Albert Museum in London is a fine example of a late thirteenth-century vestment with heraldic needlework. While secular medieval heraldic hangings and textiles have largely disappeared, the tradition continued into the sixteenth and seventeenth centuries. The remarkable collection of Elizabethan furnishing textiles at Hardwick Hall in Derbyshire has many pieces depicting the arms of Bess of Hardwick. The medieval idea of the 'cloth of state', embellished with arms, continued into the reign of

George III in the canopies with the royal arms and cyphers given to ambassadors as part of their accoutrements of office. An example from the Earl of Buckinghamshire's embassy to Russia survives re-used as the state bed at Blickling.

Heraldry provided the artist with an easy repertory of ready-made motifs and full advantage was taken of this, notably by painters and stained-glass makers, the patterns and colours of coats of arms lending themselves to glazing. Surviving medieval stained glass contains much elaborate heraldic decoration – the windows in the chapel at Petworth, for instance, had glass with the arms of the Percys. Stained glass in both secular and religious buildings has continued to be one of the most popular decorative uses of heraldry down to the present day, perhaps reaching its most extensive manifestation in the pedigrees in windows of Elizabethan houses like Montacute, Charlecote, Coughton Court and Baddesley Clinton where chronological arrangements of impaled arms recording successive marriages create a colourful family tree.

In the later Middle Ages and Tudor period the architectural manifestation of heraldry became increasingly uniform. In churches, coats of arms and crests embellished the bosses of the vault, the stained glass in the windows, the spandrels of the arches, the panels of screens, and tomb chests. In houses, colleges and secular buildings it also became the norm to have a grand heraldic display over the gatehouse, on fireplaces and on the metal vanes on the roof, as can be seen at Tattershall and Bodiam or Tudor and Elizabethan houses like Coughton Court and Charlecote. The architectural use of heraldry in Gothic architecture reached its ultimate prominence in the decoration of King's College Chapel at Cambridge. There, all the stone carving is devoted to dynastic display and there is no religious imagery in the stonework at all; everywhere six-foot-high rampant greyhounds and dragons support the royal arms. Immense and deeply undercut roses and portcullises are set off against the bare Perpendicular stone panelling. This triumphant heraldic expression on the part of the new Tudor monarchy was part of an international architectural development in the later Middle Ages.

It was echoed on a smaller scale in their country houses by supporters of the Tudors; for instance, at Cotehele and Ightham Mote where the Tudor livery colours of green and white were used and where the Tudor rose or Beaufort portcullis and the pomegranate or castle of Catherine of Aragon are incorporated in the stained glass and carved and painted ornamentations. The best example is the panelling in the Oak Gallery at The Vyne, installed by William Sandys, Lord Chamberlain of Henry VIII. It includes the royal arms and much other heraldry including the Spanish pomegranate.

There also developed a vogue for elaborately carved wooden or moulded plaster overmantels with royal or family heraldry as at Hardwick, Sizergh, Lyme or Montacute. Usually the royal arms of Elizabeth I or James I were depicted over the fireplace of the principal room, the High Great Chamber at Hardwick, for instance, expressing the formal, state character of those apartments; whereas the family arms could be found over the fireplaces of the everyday living rooms or bedchambers or sometimes in the Great Hall as at Hardwick. Something of the medieval quality of heraldry lingered on in the fantastic decorations and use of sejant beasts as finials at Knole, Blickling, Felbrigg and other Jacobean mansions.

The quartered and impaled arms of Lucy and Spencer over the Gatehouse arch at Charlecote for Sir Thomas Lucy III and his wife, Alice Spencer, who married in 1610.

The arms and crest of Sandys on roundels supported by angels who hold between them the Tudor royal arms, carved c.1527, in the Oak Gallery at The Vyne.

Heraldry was also much used in temporary decorations for royal and other pageantry, as well as being permanently executed in stone: for the marriage of Prince Arthur to Catherine of Aragon in 1501, elaborate wooden canvas arches were erected, embellished with paintings of royal arms, badges, devices and supporters. These forms of 'stage scenery' became a standard item of royal ceremonial at coronations, marriages and receptions for foreign dignitaries, and are recalled in the design of structures like the Hall screen at Knole. The apotheosis of this type of sixteenth-century temporary decoration was Henry VIII's Field of the Cloth of Gold between Guines and Ardres in northern France in 1520 where the King and Cardinal Wolsey met François I of France for a diplomatic celebration, and a whole temporary camp or village of fantastic structures, and fountains flowing with wine, was created for the reception of the two monarchs and their entourages. It is possible that the painted wooden Chapel ceiling at Ightham Mote with its Tudor heraldic decorations may have been reused from one of the pavilions at the Field of the Cloth of Gold; it is known to have come from the Royal Wardrobe.

A detail of the wooden Chapel ceiling at Ightham Mote, possibly from part of a pavilion at the Field of the Cloth of Gold (1520), showing the Tudor livery colours of green and white and English and Spanish royal badges, the castle of Castile, Tudor rose, Beaufort portcullis and quiver full of arrows of Aragon for Henry VIII and his first wife, Catherine of Aragon.

In the course of the seventeenth and eighteenth centuries the use of heraldry in architecture became more restrained and disciplined, and was curtailed to fit the proportions and forms of classicism. Certain standard conventions emerged – the carving of the family arms on the pediments of houses or in a cartouche over the front door; the embossing of the arms, crest or coronet on lead rainwater heads and downpipes, or worked in iron in the overthrow of gates. At Petworth the family arms of the Duke of Somerset with the phoenix crest and the Seymour wings form a major role in the carved stone decoration of the great baroque façade. Inside, the brass locks are all engraved with heraldry, a fashion also seen at Belton. Heraldry was much used on cast iron firebacks where, as well as the family arms, the royal arms can also frequently be found. The triumph of Palladian architecture over the native baroque saw the gradual disappearance of large-scale heraldry from external architecture, especially in the later eighteenth century. Some National Trust-owned Georgian houses such as Basildon Park in Berkshire, for instance, have no heraldry at all.

Inside late Georgian houses the convention was to confine the display of heraldry to the Entrance Hall, where the family crest was sometimes used as a decorative emblem in the plaster frieze. At Kedleston, the seat of the Curzon family since Norman times but rebuilt in the mid-eighteenth century, there is much heraldry but it is restricted to minuscule decorations, such as marble tablets in the chimneypieces of Adam's Entrance Hall. There are exceptions to this Georgian heraldic minimalism. For instance, there is a charming eighteenth-century painted secondary staircase at Knole, almost entirely decorated with the Sackville arms and the Order of the Garter, while the painted ceiling of the Gothic Temple at Stowe makes that structure into an heraldic Valhalla of the Temple family. Horace Walpole and his friends were keen revivers of heraldic architectural decoration. Their strong, if irreverent, heraldic interests can be savoured at The Vyne in Hampshire where John Chute, one of Walpole's closest cronies and a member of the Strawberry Hill Committee of Taste, executed various works in and around the late Gothic Chapel, including the erection of a fascinating antiquarian 'tomb' to his ancestor Chaloner Chute, complete with large heraldic cartouches on the sides of the tomb chest.

Although heraldry was generally used in a restrained manner in Georgian classical architecture, it continued to play its part in the embellishment of the furnishings of country houses. The family crest, or supporters, full arms or coronet can frequently be found carved on mirror and picture frames, side tables and pedestals, or embroidered on bed hangings, chair covers, screens or cushions, or painted on hall chairs.

The principal vehicle for heraldic display in the Georgian interior was, however, the family silver. Heraldry has been used to decorate gold and silver plate as far back as the thirteenth century, but in the seventeenth and eighteenth centuries its use became conventionalised, with the engraving or embossing of the full arms on larger display pieces of plate, or just the crest or cypher and coronet on flatware. Heraldic devices were also used, fully modelled, to decorate silver, the crest sometimes being employed as a finial on top, as in the instance of the Kandler soup tureens at Ickworth; or heraldic supporters doing duty as side handles, as on the wine cisterns at Belton and Dunham Massey. The collections of plate at Belton, Dunham Massey and Ickworth are extensive and allow the visitor to see the whole gamut of heraldic decoration, but heraldic silver can be found in nearly all National Trust houses. Pewter was often also engraved in the same way, as can be seen at Cotehele and Sizergh Castle.

A particular sub-theme in English ancestral plate of the late seventeenth, eighteenth and early nineteenth centuries is the ambassadorial plate, given from the Jewel House to Ministers on diplomatic missions beyond the seas, and retained by them afterwards as a perk of office. This is engraved and embellished with the royal arms as well as the family arms as can be seen at Ickworth. A good example is Lord Berwick's Regency plate at Attingham in Shropshire.

Heraldry was not confined to silver tableware. The convention passed easily to ceramics, as china came increasingly to be used for dining in the course of the eighteenth century. The use of heraldry to decorate ceramic tableware perhaps had its most attractive expression in the large services of armorial porcelain that were ordered from China in the eighteenth century by English clients. Whole dinner services were painted with coats of arms, depicted with greater or lesser accuracy. The stories of written instructions on the original sketch being painstakingly reproduced on dozens of plates are not apocryphal. The attempts of oriental painters to capture a likeness of heraldic lions, griffins, unicorns or dragons also led to some amusing hybrids – more like Pekinese than the majestic beasts of medieval heraldry. It is no exaggeration to say that nearly every National Trust house can produce examples of this type of china. Belton, for instance, has three Chinese armorial dinner services, and there are other fine examples at Osterley and Shugborough.

The arms on Chinese export porcelain were usually copied from heraldic bookplates which the client sent with his order. Bookplates themselves are an attractive heraldic form invented in Germany in the fifteenth century. The earliest English bookplate is that of Sir Nicholas Bacon of 1574, and they became increasingly popular in the seventeenth and eighteenth centuries. The National Trust has good examples of different periods in different houses, including Lady Mary Booth's early Georgian bookplate in her books at Dunham Massey, or Benjamin Disraeli's Victorian examples at Hughenden in Buckinghamshire.

Heraldry has been used to embellish book bindings since the Middle Ages. Charles I's Bible, used by his chaplain on the scaffold in 1649 and now preserved at Chastleton, still has its original binding with the royal arms. There are fine eighteenth-century armorial bindings from the famous Harleian Library on the prayer books still in the family pew in the Chapel at Wimpole in Cambridgeshire, and Waddesdon in Buckinghamshire has a particularly fine assemblage of French examples; all of the most illustrious provenance, as is only to be expected in a Rothschild house. Many country house libraries contain magnificent illuminated family trees on vellum, often prepared by the heralds; these range from a Jacobean example at Lanhydrock, through an eighteenth-century one at Coughton to a Regency example at Tatton.

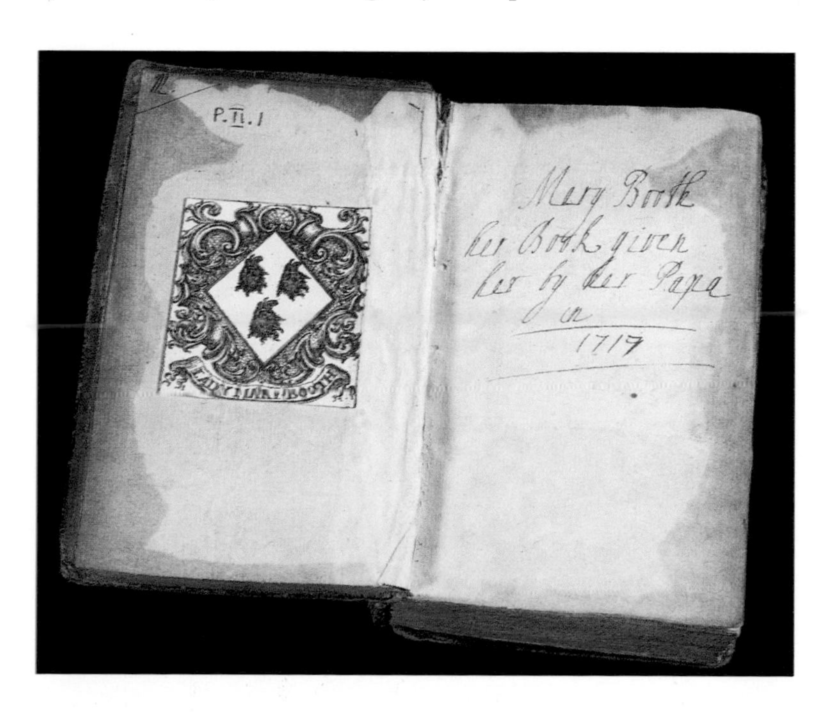

The bookplate of Lady Mary Booth (d.1772), subsequently Countess of Stamford, as a spinster, showing her arms on a lozenge.

The heraldic revival was part of the Gothic Revival from the late eighteenth century onwards. As already pointed out, Horace Walpole's circle at Strawberry Hill had a precocious interest in the subject, and from then on, the two things – Gothic and coats of arms – went hand in hand throughout the late Georgian and Victorian ages. John Ivory Talbot's Gothick Hall at Lacock has its ceiling covered with coats of arms of his friends.

Wherever mock battlements or traceried windows or pinnacled skylines raised themselves, so also could be expected a proud display of, occasionally bogus, heraldry. William Beckford's Fonthill Abbey, for instance, was bedecked with all the heraldry he could command in plaster, stone and stained glass. A table from Fonthill carved with crosses patonce from Beckford's second crest granted in 1794 can be seen in the Hall at Charlecote. The early nineteenth century saw the enthusiasm for the Middle Ages manifested in such projects as the grandiose reconstruction of Windsor Castle, combined with a more scholarly approach in the work of designers like Thomas Willement, 'Heraldic Artist to His Majesty King George IV', who was responsible for reviving medieval-style heraldic painted decoration and stained glass. Willement was also a prolific writer: his published work includes the definitive *Royal Heraldry, the Armorial Insignia of the Kings and Queens of England* (1821) and *Heraldic Antiquities* (1865). Willement's most extensive surviving heraldic display is in the rooms added to Charlecote in the 1830s, where he designed not only stained glass windows and armorial chimneypieces, but heraldic carpets and upholstery, all decorated with the *luces* of the Lucy family. The interior of Oxburgh in Norfolk is an equally important demonstration of early nineteenth-century heraldic decoration.

The revival of heraldic art pioneered by Willement was perfected by A. W. N. Pugin. Just as he introduced a note of high seriousness into the Gothic Revival, so also he helped to instil a scholarly note into heraldic decoration. His heraldic display in the Houses of Parliament is exemplary, and would have won the approval of Henry III himself. It set the standard for much of the later Victorian revival of architectural heraldic decoration, which soon outdid even the fourteenth century in scale and prolixity. To Pugin, for instance, goes the credit for reviving the heraldic encaustic tile, as well as brasses and enamelwork. Pugin's heraldic enthusiasms greatly influenced the Crace family of designers, and heraldic ornaments attributed to Crace are to be found at Knightshayes, Gawthorpe and Ickworth. Pugin himself is represented by interesting work of the 1840s at Chirk Castle and furnishings at Gawthorpe. The great Gothic Revival architects of the mid- to late Victorian period produced superb heraldic art. At its jolliest this can be seen in William Burges's work at Knightshayes and at its most progressively original in Hungerford Pollen's stained glass and firedogs in the Gallery at Blickling.

The fashion for heraldic decoration in the nineteenth century was not just an aspect of the Gothic Revival and new medieval historical scholarship; it was also a manifestation of the seigniorial pride of the English upper classes after the French Revolution and Waterloo. The early nineteenth century in England saw the manufacture of numerous Norman pedigrees, the medievalising of surnames and titles – de Freyne, de Tabley, Wyatville – and the indiscriminate enjoyment of all the trappings that went with such

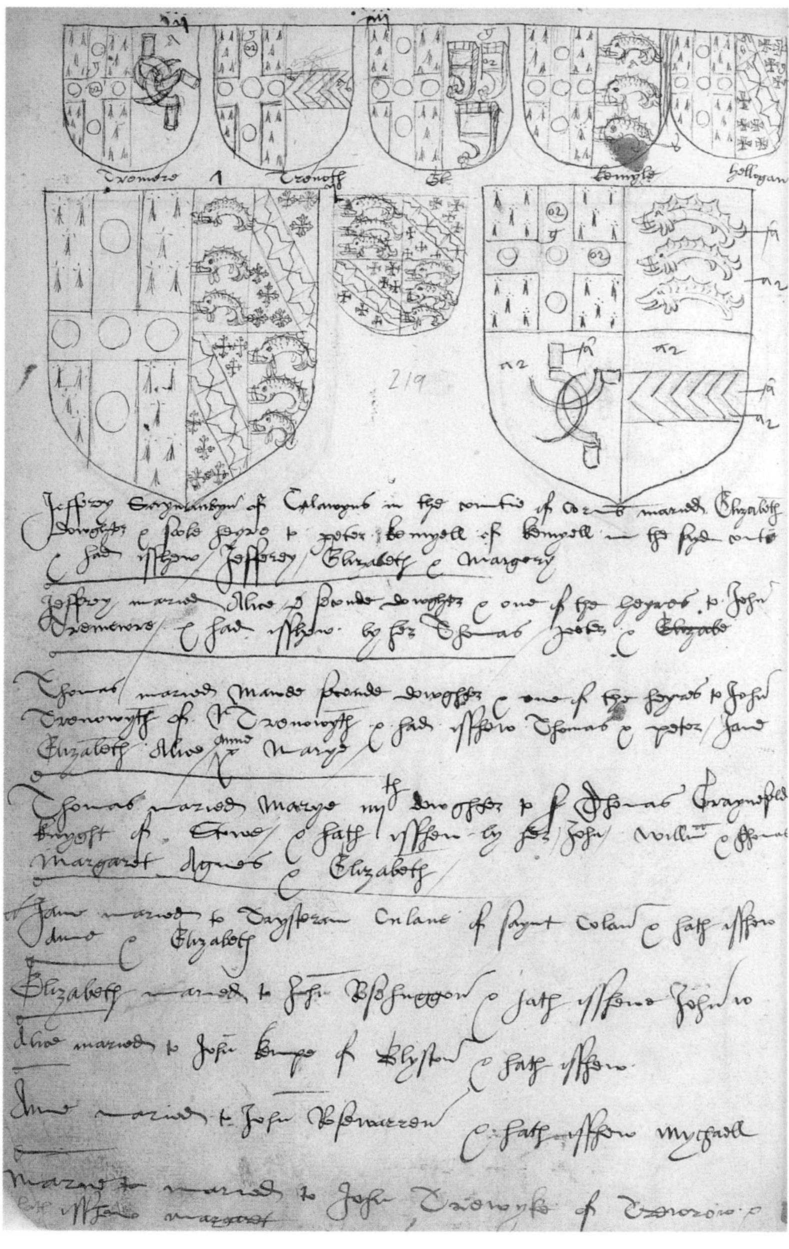

ABOVE LEFT: *A Minton floor tile c.1895 at Lyme showing the impaled arms of Legh and Wodehouse with a peer's parliamentary robe of estate for the 1st Lord Newton (d.1898).*

ABOVE RIGHT: *A pedigree of St Aubyn registered in 1531 showing impaled arms and a quartered coat incorporating the arms of heiresses (College of Arms Ms: H.18/118b).*

sonorous medievalisms. Thus, the landowner often marked all the tied cottages on his estate with tablets bearing his crest or coat of arms and these can be found surrounding many National Trust houses, for instance, in the model estate village at Belton and the lodges and cottages at Felbrigg. Humphry Repton, in the *Red Book* for improving the park at Tatton in Cheshire, advised his client there, Wilbraham Egerton, to decorate all the milestones along the public roads on the estate with the Egerton arms. The heraldic inn sign, which became widespread in this period, continues to be so common a sight in England as to be taken for granted. Nearly every village and town has at least one pub displaying the arms of a past or present local family, like the Buckinghamshire Arms at Blickling, or the Spread Eagle at Stourhead.

The use of heraldry has always been a mark of livery, and though partly practical (to enable a man's servants and dependants to be recognised) this was always largely decorative. In the Middle Ages great magnates clad their servants and followers in liveries based on their heraldic colours, despite repeated attempts by the Crown to control this. Armorial bearings were used as a symbol of a man's authority on all he owned and directed: on his seals, his plate, his horse trappings, his servants, his gaming counters, his dogs and so forth. In the eighteenth and nineteenth centuries this had its most spectacular manifestation in the decoration of carriages and footmen's livery with their silver armorial buttons, as at Lanhydrock. Whole armies of coach painters were employed in painting heraldic panels for carriages, and some well known artists began in this particular line. The architect William Kent, for instance, began life as an apprentice coach painter in Hull, before a group of local gentlemen, struck by his talent, clubbed together to pay to send him to Italy to train as a proper painter. Many heraldic coach panels survive, as they were often cut out and kept when the coach itself was broken up; an example can be seen at Hughenden. The National Trust has several superb examples of the coach painter's art, notably the Craven state carriage on display at Arlington Court, the Lucy travelling coach at Charlecote or the Egerton coach at Tatton.

Coachmen's and footmen's livery also made great decorative play on the family heraldry, usually being in the family colours, with the silver buttons bearing the full achievement, or the crest alone. Some liveries went even further in the heraldic line. The footmen of the Leghs of Lyme of Cheshire, for instance, wore a spare sleeve flapping at the back of their coats to represent the standard-bearing arm of the augmentation in the family arms. A complete set of Victorian servants' liveries is on display in the special Footmen's Livery Room at Lanhydrock in Cornwall.

Thus, throughout its history, heraldry has been primarily for display, and a decorative form of identification for families. In later centuries these ornamental forms of heraldry became increasingly standardised, and visitors will notice varied but similar examples in different National Trust houses: hall chairs, Chinese porcelain dinner services and bookplates. Such items often display only part of the family arms: the crest, say, or the motto, or the shield; or it may be the basic charge from the shield or a more elaborate example with many quarterings of arms showing the descents from heiresses. The rules governing these various components of the full achievement of arms is explained in the next chapter.

How Heraldry Works

The official registry for armorial bearings in England and Wales is the College of Arms. In this book the emphasis is on English heraldry although there are some notable Welsh examples in National Trust houses. Welsh heraldry is a complicated subject because the arms often postdate the ancestors to whom they are attributed, some of whom are legendary, and many of whom lived in a pre-heraldic period. The medieval Welsh system of dividing inherited land led to a great knowledge of their genealogy essential for proving ownership. When families of Welsh descent approached the English heralds for arms, their claim – as in the case of Walter Jones of Chastleton – was based on their ancient ancestry, and the heralds allowed them the attributed arms with small differences.

The Anatomy of Heraldry

An heraldic achievement is made up of arms, a crest, helmet and mantling, and sometimes supporters, a coronet of rank and a badge. Mottoes also appear but are not indexed in the College of Arms records, presumably because they are not technically considered something over which you can have legal rights. All eminent men and women are eligible to bear arms. This includes those with university degrees and professional qualifications, and those holding civil or military commissions.

The arms displayed on a shield pre-date the other elements and are the most important. It is possible to have arms and nothing else, but neither a crest, badge nor supporters may be borne without arms. Arms can be displayed on flags or banners and they are then redrawn to occupy the entire rectangular or square shape. Shield shapes can vary and are a matter of artistic licence, as is the depiction of charges like lions or eagles which need only follow the blazon – the written description.

Describing Arms

Blazon is the language of heraldry, which has remained largely unchanged since the sixteenth century. The standard College of Arms style of blazon used in Letters Patent since the nineteenth century omits all punctuation, like some legal documents, and all descriptions are given as though you are standing behind the shield, so that the dexter side is the left-hand side as you look at it, and sinister the right.

Crest

The crest was originally worn on top of the helm to deflect sword blows. In the thirteenth and fourteenth centuries these were fan-shaped plates which developed into panaches or bushes of ostrich feathers over which no family would dispute ownership. Subsequently the crest became a three-dimensional object made of boiled and gessoed leather and by the sixteenth century crests were the subject of complicated individual grants. They were clearly no longer intended to be worn, because in some cases part of the design was detached; the crest of Sir Francis Drake (q.v. Buckland Abbey), in which a hand emerges from clouds and holds hawsers attached to a ship on a globe, is clearly impossible to wear on a three-dimensional helmet.

Crest Wreaths

Methods of attaching the crest to the helm are first seen with ostrich feather crests which might be fixed with a chapeau or cap as in the case of Ralph, Lord Cromwell, the builder of Tattershall Castle; by a coronet as seen on the Garter Stall Plate of Sir Simon Felbrigge of Felbrigg (d.1442); and most usually with a crest wreath or torse – cloth or silk twisted into a circlet. From the seventeenth century this appeared as six visible twists alternately of the principal metal and colour in the arms commencing with the metal, but in medieval examples the number of twists and order of the metal and colour varies. Wreaths are therefore often stated to be 'of the colours', which refers to the first metal and colour mentioned in the blazon of the arms. If the field or the principal charge is Ermine, then Argent (white) is used for the wreath. Wreaths also hold the mantling to the helmet.

Mantling

Mantling is the cloth worn over armour to deflect the rays of the sun. In British heraldry it is usually shown as slashed and often stylised in the form of acanthus or other leaves that sometimes resemble seaweed. Originally a continuation of the crest, mantling developed into a decorative pattern emerging from the wreath and surrounding the shield during the fifteenth century. In the sixteenth century mantling tended to be of the national colours red and white – *Gules doubled Argent* – which did not necessarily follow the tinctures of the wreath, but since the eighteenth century it has been more usual for the mantling to be of the principal metal and colour in the arms.

In the early seventeenth century, English peers of the rank of Earl and above bore Ermine linings to their mantling. By the end of the century this practice had also been adopted by some Viscounts and Barons. But since the mid-eighteenth century only the Sovereign and Prince of Wales have an Ermine lining to the mantling which in their case is gold. Other members of the Royal Family have gold and white mantling. The mantling of peers in Scotland has developed differently.

Helm

In medieval depictions, such as on early Garter Stall Plates and heraldic seals, crests are shown on closed tilting helms, irrespective of the rank of the bearer. Different helms began to be used according to rank in the late sixteenth century and the current practice in England is:

Sovereign & Royal Princes	– gold barred helms affronty
Peers	– silver helms with gold bars in place of a visor, usually facing dexter
knights and baronets	– steel helms with the visor raised and usually affronty
esquires and gentlemen	– closed steel helms normally in profile like medieval helms

Coronets

Royal arms and those of peers are often shown with a gold coronet of rank resting on the shield beneath the helm. There are five ranks of peer in England and Wales and the dates and forms of their coronets are as follows:

Duke	– (1362) eight strawberry leaves on a gold circlet of which three and two halves are visible in two dimensions
Marquess	– (1387) four strawberry leaves and four low pearls alternately of which two pearls are visible
Earl	– (1444) eight tall rays with a pearl on each and with small strawberry leaves between them. Five rays are shown in two dimensions
Viscount	– (1626) a gold circlet with sixteen pearls of which nine are usually visible
Baron	– (1661) a gold circlet with six pearls on it. In two dimensional pictures four pearls are shown

All peers below the rank of Duke are referred to as Lord in other than formal descriptions, and the eldest son of a Duke, Marquess or Earl may use a title of a lesser rank belonging to his parent as a courtesy title. It is not correct for someone with a courtesy title to use a coronet of rank, although instances exist.

Supporters

Supporters are the beasts, birds, fish, monsters or human figures which stand on either side of a shield and in England they are always granted in pairs. Sometimes they are identical but not necessarily so: the royal supporters since 1603 have been a lion and a unicorn. Since the late seventeenth century supporters have been restricted to the Sovereign, some members of the Royal Family, Peers, Knights of the Garter, large corporate bodies and more recently to Knights Grand Cross of the other Orders of Chivalry, who, like Life Peers, may bear supporters for life. But before this, some families without a peerage bore supporters and continued to do so afterwards although with doubtful authority, like the Luttrell family of Dunster Castle who bore two swans. In the late thirteenth century supporters appear as decoration on larger circular heraldic seals, occupying the space between the sides of the shield and the edge of the seal – about a third of the surviving ninety-six seals on the Barons' Letter to the Pope of 1301 show wyverns or dragons. By the fifteenth century more distinctive supporters were used but there is only occasional evidence of grants of supporters by a King of Arms before the seventeenth century. By the late eighteenth century, grants were made by Garter alone.

Motto

Under the English Law of Arms mottoes have always been regarded as personal because the Kings of Arms do not have power to grant legal rights over a group of words. They may therefore be used by more than one family and can change from generation to generation, although in practice many are retained for centuries. The motto in England is customarily shown on a ribbon or motto scroll beneath the shield; in Scotland it usually appears above the crest. Mottoes have a number of origins. Some began as battle cries (which have been forbidden by statute since 1495): *Dieu et Mon Droit* used by Richard I at the Battle of Gisors in 1198 was adopted as the English royal motto by Edward III in 1340. Others are puns on the surname such as *Cavendo Tutus* (Safe by being cautious) of Cavendish of Hardwick, *Templa quam Dilecta* (How beloved are the temples) of Temple of Stowe, and *Festina Lente* (On slow! or Hasten cautiously) of Onslow of Clandon Park. Anagrams of the bearer's name can illustrate the personal nature of a motto: Mary Queen of Scots used *Veritas Armata* (Armed Truth) which is almost an anagram of Marie Stuarta. Later mottoes tend to be innocuous expressions of wisdom, virtue and honour.

Badges

Badges are perhaps the most nebulous part of an achievement of arms. These free-standing devices can be divided into two types. The first is the beast, which would be for personal use and might be an animal, bird, reptile, fish, monster or a human figure. Many early sixteenth-century depictions of arms on banners and, occasionally, seals show them as a single supporter holding the banner or shield. Smaller inanimate badges such as crescents and knots were for use by retainers or to mark property and appear in profusion. They vary in complexity: the crescent badge of the Percys, to be found on the hall chairs at Petworth, Sussex, is very simple, while the Bourchier knot seen at Beningbrough Hall in Yorkshire is more complicated.

The tincture – the colour, metal or fur – used for the background of the shield – or field – is mentioned first, followed by whatever is in the centre, working outwards.

TINCTURES

COLOURS	METALS	FURS
AZURE (blue)	ARGENT (silver or white)	ERMINE (black ermine tails on white)
GULES (red)	OR (gold or yellow)	ERMINES (white tails on black)
SABLE (black)		ERMINOIS (black tails on gold)
VERT (green)		PEAN (gold tails on black)
PURPURE (purple)		VAIR (blue and silver squirrel skins)

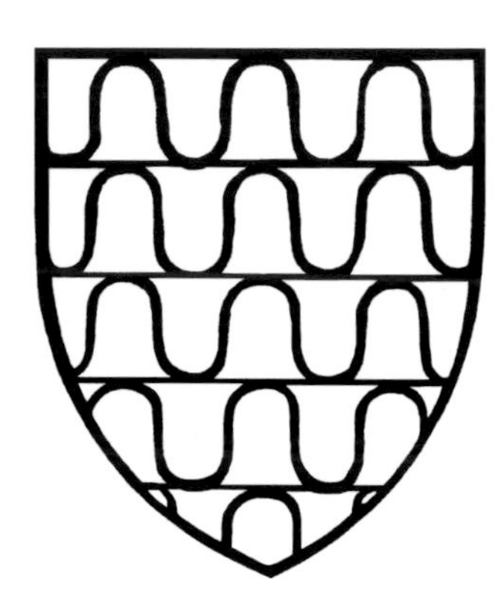

Vairy arms of Ferrers, Earls of Derby and Barons Ferrers of Chartley. Ermine and Vair are the two principal furs in heraldry. The latter is a stylized pattern derived from animal skins joined together head to tail and is termed Vair *when Argent and Azure and* Vairy *in all other tinctures.*

There are also three subsidiary colours known as stains – *Murrey* (mulberry), *Sanguine* (blood red) and *Tenne* (orange). The actual shade of a colour can vary and is a matter of artistic licence. Traditionally, there was no 'approved' shade of red for *Gules* or green for *Vert*, but in the twentieth century a sky blue termed *Bleu Celeste* was developed for the Royal Air Force, so *Azure* would not now be shown as pale blue. *Vair* also appears in other tinctures, and is termed *Vairy* with the tinctures stated. The original coat of the Ferrers family (Baddesley Clinton) of *Vairy Or and Gules*, for instance, is a gold and red arrangement of squirrel skins. Finally, anything that is described as *proper* – such as birds or beasts – appears in its natural colours.

The simplest coats of arms are those which contain geometrical patterns and nothing else. These can be achieved either by a line of partition as in the arms of Waldegrave *Per Pale Argent and Gules*, which are divided vertically with the left side (dexter) silver and the other red, or by a solid geometric shape. The eight most commonly used shapes, described as honourable ordinaries by the writers of heraldic textbooks, are listed below.

ORDINARY	DESCRIPTION	DIVISION
CROSS	divides the shield into quarters	*Quarterly*
CHIEF	created by dividing the top third or fifth of the shield from the rest	–
PALE	a single vertical stripe covering a third or fifth of the shield. A number of pales are termed pallets and are narrower	*Per Pale*
BEND	a diagonal band from dexter chief to sinister base. A *Bend sinister* goes from sinister chief to dexter base	*Per Bend or Per Bend sinister*
FESS	a horizontal band across the centre of the shield; two or more are termed *Bars* and an even number of four or more horizontal bands is described as *Barry*	*Per Fess*

Inescutcheon	a shield borne as a charge on the shield	–
Chevron	an inverted letter 'V'	*Per Chevron*
Saltire	St Andrew's Cross	*Per Saltire*

Other shapes are termed sub-ordinaries or plain ordinaries, and include the Gyron, Orle, Pile, Quarter, Canton, Flasque, Flaunch, Fret, Lozenge, Fusil and Mascle, which are described in the glossary. Like tinctures and charges, ordinaries and sub-ordinaries are given capital letters in the blazon. Often both the edges of the shapes and the lines of partition which derive from them are decoratively modified and, again, terms like engrailed, invected, wavy, dancetty, nebuly and embattled are explained in the glossary.

The arms granted in 1627 to Sir William Craven when he was created 1st Baron Craven.

Most coats of arms include a combination of ordinaries or sub-ordinaries and charges. The number of possible charges is limitless, but as arms were intended as a means of identification, complicated designs were initially rare. Charges can be just about anything: beasts, birds, reptiles, monsters – and parts of them – all appear; many were derived from medieval bestiaries (natural history books), and some were the heralds' own inventions, particularly from Tudor times onwards. Flowers, including fleurs de lys, roses and trefoils were also popular, as were inanimate charges like suns, crescents and stars. In heraldic blazon, tinctures come after what they describe, and they refer to everything before them until another tincture is reached. The arms of Craven of Ashdown House are blazoned *Argent a Fess between six Cross Crosslets fitchy Gules*. This means that the shield is silver or white with a horizontal band across the centre and both it and the pointed (fitchy) Cross Crosslets are red. The next stage in complication is to have charges both on an ordinary and on either side of it, as in the arms of Blackett of Wallington *Argent on a Chevron between three Mullets Sable three Escallops Argent* – three white escallops are on a black chevron, which is between three black mullets (stars) on a white field.

The purpose of blazon is to enable the reader to draw a coat of arms and it should therefore be as simple as possible, although there are more complicated styles. The arms of Blackett described above could also be blazoned *Argent on a Chevron between three Mullets Sable as many Escallops of the field*, which means that there are as many escallops as there are black mullets, and that the escallops are the same tincture as the field. Another form of blazon describes charges and ordinaries as 'of the first' or 'of the second', referring to the first or second tincture mentioned. The arms of Hardwick of Hardwick Hall *Argent a Saltire engrailed Azure on a Chief also Azure three Roses Argent barbed and seeded proper* could be written *Argent a Saltire engrailed Azure on a Chief of the second three Roses of the first barbed and seeded proper*.

Heraldry is, however, a visual subject, and the records at the College of Arms of the Visitations which regulated heraldry in the sixteenth and seventeenth centuries do not give blazons but show pictures of the arms to which families were entitled. Some of these are in colour, but the majority are tricks of arms – pen and ink sketches with the tinctures indicated by abbreviations like G or Gu for Gules and so on. The disadvantage of visual records like this is that sometimes the identity of charges can be lost: the birds in the arms of Onslow of Clandon Park seem to have started as sparrowhawks, had a period as falcons and ended up as Cornish choughs. This problem does not arise where an original grant of arms survives. The College has the complete text of grants by the English Kings of Arms since 1673, but before that date information exists in varying degrees of detail. Many of the arms that were assumed and simply

A verre églomisé *panel with two shields of Talbot impaling Hardwick beneath an earl's coronet for the 6th Earl of Shrewsbury (d.1590) and his wife Elizabeth (Bess of Hardwick d.1607/8) and in the centre a full achievement of the arms and crest of Hardwick.*

confirmed in Heraldic Visitations were never the subject of a formal grant and therefore never officially blazoned.

Tinctures in monochrome sketches can also be recorded by a system known as hatching, which was devised by Sylvester Petra Sancta and published in *Terrerae Gentilitia* in 1638.

Azure	– horizontal lines
Gules	– vertical lines
Sable	– cross-hatched vertical and horizontal
Vert	– diagonal bendwise
Purpure	– diagonal bendwise sinister
Or	– small dots
Argent	– unhatched

This system also covers the furs: *Ermine* is shown as a black ermine spot on white, and *Vair* appears in the tinctures Azure and Argent. Heraldry in bookplates and engraved on silver is often hatched, but it also appears in this form on glass, seals and stamped into book bindings.

A silver gilt dessert dish by Paul de Lamerie for the 2nd Earl of Bristol with the hatched arms at Ickworth. The quarterings are in the wrong order. Felton should be in the second quarter and Howard should precede Brotherton. Arms, supporters and motto are shown on a peer's parliamentary robe of estate not with mantling, and there is an earl's coronet of rank.

Interpreting heraldry

Honourable exploits, illegitimacy and a man's place in the family can all be recorded on a coat of arms, as can the status of his wife – whether she is entitled to arms or not and, if she is, whether or not she is an heraldic heiress, or even a peeress in her own right. An heraldic heiress is a woman entitled to arms whose father is dead and who has no brothers. Under the English Law of Arms, sisters rank equally, so any number of sisters would be equal coheirs. It is sometimes wrongly stated that if a woman has a brother who dies without male issue, she and her niece are equal coheirs. This is nonsense. The niece alone is an heraldic heiress and the aunt would only become an heraldic heiress on the extinction of the niece's issue. It follows from this that a woman can become an heraldic heiress long after her own death.

In the medieval period different members of a family would personalise or difference their arms by varying them in some way, even reversing the tinctures. Around 1500 John Writhe, Garter King of Arms, invented a system to indicate a son's place in the family by putting small marks, known as cadency marks, on the shield as follows:

LABEL – eldest son in the lifetime of his father
CRESCENT – second son
MULLET – third son
MARTLET – fourth son
ANNULET – fifth son
FLEUR DE LYS – sixth son
ROSE – seventh son
CROSS MOLINE – eighth son

Cadency marks should be of an appropriate tincture, and can be placed anywhere on the shield, depending on the design of the arms. The system only indicates the position within the immediate family – an uncle and a nephew who are both second sons would also both difference their arms with a small crescent. Cadency marks occasionally appear on Letters Patent of Arms, for instance the 1603 patent to Walter Jones subsequently of Chastleton, which confirms his right to ancient Welsh arms but differences them with a crescent on a mullet appropriate for the second son of a third son or his descendant. The arms borne by Sir Winston Churchill of Chartwell are those of the Dukes of Marlborough differenced in the centre point by a crescent, as his father was the 7th Duke of Marlborough's second son. In the sixteenth and seventeenth centuries cadency marks were used as a matter of course. Today they are optional, although the strict legal position is outlined by Sir Edward Coke in his *Commentary on Littleton* (1628), Section 210: 'The eldest shall beare as a badge of his birthright his father's arms without any differences for that as Littleton saith sectione 5 he is more worthy of blood but all the younger brethren shall give several differences.' In English law, and excepting royalty, daughters rank equally, so do not use cadency marks other than those used by their father.

Since the sixteenth century a label – a thin bar with dependent points (lambeaux) – is the cadency mark for an eldest son in his father's lifetime when it is shown with three points. If the label has five points it is the cadency mark for the eldest son of an eldest son in the lifetime of his grandfather. This is the only cadency mark which indicates that three generations of a family are alive. In royal heraldry both Princes and Princesses have labels on their arms with different charges on the points which are specifically assigned to them. Children of the Sovereign have three-point labels and grandchildren have five points. Only the Prince of Wales has a plain, i.e. uncharged, label.

Differencing of arms also occurs as a result of illegitimacy, although this is not automatic. Since the fifteenth century, in England most grants of arms other than to illegitimate children have been made directly by the Kings of Arms. Illegitimate children are not entitled to their family's arms and can only acquire them directly from the Crown by Royal Charter; by Royal Licence and a subsequent grant from the Kings of Arms; by an Act of Parliament; or occasionally by grant from the Kings of Arms without a Royal Licence. The traditional mark of illegitimacy is the bend sinister. In practice a baton sinister, a narrow bend sinister that does not reach the edges of the shield, is used, particularly for royal illegitimacy. An example is shown in the painting of the arms of Henry FitzJames, second illegitimate son of James II and Arabella Churchill, at Dunster Castle. These were granted by Royal Warrant in 1686 and are the royal arms of James II and over all (or debruised by) *a Baton sinister Azure charged*

The arms and crest granted by Royal Warrant of James II to his illegitimate son Henry FitzJames (College of Arms Ms: I.26/110). They appear in a painting at Dunster Castle.

with three Fleurs de lys Or. The crest granted at the same time bears no resemblance to the royal crest; the crests of illegitimate children were usually those of the father, suitably varied.

The other most usual form of differencing arms for illegitimacy is by adding a border. In 1543 Sir William Herbert, who was created Earl of Pembroke in 1551, was granted the arms of Herbert within a *Bordure gobony Or and Gules*. His father Richard Herbert was an illegitimate son of an earlier Earl of Pembroke. Borders can be plain, engrailed or wavy, like the grants in 1806 to Thomas Peter Legh's seven illegitimate children (q.v. Lyme Park). The wavy borders for the sons were Argent, Or and Ermine. Those for the daughters were all Argent but charged with Roses, Trefoils, Quatrefoils and Cinquefoils. The crest was differenced for the sons by different colours of wavy pallet charged on the ram's head.

The appearance of a shield can also be altered by an addition or augmentation of honour. Armorial bearings can be augmented in a number of ways, most usually by an addition to the arms and occasionally by the grant of an additional crest or even a whole coat of arms. The Seymour family, Dukes of Somerset, have borne an additional coat of arms composed of elements from the royal arms of England and France since the marriage in 1536 of Jane Seymour to King Henry VIII. It is blazoned *Or on a Pile Gules between six Fleurs de lys Azure three Lions passant guardant Or* and appears in the first quarter before the paternal arms. Examples can be seen at Petworth.

Charles II rewarded many Royalists after the Restoration with augmentations to their arms. A Royal Warrant of 3 September 1660 gave Sir Edward Walker, Garter, 'full power and authority to give grant and assigne unto any person of eminent quality fidelity and extraordinary merit that shall desire it such augmentation of any of Our Royall badges to be added unto his Armes as you shall judge most proper to testify the same'. About fifty grants were made under both this general warrant, and another in the same terms from Charles I to Walker given at Oxford in 1645. Augmentation can take place some time after the event to which it relates. Thomas Whitgreave of Moseley, who sheltered Charles II after the Battle of Worcester in 1651, did not apply for an augmentation under the 1660 Warrant – possibly because he received a pension – but almost two centuries later in 1838 his descendant, George Thomas Whitgreave, was granted an augmentation of *A Chief Argent thereon a Rose Gules irradiated Gold within a Wreath of Oak proper* with an additional crest for the service performed. Usually grants to military or naval heroes occur closer to the time of the heroic action, such as that granted following a Royal Licence to Sir George Eliott, 1st Lord Heathfield in 1787 which commemorated his defence of Gibraltar against combined French and Spanish forces between 1779 and 1783 with a *Chief of the Arms of Gibraltar*. These arms were borne as a quartering by his descendants the Fuller-Eliott-Drakes of Buckland Abbey.

Much of the usefulness and enjoyment of heraldry depends on understanding how and why coats of arms are combined together. Compounding, dimidiating, impaling, quartering and bearing arms in pretence are different ways in which more than one coat of arms can be borne on a single shield.

Compounding arms means that elements are taken from two shields and put

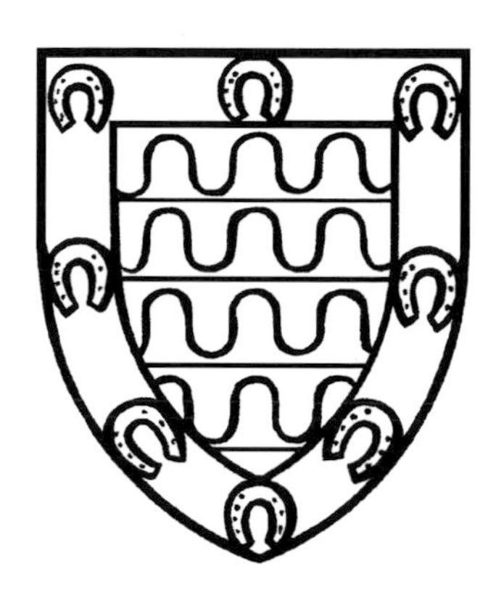

Compounded arms of William Ferrers, Earl of Derby (d.1254).

together to form a new design. This occurred in the thirteenth and fourteenth centuries so that different members of a family bore distinct arms before cadency marks evolved. William Ferrers, Earl of Derby (d.1254) and ancestor of the Ferrers family of Baddesley Clinton, altered the Vairy coat borne by other members of the family by adding a bordure charged with horseshoes. If the horseshoes are derived from a coat of *Argent six Horseshoes Sable* – reputedly the earliest Ferrers arms – the result is a compounded coat.

Dimidiation was a medieval and now obsolete way of combining two coats of arms usually to denote husband and wife. Each shield was divided vertically and the dexter side of the husband's was attached to the sinister side of the wife's. The disadvantage was that some designs could become unidentifiable – a coat with three chevrons, for instance, would be transformed into one with three bends. The arms of Great Yarmouth are dimidiated with the English royal arms in the dexter half of the shield and three herrings in the sinister half, so the shield shows the front half of three lions attached to the back half of three herrings. A horizontal dimidiation can be seen in the arms granted in 1514 by the Emperor Maximilian to William Knight whose arms appear over the entrance doorway to Horton Court in Gloucestershire.

Arms granted by the Emperor Maximilian to William Knight (d.1547), Ambassador from King Henry VIII, which consists of two coats dimidiated horizontally.

Since the early fifteenth century the usual way to show the arms of husband and wife is by impalement. The shield is divided vertically and both coats of arms are redrawn to occupy one half each. If either coat is *within a bordure*, the border is only shown around the edges and not down the vertical division to leave more room for the design. Arms of office and the personal arms of the office holder can be similarly impaled with the arms of office being shown to the dexter.

When a marriage is commemorated, the husband's arms are shown to the dexter, and the wife's to the sinister. If a wife is an heraldic heiress then her arms can be shown on an escutcheon of pretence – a small shield in the centre of her husband's arms. All legitimate children of a man entitled to arms are themselves armigerous, but only sons pass the right to arms on to their children unless the daughters become heraldic heiresses.

The children of an heraldic heiress may quarter her arms with their paternal arms. Quartering means dividing a shield into four or more equal parts – always termed quarters no matter how many there are. The paternal arms are always placed in dexter chief – the top left-hand corner. Next to it, in the second quarter, are the arms of the first heraldic heiress in the male line, followed by her own quarterings, which begins a chronological sequence of heraldic heiresses who married into the family and from whom subsequent generations are descended.

In the simplest quartered coat the paternal arms are shown in the first and fourth quarters (top left and bottom right as you look at the shield) and the arms of the heiress from whom there is a descent in the second and third quarters. If an heraldic heiress is entitled to a coat of twenty quarters her children may add all twenty quarters to their paternal arms, each quarter being the same size. Arms are only quartered within a quarter when they are quartered as a result of a Royal Licence which is deemed to create an impartible coat. The arms of Percy and Lucy (q.v. Petworth) are treated as an impartible quarter as are the 1688 arms of Temple of Stowe.

The quartered arms and crest of Sir John Cust, 3rd Bt. of Belton (1718-70) (College of Arms Ms: 5D.14/157).

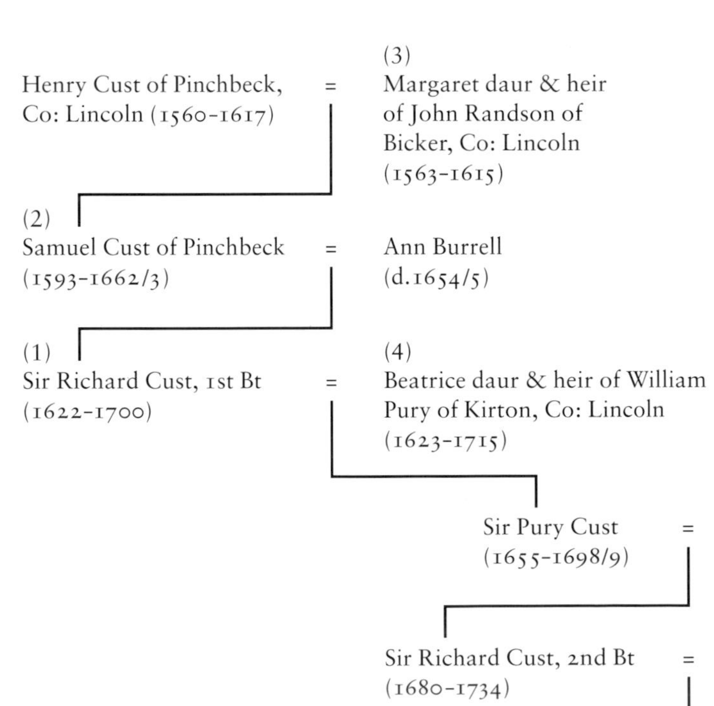

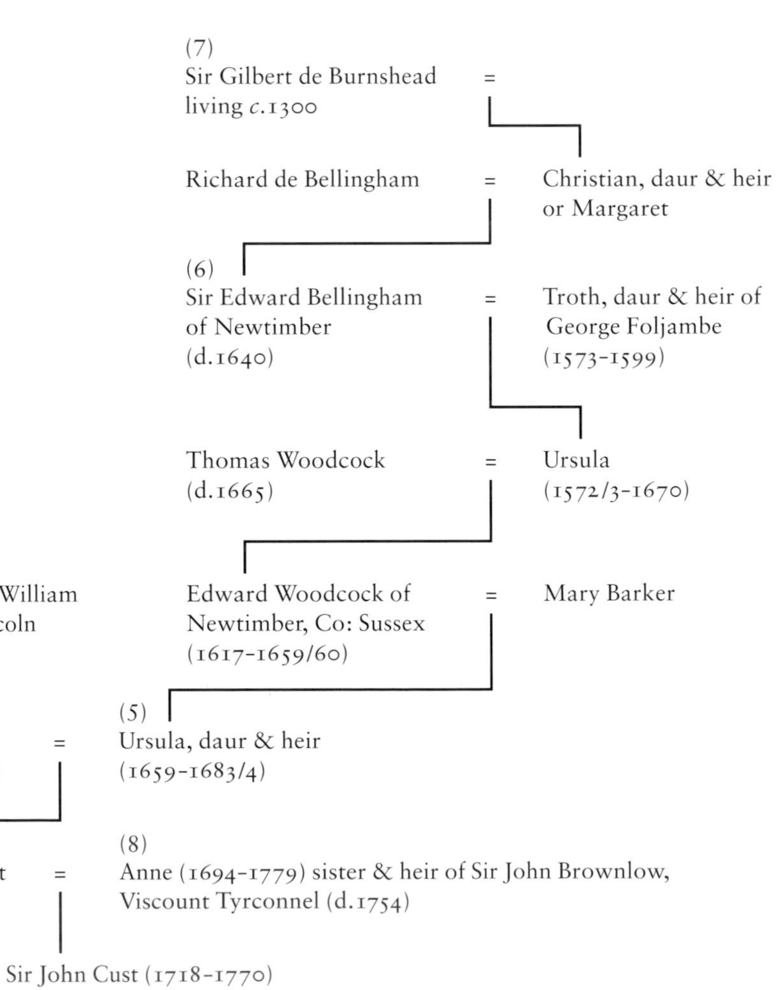

The best way to understand the order in which quarterings should be arranged is to look at an example. The scheme of quarterings recorded in 1763 at the College of Arms by Sir John Cust, Bt. (d.1770) of Belton, Speaker of the House of Commons shows:

(1) Cust [granted 1663]	(2) Cust [granted 1649]	(3) Randson	(4) Pury
(5) Woodcock	(6) Bellingham	(7) Burnshead	(8) Brownlow

The source of the quarters is shown on the pedigree opposite:

(1) The paternal arms are correctly shown in the first quarter.

(2) In the second quarter is the coat granted to Samuel Cust in 1649. This, like all other grants by the Commonwealth Kings of Arms, was declared void by a Royal Warrant in 1660. Therefore it should not be included, but it appears not only in this 1763 entry but also in the 1666 Lincolnshire Visitation. It was probably included in 1660 because both grants and the Visitation were made by the same man, Sir Edward Bysshe.

(3) The third quarter shows arms for Randson. Samuel Cust's mother was the daughter and heir of John Randson. However, the Randson arms should not have been included because her husband, Henry Cust, was never entitled to arms, so her arms could not be transmitted to the next generation. Nevertheless, they appear in the 1666 Visitation and the error was perpetuated in 1763.

(4) In the fourth quarter are arms for Pury for the 1st Baronet's wife. These appear on an escutcheon of pretence in the 1666 Visitation entry. However, they seem to be the wrong Pury coat as her family recorded arms of *Argent on a Bend Sable three Pears Or* at the 1634 Lincolnshire Visitation. The arms shown here were recorded for Pury in sixteenth-century Visitations of Devonshire.

(5,6,7) The fifth quarter shows the arms of Sir Pury Cust's wife, Ursula Woodcock, who brought the sixth and seventh quarters with her. Her arms are entered in the 1662 Visitation of Sussex with Bellingham quartering Burnshead – the sixth and seventh quarters – on an escutcheon of pretence. If her Bellingham ancestor did marry the Burnshead heiress *c.*1300, these quarters are shown correctly. She could have brought in an eighth quarter for her great-grandmother Troth Foljambe, but did not do so.

(8) Finally, the eighth and last quarter in this scheme shows the arms of Brownlow which Sir John Cust was entitled to quarter after the death of his uncle, Viscount Tyrconnel, in 1754. It is sometimes suggested that arms may not be quartered till the heraldic heiress is dead. This is not now the practice in England and has not been followed in this case as Sir John Cust's mother outlived him.

The correct scheme of these quarterings in 1763 would seem to be: (1) Cust 1663; (2) a different coat for Pury; (3) Woodcock; (4) Bellingham; (5) Burnshead; (6) Brownlow. The void 1649 grant for Cust and the Randson quarter are omitted.

(1) Cust [1663]	(2) Pury [a different coat]	(3) Woodcock
(4) Bellingham	(5) Burnshead	(6) Brownlow

Schemes displaying every quartering to which a family is entitled can become very complicated and show even hundreds of quarters. Often a selection is made to record the most significant heiresses married by the family. An example is the 9th Earl of Stamford's (d.1910) quartered coat shown above the Dining Room fireplace at Dunham Massey. Although erected in 1905, this shows (1) Grey, the paternal arms; (2) Bonville, for Cicely, Baroness Bonville and Harington in her own right (m.1474); (3) Cecil, for Lady Anne Cecil (m.1620), daughter and coheir of the 2nd Earl of Exeter who brought the Manor of Stamford into the family; (4) Booth, for Lady Mary Booth (m.1736), heiress of Dunham Massey.

Although the terminology and rules of heraldry may seem obscure and complex, an understanding of them provides a fascinating insight into the way previous generations regarded themselves and their lineage. The distinct quarterings, impalements and escutcheons of pretence act like hallmarks on objects, tying them down to a particular date. The heraldry in a house provides the visitor with a guide to the history of the family and is an undervalued key to the past which can date and explain many forms of decoration.

The Houses

Baddesley Clinton

WARWICKSHIRE

Ferrers

Arms: Gules seven Mascles conjoined 3,3&1 Or a Canton Ermine

Crest: On a Wreath of the Colours (Or and Gules) A Unicorn passant Ermine

Badges: (1) A Unicorn courant Ermine charged on the shoulder with a crescent Sable
(2) A Mascle Or

Motto: *Splendeo Tritus* [I shine though worn]

The moated manor house of Baddesley Clinton was bought in 1438 by John Brome, M.P. for Warwick, and belonged to his descendants, the Ferrers, down to the twentieth century.

John Brome's granddaughter married Sir Edward Ferrers, a member of the junior branch of the Ferrers of Groby, whose ancestors had come to England at the Norman Conquest. The Ferrers were very proud of their Norman ancestry, and successive generations at Baddesley Clinton were remarkable for their antiquarian and heraldic enthusiasms, most notably the Elizabethan Catholic, Henry Ferrers (d.1633), known as 'the Antiquary'. He inherited Baddesley in 1564 and presided over it for nearly seventy years, building the Great Hall and filling the house with oak panelling, carved heraldic overmantels and armorial glass, as the money was available.

The large carved stone chimneypiece in the Great Hall is an example of the Antiquary's heraldic interests. In the centre of the overmantel is a shield of the quartered arms of Ferrers of Baddesley Clinton: Ferrers; Brome; Hampden; and White. Six shields of impaled arms showing the marriages of successive ancestors surround it. The heraldic theme continues in the Hall windows, installed by Henry the Antiquary, which contain fine late sixteenth-century armorial glass, possibly made by Nicholas Eyffeler of Stratford (q.v. Charlecote). On the courtyard side, shields with impaled arms and coronets represent the history of the Ferrers family from the Norman Conquest as far as the 5th Lord Ferrers of Groby (d.1445), the great-grandfather of Sir Edward Ferrers who came to Baddesley in 1517. The windows flanking the chimneypiece contain impaled arms commemorating the ancestors of the Antiquary's wife, the Whites; his own; and the Bromes.

Some Victorian glass added in 1894 displays the arms of Edward Ferrers (d.1830), his son Marmion Edward Ferrers (d.1884) and Edward Heneage Dering (d.1892). It recalls the most extraordinary episode in the life of Baddesley Clinton, when Georgiana, Lady Chatterton, her niece Rebecca Dulcibella Orpen and their husbands, Edward Heneage Dering and Marmion Edward Ferrers, all lived in the house together.

The story is that Dering went to Lady Chatterton to ask permission to marry her niece Rebecca. She misunderstood him, and accepted the proposal for herself. He was too chivalrous to disabuse her and they married in 1859. Rebecca herself married Marmion Edward Ferrers in 1867. After Lady Chatterton's and Marmion Ferrers' deaths, Dering and Rebecca Dulcibella finally married in 1885. All four had a romantic interest in the past and contributed to the antiquarian heraldic decorations of the house. Rebecca Dulcibella painted one wall of the Hall with Dering heraldry, and many of the 'ancestral' portraits in the house are the product of her brush.

In the Dining Room, the Jacobean chimneypiece – part of Henry the Antiquary's scheme – is carved with the Ferrers arms, while the big Charles I cupboard introduces a more modern heraldic note; it was restored in the 1940s and embellished with the

The carved stone chimneypiece in the Great Hall at Baddesley Clinton. In the centre is a shield showing quartered arms of (1) Ferrers (2) Brome (3) Hampden (4) White.

Nineteenth-century heraldic glass at Baddesley Clinton showing the Ferrers arms, derived from de Quincy, quartering an earlier attributed Ferrers coat with Townshend in pretence for the parents of Marmion Edward Ferrers, and his own arms showing the medieval Ferrers coat impaling Orpen and wrongly surmounted by a baron's coronet as, though he was a coheir to the Barony of Ferrers of Chartley, it was not called out of abeyance in his favour.

Ferrers-Walker arms of the family who bought the house in 1940. The Drawing Room is an eighteenth-century antiquarian ensemble fitted up with old oak panelling transferred from elsewhere in the building. The carved panel in the chimneypiece, another production of Henry the Antiquary, displays the quartered arms of Ferrers and White – the arms of his son Edward. The stained glass shields in the windows depicting sixteenth-century Ferrers marriages also date from the time of the Antiquary, but are *ex situ* and, accompanied by the arms of Marmion Edward Ferrers and Edward Heneage Dering, were installed by Rebecca Dulcibella in 1895.

Hanging on the staircase is a fine late eighteenth-century pedigree roll showing the ancestry of the Townshends, the family of Marmion Edward Ferrers' mother, through whom he was a coheir to the Barony of Ferrers of Chartley. Upstairs, the former State Bedroom contains another of Henry the Antiquary's carved oak heraldic chimneypieces. In his diary of 1629, he recorded its construction and how he constantly visited 'the Radclifs', the joiners, to supervise the heraldry and ensure that it was correct. The carved arms, Ferrers of Groby quartered with Hampden, bearing White on an escutcheon of pretence, are those of the Antiquary himself and his wife Jane, daughter and heiress of Henry White. The Antiquary's paternal grandmother was the daughter and coheir of Sir John Hampden of Hampden, Buckinghamshire.

It is clear that Henry the Antiquary's heraldic decoration at Baddesley, executed in stained glass or carved in wood and stone, formed part of a carefully considered scheme, devised to show his family descent, culminating in his own arms and those of his son Edward. The stained glass in the Hall, for instance, traces the Ferrers descent to the fifteenth century, while that in the Drawing Room continued the story through the sixteenth century down to the Antiquary himself.

The main charge of the Ferrers arms – seven mascles – is laid out in the courtyard lawn and planted in the correct tinctures in summer, an unusual example of an heraldic flower-bed dating from late Victorian times.

Belton House

LINCOLNSHIRE

Brownlow

Arms: Or an Inescutcheon in an orle of Martlets Sable

Crest: On a Chapeau Gules turned up Ermine a Greyhound passant Or plain collared Gules

Supporters (as Viscount Tyrconnel): On either side a Lion reguardant Argent plain gorged Gules

Motto: *Esse Quam Videri* [To be rather than to seem to be]

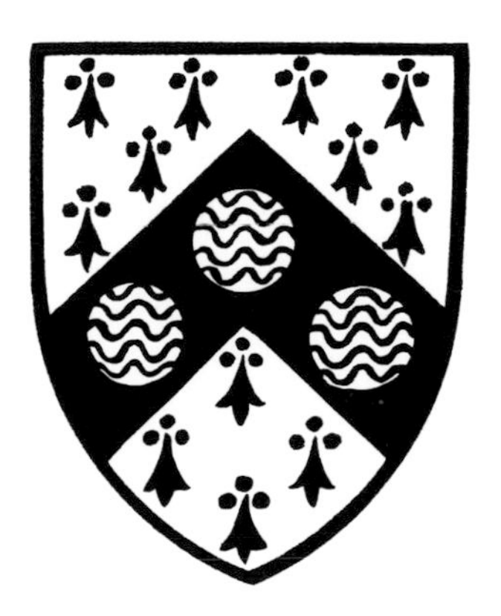

Cust

Arms: Ermine on a Chevron Sable three Fountains

Crest: On a Wreath of the Colours (Argent and Sable) A Lion's Head erased Sable plain collared gobony Argent and Azure

Supporters (as Lord Brownlow): On either side a Lion reguardant Argent collared paly wavy Argent and Azure

Motto: *Opera Illius Mea Sunt* [His works are mine] *Esse Quam Videri* [To be rather than to seem to be]

At first glance, the perfect Anglo-Dutch architecture of Belton might not seem a good vehicle for heraldic decoration. But in fact, few English houses are as rewarding for the heraldry enthusiast, and it will be seen that the arms of the two successive, interrelated families who owned the Belton estate for twelve generations from the seventeenth to the twentieth centuries are to be found everywhere, in wrought and cast metal, carved and inlaid in wood, moulded in plaster, engraved on silver and brass, painted on wood, canvas and china. The inheritance of the 7th Earl of Bridgwater's estates in the nineteenth century, which was conditional on assuming the name and arms of Egerton, further enrich the heraldic quarry.

The founder of the family, Richard Brownlow (d.1638) who purchased Belton, was Chief Prothonotary of the Common Pleas and made a huge fortune from the law. He received a confirmation of arms and grant of a crest in 1593 with a greyhound on a cap of maintenance, and the greyhound pervades Belton from the weather vane on top of the cupola downwards. In the eighteenth century, Lord Tyrconnel was particularly proud of his noble status as a Viscount and as a Knight of the Bath, and this was reflected in his embellishments at Belton, and also in his funeral in 1754, which was a late example of full-scale heraldic ceremonial; it included a procession of armorial banneroles, spurs, gauntlets, a standard, helmet, shield and sword, just as in the Middle Ages.

The Custs were a much older family than the Brownlows and could trace their ancestors in Lincolnshire back to the fifteenth century. They were given a peerage in 1776 in recognition of Sir John Cust's services as Speaker of the House of Commons; though, as the Speaker himself died of overwork in 1770, his son, Sir Brownlow Cust, was ennobled in his place.

An exaggerated interest in heraldry and family seems to have been a continuing trait, for Viscount Alford, the eldest son of the 1st Earl, was an enthusiastic devotee of the early nineteenth-century chivalric revival and a leading participant in the Eglinton Tournament, the famous recreation of a medieval joust in Ayrshire in August 1839 where the participants wore armour and in which Lord Alford was called the Knight of the Black Lion from his crest. The Eglinton Tournament is recorded in an illustrated book in the library at Belton, John Richardson's *The English Tournament* (1843).

The visitor approaching the house receives a first taste of heraldry in John Warren's wrought iron gate-screen to the West Court. The gate piers are topped with the Brownlow greyhound standing on a cap of maintenance, and in the overthrow is an oval cartouche with the Brownlow arms. Beyond, over the family porch, is a large Coade stone relief of the arms of Lord Brownlow; Cust with lion supporters and lion's head crest. Both the main pediments of the house have the Brownlow arms in baroque cartouches, part of 'young' Sir John's original design and structure.

The greyhound makes his appearance again in the Marble Hall: in gilded wood

BELOW LEFT: *A lock plate showing the crest of Brownlow on a door in the Marble Hall at Belton.*

BELOW RIGHT: *A Chinese armorial plate at Belton showing on the helm the crest of Cust and below the impaled marital arms of Sir Richard Cust, 2nd Bt. and his wife, Anne Brownlow, whom he married in 1717.*

The crest of Brownlow painted on the floor of the Tyrconnel Room at Belton.

supporting the Regency console tables and, superbly engraved in brass, on the seventeenth-century lock plates. The wheel-back hall chairs (possibly designed by James Wyatt) have painted heraldry on their backs as was customary – in this case the quartered arms of the 1st Lord Brownlow, with the arms of his first wife Jocasta Drury in pretence. Another set of Wyatt hall chairs on the staircase have the Cust lion's head crest painted incorrectly.

In the Saloon, Chapel and Staircase Hall the richly moulded stucco ceilings are all embellished with the family arms or crest. In the Saloon are the Cust arms with an earl's coronet indicating that the ceiling is a clever pastiche probably made by Jacksons for the 3rd Earl Brownlow in 1873. In the Chapel and Staircase Hall, Edward Goudge's masterly original seventeenth-century work is dated by the Brownlow greyhound crest, more prominent in the latter than the former.

The Tyrconnel arms – the quartered arms of Brownlow within the circlet of the Order of the Bath with supporters and a viscount's coronet – can be seen in the Tapestry Room, woven into the borders of the early eighteenth-century English tapestries which were rescued from the attics and hung here by the 3rd Earl Brownlow.

The Tyrconnel Room is dominated by the Brownlow arms painted on the floor, with the greyhound crest; this helps to date this rare scheme of decoration to the eighteenth rather than the early nineteenth century. The pier glass in here, and its pair in the Chapel Drawing Room, display the impaled arms of 'young' Sir John Brownlow and his wife, Anne Sherard, on a lozenge; presumably these were made for Lady Brownlow after her husband's death in 1697.

Upstairs, in the Ante Library, are parts of three eighteenth-century armorial Chinese export services. Two of these were made in the 1730s for Viscount Tyrconnel and have the impaled Brownlow arms and the insignia of the Order of the Bath. A third has the impaled arms of Cust and Brownlow, commemorating the marriage of Sir Richard Cust to Anne Brownlow in 1717, by which Belton came to the Custs. Their eldest son John was the Speaker of the House of Commons who acquired the superb silver dining plate at Belton.

The famous Belton silver has a strong heraldic interest. In addition to the Brownlow and Cust arms, some of the pieces, such as the silver gilt candelabra by Paul Storr in the Hondecoeter Room, have the Egerton crest. Other pieces have the royal arms, notably Speaker Cust's great silver wine cistern with its lion and unicorn handles derived from the royal supporters. An earlier set of royal arms can be found hanging on the back stairs. This very fine piece of carving is the oldest display of heraldry at Belton and shows the arms of Charles I. It probably comes from the church where, no doubt, it was placed in 1638 when Richard, the Prothonotary, carried out alterations and rebuilt the tower after he purchased the Belton estate.

The church, though not the property of the National Trust, is accessible from the garden and contains a tremendous display of Brownlow and Cust heraldry in the serried tombs, memorials and hatchments of successive generations of the family. Harry Cust quipped that the church seemed dedicated 'to the glory of the Cust family and the memory of God'. There are forty monuments and an armorial window dated 1823 which is almost certainly by Thomas Willement (d.1871), 'heraldic artist' to George IV, who was also responsible for the interiors of Charlecote (q.v.).

BENINGBROUGH HALL

YORKSHIRE

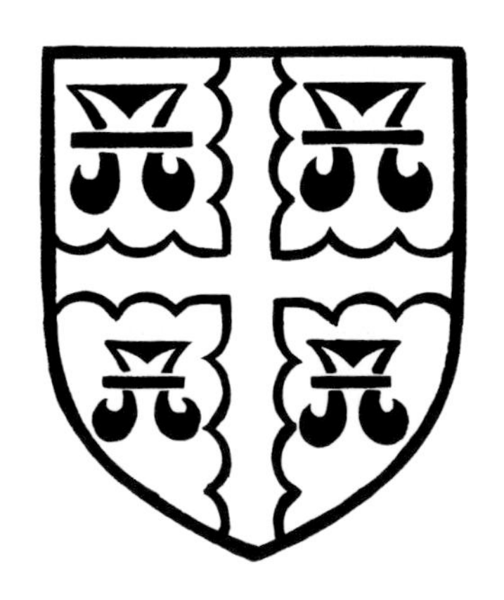

BOURCHIER

ARMS: Argent a Cross engrailed Gules between four Water Bougets Sable

CREST: On a Wreath Or and Vert An Old Man's Head couped at the shoulders habited Vert collared Or the beard and hair proper on his head a crest Coronet Or issuing therefrom a long pointed Cap Gules ending in a tassel hanging forward Or

BADGE: A Bourchier Knot Or

The Bourchiers of Beningbrough were descended from James, the bastard son of John, 2nd Lord Berners by Elizabeth Bacon. He married Mary Banester, heiress of the Beningbrough estate. Though illegitimate, James Bourchier was a blood-line descendant of one of the greatest late medieval families, Counts of Eu in Normandy

RIGHT: *The impaled arms of Bourchier and Bellwood with the crest of Bourchier over the garden door at Beningbrough.*

and Earls of Essex and Bath, Barons Bourchier, Fitzwarine and Berners in England, while in the female line through Anne Countess of Stafford, he could claim a Plantagenet descent from Edward III.

Later generations, however, intermarried almost solely amongst the middling rank of gentry, and all the glory was firmly in the past by the time that John Bourchier and his wife, Mary Bellwood, built the present house under the supervision of William Thornton of York in the opening years of the eighteenth century. It is an English baroque masterpiece with brick and stone façades based on engravings of Roman *palazzi*, while the interior is noted for his virtuoso wood carving. With one notable exception, however, the deployment of heraldry is conventional. Over the garden door is a magnificent carved cartouche on the keystone with the Bourchier arms impaling Bellwood. The arms of Bellwood, although often blazoned *Gules 3 Caltraps Argent*, are always depicted as *Gules 3 double Cronels Argent*. The head of the door above the main entrance is carved with the Bourchier knot.

BELOW: *A detail of a sixteenth-century panel at Beningbrough showing the initials of Sir Ralph Bourchier (d.1598) on either side of the Bourchier knot badge.*

The exception is the wonderful staircase, a *tour de force* of early eighteenth-century joinery. Both the half landings have fine displays of marquetry, inlaid with the impaled arms of John Bourchier and Mary Bellwood, and delightfully sinuous versions of the Bourchier knot, the family badge which recalled their medieval, albeit illegitimate, descent. Interestingly, this marquetry decoration repeated an idea from the Elizabethan house on the site, some of the panelling of which was inlaid with the initials of Sir Ralph Bourchier (d.1598) and the Bourchier knot; one of these old panels is preserved on the upper landing of the Great Staircase.

In the nineteenth century Beningbrough was inherited by the Dawnay family. Their arms (impaled with Grey) can be found incorporated in the design of the Victorian wrought iron gates in front of the house and in the garden. In 1917 the property was acquired by the 10th Earl and Countess of Chesterfield who brought with them some of the splendid seventeenth-century furniture from Holme Lacy in Herefordshire. In the Hall is a mid-eighteenth-century high-backed chair with the later quartered arms of the Earl of Chesterfield's grandfather, Sir Edwyn Scudamore-Stanhope, 2nd Bt., impaling those of his wife, Mary Dowell (whom he married in 1820), and supporters. The state bed in the Blue Bedroom has a baron's coronet.

Blickling Hall

NORFOLK

Hobart

Arms: Sable an Estoile of six rays Or between two Flaunches Ermine

Crest: On a Wreath of the Colours (Or and Sable) A Bull statant per pale Sable and Gules both bezanty armed and in the nose a ring Or

Supporters: (Dexter) A Buck reguardant proper attired and gorged with a radiant collar and a cordon passing between the forelegs and reflexed over the back Or; (Sinister) A Talbot reguardant proper langued Gules with the like collar and cordon

Motto: *Auctor Pretiosa Facit* [The giver makes them valuable]

Like so many English families, the Hobarts who created the present Blickling owed their rise in the world to successful lawyer-ancestors. They came originally from Suffolk and had been lawyers for a century before Henry Hobart became Lord Chief Justice of the Common Pleas in the reign of James I, and one of the baronets created on 22 May 1611 when the hereditary dignity of baronet was instituted by James I. The earliest Hobart lawyer of note was Sir James (d.1517), who was Henry VII's Attorney General. He is depicted in an interesting, probably seventeenth-century, ancestor portrait over the Great Staircase, which shows Sir James and his second wife, he in a tabard, she in a cloak, made up of their respective heraldry. In the centre are shields of the Hobart arms and the royal arms of Henry VII. It is reputed to be a copy of a lost stained glass memorial window in Loddon church.

The Lord Chief Justice and 1st Baronet bought Blickling in 1616 from Robert Clere who like others in the sixteenth century, with its galloping inflation, had come a financial cropper. Upon completing the purchase of the estate, Sir Henry Hobart began the existing Blickling Hall to the design of Robert Lyminge, the architect of Hatfield House. It was completed after Sir Henry's death in 1625 by his son John, 2nd Bt. In 1746 their direct descendant, Sir John Hobart, 5th Bt., who had been elevated to the peerage as Baron Hobart of Blickling in 1728, was created 1st Earl of Buckinghamshire

The carved stone heraldic decoration over the Entrance Front at Blickling showing in the centre the quartered arms of (1 & 4) Hobart (2) Lyhart and (3) Hare with the badge of the baronetage and a bull's head crest on the helm. On either side sejant erect heraldic bulls hold cartouches of impaled arms.

by George II. The Buckinghamshire peerage is commemorated in the name of the pub at Blickling, the Buckinghamshire Arms; it has a modern painted signboard with the full achievement, including supporters and earl's coronet and the motto *Auctor Pretiosa Facit*. The elevation was due to the influence of the 1st Earl's sister, Henrietta Countess of Suffolk, who was the King's mistress and one of the brightest spirits of the day – a friend of Walpole, Pope, Swift, Burlington and everybody amusing or clever.

Sir Henry Hobart, the Lord Chief Justice, like many Elizabethan and Jacobean 'new men' indulged in a grand display of heraldry in his new house to emphasise the respectability of his family, and to an unusual degree used his heraldic emblems in an incorrect manner. A positive armorial fanfare greets the visitor to Blickling. The bridge leading to the front door is flanked by sejant erect Hobart bulls holding heraldic cartouches. Shields of the quartered impaled arms of Hobart and Bell, representing the builder, Sir Henry Hobart, 1st Bt., and Hobart and Sydney for his son, Sir John, 2nd Bt., plus a large central shield of the quartered Hobart arms and the Hobart bull's head crest and motto contribute a rich top-frill to the front door. The Lord Chief Justice married the daughter of Sir Robert Bell, Chief Baron of the Exchequer, while his son added an aristocratic tone to the family by marrying the daughter of Robert Sydney, Earl of Leicester, for his first wife and Frances Egerton, daughter of the Earl of Bridgwater (q.v. Tatton Park), for his second. These shields are accompanied by two more sejant bulls. The Hobart bull appears everywhere at Blickling in a variety of forms, but rarely in the correct form of the crest. It can be seen, together with the estoile of the Hobart arms, on the lead side flaps of the seventeenth-century rainwater pipes on the Entrance Front, in the Courtyard and on the Garden Front. It appears on the gilded weather vane of the central cupola, and over the front door in the Courtyard, looking very realistic and fierce with a ring in its nose.

The interiors which survive from the Lord Chief Justice's time likewise bristle with armorial achievements and bull crests, notably the ceiling of the magnificent Long Gallery. The wonderfully elaborate moulded plaster by Edward Stanyon contains no fewer than five large central panels of the quartered arms of Sir Henry, with the baronet's badge (the red hand of Ulster) on an escutcheon, the statant bull, and the motto *Quae Supra*. The contemporary plaster frieze incorporates a bull's head crest, the statant bull and the estoile. The heraldry in the Long Gallery is continued in the richly tinted arms of the Marquess of Lothian's family: Jedburgh, Ancram, Lothian, Hobart and Britiffe, which fill the five upper panels of the large mullion and transom window at the north end. These are very high quality Victorian work and were designed by Hungerford Pollen in 1861 as part of his redecoration of the Gallery for the 7th Marquess of Lothian, who inherited Blickling through his mother, Henrietta, eldest daughter of the 2nd Earl of Buckinghamshire. They were made by Powells of Whitefriars, and from the artistic point of view, this is among the finest heraldic glass of its date in England. Pollen also designed the fireback in this room with the Lothian arms (1&4 *Azure a Sun in Splendour proper*; 2&3 *Gules on a Chevron Argent three Mullets Gules*) and steel firedogs topped by Lothian suns. The books themselves form one of the best libraries in any National Trust house. Many of the volumes are illustrated with heraldry, including a 1485 edition of Suetonius's *Lives of the Twelve Caesars* which has the arms of the d'Este family.

The Jacobean plaster ceiling in the nearby South Drawing Room (originally the Great Chamber) is also decorated with two different bull's head crests, statant bull and the estoile. The iron fireback in this room has the royal arms of Elizabeth I with unusual supporters. In the Dining Room on the ground floor the carved wooden overmantel, dated 1627, has two shields of arms. That on the left is Hobart quartered, for the 2nd baronet who completed the house after the death of his father, while on the right-hand side is Bell for his mother, with their respective family crests.

Later heraldry at Blickling is a testament to the career of the 2nd Earl of Buckinghamshire who was the most eminent of the Hobarts. Due, no doubt, to the influence of his aunt, he served at Court as Comptroller of the Household and a Lord of the Bedchamber to George II and George III. In 1762 he was appointed Ambassador to St Petersburg, and from 1776 to 1780 he was Lord-Lieutenant of Ireland. With the architects Thomas and William Ivory, he remodelled the house, keeping its Jacobean exterior and extending the Jacobean staircase sympathetically but providing some

OPPOSITE: *The quartered arms of (1&4) Hobart (2) Lyhart and (3) Hare with a bull's head crest and the motto* Quae Supra *in plaster on the ceiling of the Long Gallery at Blickling.*

QVÆ
SVPRA

The painted and quartered arms of Hobart and Bell for Sir Henry Hobart, 1st Bt. (d.1625), and his wife, Dorothy Bell, on the Dining Room overmantel, dated 1627, at Blickling.

up-to-date neo-classical interiors. The alteration of the Staircase Hall is signed by the moulded plaster statant bull in the middle of the ceiling, and in the Tapestry Room the statant bull appears in the carved rococo entablatures over the three doors inserted in the eighteenth century.

The new classical rooms included the Peter the Great Room, designed to house a large tapestry presented to Lord Buckinghamshire by the Empress Catherine the Great while he was ambassador in Russia. In the border is a rare display of Russian heraldry. The imperial arms with a double-headed eagle appear in the middle at the top while round the sides are shields of arms of Russian noble families. Russia had no indigenous heraldry of its own and Peter the Great introduced it wholesale as part of the modernisation of his empire, ordering his nobles to adopt shields with symbols.

This room is also embellished with a fine set of three large gilt-framed looking glasses in the Adam taste provided by Solomon Hudson of London in 1779. They are surmounted by the full achievement of Lord Buckinghamshire's arms with supporters and an earl's coronet. An earl's coronet and the Hobart arms can also be seen moulded in plaster in the central oval of the ceiling.

The State Bedroom was also designed in 1779 (on the site of the Jacobean chapel) to house a magnificent crimson-upholstered bed. It is made up of a cloth of state issued to the 2nd Earl in 1763 as ambassador. The back cloth is filled with a lively embroidery of the arms of George III including the tierced arms of Hanover in the fourth quarter.

The back cloth of the bed in the Chinese Bedroom at Blickling shows the impaled arms of Hobart and Conolly with supporters for the 2nd Earl of Buckinghamshire and his second wife, Caroline Connolly, who married in 1770.

The bedcover is embroidered with the post-1707 arms of Queen Anne who until the Act of Union had borne the traditional Stuart arms of Great Britain – (1&4) France and England, (2) Scotland and (3) Ireland. This bed at Blickling is the only place in a National Trust house where the Stuart and Hanoverian royal arms can be compared in such close juxtaposition. The valance of the bed is embroidered with the crowned rose, crowned thistle, crowned fleur de lys and crowned harp, and the English and Scottish royal crests.

The bed in the Chinese Room is an even more extravagant heraldic piece. The back cloth is embroidered with the full impaled arms of the 2nd Earl of Buckinghamshire and his second wife, Caroline Conolly. The valence is made up of Norwich shawl material, embroidered with the arms of Conolly and other families. This embroidery is an excellent example of the delicate, elegant depiction of heraldry in the eighteenth century and makes an instructive contrast with the bold, masculine stained glass in the Long Gallery.

A rare example of medieval heraldry, unconnected with the Hobarts, can be seen in the Brown Drawing Room. The carved stone Gothic chimneypiece was brought from Caistor Castle near Lowestoft. This was built in the fifteenth century by Sir John Fastolfe who had made his fortune fighting in France during the Hundred Years War. In the spandrels are carved a shield of the Fastolf arms impaling Tibetot and the Fastolfe panache crest.

Buckland Abbey

DEVON

Drake

Arms: Sable a Fess wavy between two Estoiles Argent

Crest: On a Wreath of the Colours (Argent and Sable) On a Terrestrial Globe a Ship proper trained about the said Globe with hawsers Or by a Hand issuing out of Clouds on the dexter all proper and on an Escroll this Motto *Auxilio Divino* [By divine aid]

Motto: *Sic Parvis Magna* [Thus great things arise from small]

Fuller-Eliott-Drake

Arms, Quarterly: (1&4 Drake) Sable a Fess wavy between two Estoiles Argent; (2 Eliott) Gules on a Bend Or a Baton Azure on a Chief the arms of Gibraltar (Azure between two Pillars a Castle Argent from the Gate a Golden Key pendent subinscribed *Plus Ultra* [More beyond]); (3 Fuller) Argent three Bars and a Canton Gules

Crests: (1 Drake) On a Wreath of the Colours (Argent and Sable) On a Terrestrial Globe a Ship proper trained about the said Globe with hawsers by a Hand issuing out of Clouds on the dexter all proper and on an Escroll this Motto *Auxilio Divino*

(2 Eliott) On a Wreath of the Colours (Argent and Gules) A dexter Hand in armour couped above the wrist proper grasping a Scymitar Argent pommel and hilt Or the wrist charged with a Key Sable (3 Fuller) Out of a Crest Coronet Gules A Lion's Head Argent charged with a Crescent Azure

Buckland was a Cistercian abbey in the Middle Ages, a daughter house of Quarr on the Isle of Wight. After the Dissolution Henry VIII sold the abbey and part of its estate to Sir Richard Grenville in 1541. In most abbeys which were converted to houses in the sixteenth century, the church was demolished and the domestic buildings adapted. The Grenvilles at Buckland did the opposite, sweeping away the conventual buildings and carving the house out of the church itself by inserting floors and adding a new kitchen wing. The Grenville work is commemorated in the so-called Drake Chamber where the spandrels of the fireplace are carved with their badge of a clarion derived from their arms.

In 1581 Buckland was purchased by Sir Francis Drake and the estate belonged to descendants of his family down to the twentieth century. Drake's origins are obscure; he claimed an unproved connection with the Drakes of Ash near Axminster, an older

The full achievement of Sir Francis Drake's arms on his drum at Buckland Abbey, showing arms, crest, helm, mantling and motto.

established Devon family, but when he improperly quartered their arms with his own, Sir Bernard Drake of Ash reputedly gave Sir Francis a box on the ear, according to John Prince in *The Worthies of Devon* (1701).

Sir Francis made his fortune in the late 1570s by his great voyage round the world. He was knighted by Elizabeth I and received a grant of arms on his return in June 1581 in recognition of his achievement in being the first Englishman to circumnavigate the globe. His feat is reflected in the arms; the estoiles represent the Arctic and Antarctic pole stars, and the fess wavy signifies the oceans of the world. 'This Knight for his special merit toward his Country, both well deserved to beare in a feeld ... a fesse wayvee between two starres Artick and Antiartick ...' as John Ferne put it in his *Blazon of Gentrie* (1586). The arms can still be seen in various places at Buckland. The three-light Gothic window on the staircase was embellished with engraved glass by Simon Whistler in 1988 to commemorate the 400th anniversary of the defeat of the Spanish Armada, and the central pane contains Drake's arms. There is a set of colourful Festival of Britain murals of the Armada in the Pym Gallery, painted by Roland Pym in 1951, which depict the arms of Sir Francis Drake, Elizabeth I and Lord Howard of Effingham.

An early depiction of Sir Francis Drake's arms can be seen moulded in plaster in the principal panel over the chimneypiece of the Tower Room, and on his portrait by Marcus Gheeraerts the Younger in the Drawing Room in the West Wing. The Tower Room chimneypiece also has smaller shields on the sides of the arms of Drake of Ash quartering Drake and Gregorie (for the wife of Sir Francis's brother Thomas) together with an imaginary coat of arms showing a drake swimming.

The most evocative object at Buckland is Drake's drum, painted with his arms and crest. Drake's crest is interesting as it is an early example of 'bad' heraldry of the type usually associated with the Georgians. The need for a crest to be a three-dimensional object which (in theory) could be worn on top of a helmet has been forgotten. The hand appearing out of the clouds holding a golden hawser, tied to a galleon like a dog on a lead, could not easily be attached to a helmet in three dimensions. The ship perched on top of a globe, however, is a graphic memorial of Drake's great achievement in sailing round the world.

Just as rare as the drum are the set of six Elizabethan regimental colours used by Drake's regiment, his own, as colonel, bearing his estoile. The pair of well preserved standards with the royal arms may have been flown at the Royal Dockyard in Deptford when Drake was knighted by Elizabeth I on 4 April 1581.

Castle Drogo

DEVON

DREWE

ARMS: Ermine a Lion passant per pale Gules and Or in chief three Ears of Wheat stalked and bladed of the last (i.e. Or)

CREST: On a Wreath of the Colours (Argent and Gules) In front of a Bull's Head Sable gorged with a collar gemel and holding in the mouth three Ears of Wheat a Garb fesswise all Or

MOTTO: *Drogo Nomen et Virtus Arma Dedit* [Drogo is my name and valour gave me arms]

Julius Drewe, the son of a clergyman, founded Home & Colonial Stores in 1878 to buy goods more cheaply direct from their country of origin and sell them at a profit. In only six years he had made a large fortune, and was able to retire at the age of thirty-three to set himself up as a country gentleman in Kent and Sussex. By 1900 he had entered the pages of Burke's *Landed Gentry*. His elder brother, William, a barrister of the Inner Temple, had a romantic interest in genealogy and produced a Drewe family tree showing a descent from Drogo or Dru, a Norman knight whose family gave their name to Drewsteignton in Devon.

William's genealogy inspired Julius to buy an estate there by 1910 and to build a castle on the site. Such interest in legendary ancestry was similar to that of many of the new landowners of the Tudor period. In Julius Drewe's case, however, it provided the cue for the creation of a masterpiece by Edwin Lutyens at Castle Drogo which is one of the most original houses of the twentieth century. The Entrance Front has a

ABOVE LEFT: *A lion passant derived from the arms of Drewe over the Entrance Front of Castle Drogo.*

ABOVE RIGHT: *Two lions passant taken from the arms of Drewe on the front door latch at Castle Drogo.*

magnificent display of Drewe heraldry, but like all Lutyens' architectural detail, it is abstracted and subsumed in the overall, organic design. The result is remarkably impressive. Over the front entrance is a large rectangular panel, larger than the door itself, containing the medieval Drewe lion but without a field of Ermine spots. Lutyens took infinite trouble over the precise design of 'Mr Drewe's Lion', providing full-scale drawings to guide the carver, Herbert Palliser.

The low relief is admirably suited to the massive Devon granite from which the castle is built and shares the same illusory simplicity. Beneath the lion is inscribed the Drewe motto, *Drogo Nomen et Virtus Arma Dedit*. By a stroke of Lutyens' genius however this is not written on a conventional scroll but is inscribed in Trajan lettering on the string course of the projecting tower-porch. The Drewe lion reappears, in wrought iron, on the front door latch. There is a similar latch on the back of the Library door.

Other, more conventional heraldry can be found on the collars of the lead rainwater pipes which are embossed with the bull's head and roe buck crests. Inside the house, there is a representation of the full coat of arms over a bedroom fireplace.

The largest display of heraldry is carved on the back of the pews in the Chapel. If you stand facing the pews, the arms from left to right are Drewe of Killerton; Prideaux; French; Wynard; a coat with eight quarters showing (1) Drewe of Killerton (2) Prideaux (3) French (4) Wynard (5) Hockmore (6) Folkeroy (7) Baron (8) Champernowne, which are all arms of Devonshire families, and was that of Edward Drewe of Killerton, the Serjeant at Law and Recorder of London (d.1598) and are therefore arms to which Julius Drewe would have been entitled if he had descended from Edward Drewe – a claim dropped in 1914. This coat of eight quarters appears in the alternative sketches for the panel over the front door. The single shields then continue with Hockmore, Folkeroy, Baron and Champernowne. Hockmore is the most distinct coat, with two pairs of reaping hooks resembling sickles in chief and a moorcock in base. The back row of pews on which the heraldry appears has arms forming individual seats. There are two shields per seat with the full achievement alone in the centre.

Sadly, in the light of all this dynastic feeling, the Drewes' eldest son, Adrian, was killed in the First World War at the Battle of Ypres in 1917, aged twenty-six. His room at Castle Drogo is preserved as a shrine to his memory. It contains a firescreen with the arms of Eton College and the arms also appear on a great many school photographs in the room.

Charlecote Park

WARWICKSHIRE

Lucy

Arms: Gules semé of Cross Crosslets three Lucies haurient Argent

Crest: Out of a Crest Coronet Gules A Boar's Head Argent gutty Sable between two Wings displayed also Sable billetty Or

Badge: A Lucy haurient Argent

Motto: *By trwt be Delegence*
Semper Melita Virtus [Virtue is always sweet]
By Trwthe And Diligence

Charlecote is a particularly fine example of heraldic display with interesting armorial decoration from both the Elizabethan and the Victorian periods, the Lucy family and their descendants having been obsessed by their lineage and heraldry for centuries. The fact that their arms were charged with pike or luces, a pun on the family name, helped to give their heraldry a decorative quality and an exceptionally personal character which appealed to successive generations.

The visitor is immediately greeted by the Lucy crest on top of the nineteenth-century gateposts at the entrance and then by the richly coloured Jacobean panel of impaled and quartered arms over the archway of the Gatehouse. The latter depicts the arms of Sir Thomas Lucy III (d.1640) and his wife Alice, daughter of Thomas Spencer of Claverdon. This Sir Thomas inherited Charlecote in 1605. If the heraldry is contemporary with the building it confirms the tradition that the Gatehouse is Jacobean and later than the main house, which was built by Sir Thomas Lucy I between 1551 and 1558. This is a good example of how heraldry can be brought to the aid of historians to date buildings.

The heraldic display continues on the outside of the house: the boar's head crest is embossed on the lead rainwater hoppers, and the gilded vanes on the turrets display three luces (pike) interlaced between cross crosslets. Such gilded vanes representing small banners were a medieval convention, probably of French derivation. In the late Middle Ages, their display on a house was considered to be one of the distinguishing marks of nobility.

At Charlecote, however, they form part of the amazing nineteenth-century decoration of the house by George Hammond Lucy and his wife Mary Elizabeth Williams who employed the architect Charles Smith (a pupil of Jeffry Wyatville) and the heraldic artist and designer Thomas Willement (q.v. Belton) to advise on the work. The main Lucy line had died out with George Lucy in 1786, and the estate was then inherited by his cousin, the Rev. John Hammond, who took the name and arms of Lucy. His son George Hammond Lucy and his wife Mary were responsible for Charlecote as it is today – an early nineteenth-century revival of the age of Shakespeare and Good Queen Bess.

The Entrance Porch survives from the Elizabethan house. Over the front door is a carved panel of the royal arms of Elizabeth I. On the parapet are two figure of bears squatting upright on their haunches and holding tall staves. These are the badge of the Dudleys, Earls of Leicester, and by family tradition they are supposed to have been put up in honour of Robert Dudley, the Queen's favourite. He knighted Sir Thomas Lucy I, deputising for Elizabeth I at Charlecote in 1565, so the bears are a discreet reference to this notable occasion in the history of the Lucys.

The Great Hall continues the combination of Elizabethan and nineteenth-century heraldic decoration which is such a distinctive and fascinating feature of Charlecote. The stained glass in the windows is of outstanding importance. It is dated 1558 and depicts the family genealogy from the early Middle Ages up to that date in the form of the impaled arms of successive heads of the family and their wives. It was commissioned by Thomas Lucy I and made by a German from Osnabruck, Nicholas Eyffeler (q.v. Baddesley Clinton), who had settled in London. Sir Thomas, like all the Lucys, was very proud of his medieval heraldry and would always remark of his arms 'and a very old coat too'. This was an aspect of his character which Shakespeare caricatured in Justice Shallow, also making great play on old pike (luces). The stained glass was restored and extended for the Hammond Lucys by Thomas Willement, who also extended the sequence in the windows of the new Dining Room and Library which they built onto the West Front.

Lucy
CAMPBELL
CAMERON
FASSIFERN
GLENCOE
ERSKINE
LOCHNELL
ACHALADER
CAMPBELL BARCALDINE
GORDON
LOCHIEL
DAVENPORT
MACLEAN of DOWART
LENNOX
GLENORCHY
SPENSER
MAINWARING
ARGYLL
HUGFORD
STEWART
BRUCE
ERLES of Chester
SAXON EARLS
KINGS of FRANCE
EARLS of FLANDERS
MESCHINES
AMOR OMNIA VINCIT
LOVE
TIME AND DEATH
LIFE
Call it not ill done to strive to lay The ghosts that crowd about life's empty day Then let the others go! And if indeed, In some old garden thou and I have wrought And made fresh flowers to grow from hoarded seed, And fragrance of old days & deeds have brought Back to folk weary, All was not for nought.

A display of family heraldry in the Hall is the series of shields in the top of the panelled dado depicting all the major quarterings inherited by the Lucys through the centuries. These were painted by the present Sir Edmund Fairfax Lucy's aunts Joyce and Linda and his grandmother Ada with help from Miss E. M. Hinckley, an amateur genealogist. The shields were derived from the 'Lucy Pedigree Book' in the Library at Charlecote. This is a splendid affair illuminated on vellum in 1836 under the direction of Francis Martin, Windsor Herald, and George Rogers-Harrison, Bluemantle Pursuivant. It traces the family tree from the Norman de Montforts, Earls of Leicester, via Thurstane de Charlecote who was given Charlecote by Henry de Montfort in the twelfth century. Thurstane's great-grandson Sir William, who inherited Charlecote in 1247, was the first of the family to adopt the name of Lucy. The Pedigree Book was compiled at a time when the squire of Charlecote was even more obsessed with his lineage than usual, in the hope of claiming the abeyant medieval barony of Lucy. Although this failed to materialise, the research produced a rich field for the redecoration of Charlecote in the nineteenth century.

An heraldic detail to note, though not directly connected with the Lucys, is on the *pietra dura* table from Fonthill in the centre of the Hall. The frame, designed by William Beckford himself, is embellished with the cross patonce from Beckford's second crest (granted in 1798). Beckford, whose paternal ancestry from Jamaican slave owners was relatively parvenu, took great pride in his distinguished maternal ancestry, and recorded a scheme of thirty quarterings at the College of Arms in 1808 which formed the basis for a rich heraldic overlay at Fonthill Abbey in Wiltshire, his eccentric Gothick house, designed by James Wyatt.

Another heraldic detail of some interest can be found in the large late seventeenth-century painting of Charlecote from the west which hangs on the fireplace wall. On the Gatehouse can be seen a hatchment. As it was the tradition to hang a hatchment with the arms of the deceased over the entrance to his house for a year after death, this would seem to date this picture to 1690, the year that Col. George Lucy died, another example of how heraldry can help to date things.

The Dining Room and Library which were added to Smith's design for the Hammond Lucys between 1829 and 1834 are remarkable examples of early nineteenth-century revivalism. Here is Willement's continuation of the Hall's heraldic stained glass in the upper lights of the mullion and transom windows. Their design is based on the Elizabethan originals, but their colours immediately mark them out as products of the early nineteenth century. Thomas Willement (d.1871) was a key figure in the nineteenth-century revival of heraldic decoration, foreshadowing the work of A.W. N. Pugin. He was a prolific writer as well as a designer of stained glass. A Victorian obiturist commented: 'to him modern glass-painters are to a considerable extent indebted for the revival of their art'.

Not that Willement's genius for heraldic design was confined to stained glass, as the carpets in the Dining Room and Library at Charlecote demonstrate. They were devised by Willement and sport an overall pattern of luces and cross crosslets. Over the Library fireplace the carved overmantel displays the Lucy arms impaled with Hammond and Williams. The firedogs and even the iron doorstops sport the winged boar's head crest.

The heraldic pedigree of Lucy in the form of an oak tree painted on deerskin by Constance Linda (1867-1955) and Joyce Alianore (1871-1948), daughters of Henry Spencer Lucy.

The Library at Charlecote showing the carpet designed by Thomas Willement. The impaled arms of Lucy and Williams on the chimneypiece are for George Hammond Lucy and his wife, Mary Elizabeth Williams (married 1823).

Charlecote is saturated with heraldry: blotters, firescreens, stair newels, fireplace tiles, all bristle and glow with luces, cross crosslets, winged boars' heads and the family mottoes. Nor does the almost obsessive armorial display end there. The visitor should not miss the Lucys' travelling coach in the stables. It was built *c.*1840, and the interior has wonderful heraldic upholstery as well as the arms painted in the usual manner on the outside of the doors. Also not to be missed is the unique family tree, painted on deerskin, which is exhibited in the museum in the Gatehouse.

Chastleton

OXFORDSHIRE

Jones

Arms: Gules a Lion rampant within a Bordure indented Or with a Crescent Sable on a Mullet Or in dexter chief for difference

Crest: On a Wreath of the Colours (Or and Gules) A demi Lion rampant Or armed and langued Azure holding a Mullet Gules

Whitmore-Jones

Arms, Quarterly: (1&4 Jones) Gules a Lion rampant within a Bordure indented Or and for distinction a Canton Ermine; (2&3 Whitmore) Vert fretty Or

Crests: (1 Jones) On a Wreath of the Colours (Or and Gules) A demi Lion rampant Or holding between the paws a Mullet Gules and for distinction charged on the body with a Fret Gules

(2 Whitmore) On a Wreath of the Colours (Or and Vert) A Falcon standing on the stump of a tree with a branch springing from the dexter side all proper

The house was built between 1607 and 1612 by Walter Jones, a lawyer of Welsh descent who had been M.P. for Worcester and had bought the Chastleton estate in 1602. He was the son of Henry Jones of Witney who had made the family fortune as a wool merchant in the sixteenth century. Many Welsh families had come to England to seek their fortune in the wake of the Tudors, of whom the Cecils were the most prominent. Walter Jones's social success was completed when his children married into old established local gentry families, and these alliances provided grist for the scheme of heraldic decoration in the carved chimneypieces and decorative plasterwork at Chastleton, as well as his own brand new arms. A rare copy from the College records confirming the Jones arms made at the 1634 Visitation of Oxfordshire hangs on the Hall screen. Also hanging in the bay window in the Hall at Chastleton is a seventeenth-century hatchment. Now much restored and repainted, it is that of Henry Jones I (son of Walter) who died in 1659 – a rare survival of an early hatchment. The Jones arms are impaled with Fettiplace for his wife, Anne Fettiplace.

The Great Chamber on the first floor is the most elaborately decorated room in the house with a splendid plaster ceiling and richly carved panelling incorporating the Tudor royal badge of a crowned rose – the Rose and Crown of many pub names. There is also a huge carved stone chimneypiece. It sports a proud shield of Walter Jones's arms

The carved stone chimneypiece in the Great Chamber at Chastleton with the impaled arms of Walter Jones (d.1632) and his wife, Elinor Pope.

impaling those of his wife, Elinor Pope, in the centre of the overmantel. The latter arms are those of Sir Thomas Pope of Wroxton, to whom Elinor was probably not related, as her father was Flemish (the English cloth trade had close associations with Flanders) but the display of these arms indicates Walter Jones's social ambitions.

The chimneypieces in the other principal rooms also display arms. In the Fettiplace Room, the chimneypiece heraldry, a shield of the Fettiplace arms crisply carved in wood, commemorates the marriage of Walter's son Henry to Anne Fettiplace in 1609. The moulded plaster lion and griffin on the soffit of the window in this room may also be heraldic, though they do not have crest wreaths. The arms of Jones impaling Fettiplace decorate the overmantel of the Middle Chamber as a further celebration of this welcome dynastic marriage.

The painted stone overmantel in the Sheldon Room at Chastleton showing the arms of Sheldon quartering Ruding.

The Jones family's keenness to associate with and be accepted by the older families in the area is also demonstrated in the Sheldon Room, where the painted stone overmantel bears the Sheldon arms quartering Ruding. The Sheldons were near neighbours, living at Weston over the Warwickshire border. Ralph Sheldon was a friend of Walter Jones. The sheldrakes of the Sheldon arms are also incorporated as a motif of the plaster frieze in this room, a nice decorative touch.

The great treasure of Chastleton is displayed in the Library. This is the Bible of Charles I which the doomed King is supposed to have used in his last days, after being condemned to death by Parliament, and from which William Juxon, Bishop of London, read to him before his execution in Whitehall in 1649. It descended in the Juxon family who gave it to Chastleton in the late eighteenth century. The splendid gilt leather binding has the arms of Charles I with crown and supporters, and his cypher 'CR'.

The interior of Chastleton was much titivated in the early nineteenth century. The Whitmore-Joneses aimed to enhance its 'olden tyme' atmosphere, and the Great Parlour, or Dining Room, on the ground floor was remodelled. The carved oak sideboard in the window bay in here has the Whitmore-Jones arms and the two crests: the demi lion and the falcon.

The Long Gallery which runs the full width of the top floor of the house has a beautiful Jacobean barrel-shaped plaster ceiling, the decoration of which is modelled with remarkable delicacy. When it was repaired in 1904-5, the arms of Miss Mary Whitmore-Jones (on a lozenge) and of Whitmore-Jones impaling Dickins for her nephew, Thomas Whitmore (Harris)-Jones, were added on either side of the large mullion window at the east end. It is possible that the boxwood carving of Mary Whitmore-Jones's arms, lying on a table in the Hall, is the mould for the lozenge in here.

The last private owners of Chastleton, the Clutton-Brocks, were descended from the brother of Dorothy Clutton, the wife of John Whitmore-Jones who inherited Chastleton in 1828. There is a portrait of her ancestor, John Clutton (d.1669), hanging in the Screens Passage, with the Clutton arms painted in a corner of the canvas.

The exterior of Chastleton is a splendid, sophisticated design, flanked by two tall symmetrical staircase towers. These are topped with gilded iron vanes, depicting the lion rampant of the Jones arms. The Jones arms are also the last thing that a visitor sees as he leaves, as they are carved on the back of the pediment over the gateway to the front courtyard.

Chirk Castle

DENBIGHSHIRE

MYDDELTON

ARMS, Quarterly: (1&4 Rhirid y Pothan Flaidd) Argent on a Bend Vert three Wolves' Heads erased Argent; (2&3 Rhirid Flaidd) Vert a Chevron between three Wolves' Heads erased Argent

CREST: On a Wreath of the Colours (Argent and Vert) A dexter human Hand couped proper

MOTTO: *In Veritate Triumpho* [I triumph in the truth

Chirk is one of a chain of border castles built in the late thirteenth century to maintain the conquests of Edward I in Wales. In the Middle Ages it belonged to various families beginning with the Mortimers, and after changing hands several times during the Wars of the Roses, ended up in the hands of Sir William Stanley, a supporter of the

The Cromwell Hall at Chirk with shields attached to the panelling showing the arms of the Noble and Royal Tribes of Wales.

Tudors. None of them left their heraldic mark. For much of the sixteenth century the castle was held by the Crown, but in 1595 it was purchased by the Elizabethan merchant venturer and a founder of the East India Company, Thomas Myddelton, whose descendants have lived there ever since.

The ancestry of the Myddeltons, who adopted the English surname in the fourteenth century after marriage to a Myddelton heiress from Shropshire, is lost in the mists of Celtic tradition. They claimed descent from the twelfth-century Rhirid Flaidd (the Wolf), Lord of Penllyn whose maternal grandmother Haer was granddaughter of Blaidd Rhudd or the Bloody Wolf of Gest, a township in Eifionydd, from whom Rhirid inherited his appellation of the wolf, which accounts for the wolves' heads in the arms of his descendants. The family was exceedingly proud of their wolf ancestor and heraldry. This enthusiasm was carried to extremes in the seventeenth and eighteenth centuries when successive owners kept a live wolf at the castle. Thomas Dineley's manuscript account of the Duke of Beaufort's progress through Wales in 1684 records that 'In that part of ye dry ditch of Chirke Castle marked M. Sr Richard Middelton keepeth a living wolf'. The wolf was presented to the 2nd Baronet in 1680. The 3rd and 4th Baronets continued to keep a live wolf at the castle. The 4th Baronet's was reputed to be 'perfectly tame'. Living heraldry indeed.

The 4th Baronet died unmarried; the baronetcy – created by Charles II for the son of the Civil War general Thomas Myddelton (whose Parliamentarian sympathies changed in 1651 when he came out for Charles II and the Restoration) – became extinct in 1718, and the estate passed to cousins descended from the 1st Baronet's younger brother. The estate was divided between Richard Myddelton's three daughters after the premature death of his only son in 1796. Charlotte, the eldest, inherited the castle and married Robert Biddulph of Ledbury who took her name in 1801 in addition to and before his own. Their son, Col. Robert Myddelton Biddulph, was responsible for the remodelling of the castle, by now a comfortable country house, in the 1840s and the introduction of so much of heraldic interest. This last major phase of work was executed under the direction of A.W.N. Pugin by the decorator J.G. Crace.

Chirk is the only example in National Trust hands of the work of Pugin himself, the master of the Victorian heraldic revival. Pugin, for instance, inserted the carved stone achievement of the Myddelton Biddulph arms over the castle gateway, commemorating the 1840s gothicisation. Inside, the Cromwell Hall is a complete example of Pugin's work – replacing an incongruous Georgian room. The characteristic medievalising stone chimneypiece has the arms of Col. Robert Myddelton Biddulph and his wife, Fanny Mostyn-Owen, not impaled, but as two separate shields. The oak screen has the Myddelton motto *In Veritate Triumpho* and the Biddulph motto *Sublimiora Petamus* [Let us seek higher things]. Pugin was also responsible for the heraldic stained glass in the upper lights of the windows which include the arms of Mortimer and the colourful shields attached to the panelling, possibly copied from the Tribes Room at Erddig (q.v.) as they show the arms of the Noble and Royal Tribes of Wales. Among the old arms and armour in the Hall are two funerary helmets, probably brought from the church, including that used at the funeral of General Thomas Myddelton.

Other objects of heraldic interest add to the antiquarian *mise en scène*, including a drum painted with the Myddelton arms, purchased in 1679 for the use of the Denbighshire militia with which the Myddeltons were closely connected, and the patent of the baronetcy granted by Charles II. The Staircase Hall, by contrast, is entirely neo-classical, having been reconstructed under the direction of Joseph Turner of Chester in 1777-8. On the landing is a set of eighteenth-century hall chairs which were used in the Georgian Entrance Hall, before Pugin altered it into the Cromwell Hall. They date from the 1770s and have the arms of Myddelton impaled with Rushout; Richard Myddelton married Elizabeth Rushout in 1761 and they modernised the castle and landscaped the park. Their arms also appear on the silver rococo cup and cover by Edward Wakelin in the Dining Room.

The late seventeenth-century Long Gallery with bold oak panelling was also altered

The wrought iron gates at Chirk of c.1715 with the arms, including the badge of the baronetage, crest and motto of Myddelton, above the gates and sejant wolves on the gate piers.

in the 1840s, probably by Pugin, when the ceiling was ornamented with a series of painted panels of the arms of the ancestors of the Myddeltons. Pugin was also responsible for the cast iron fire grates and firedogs with bronze finials and shields. The encaustic tiles in the fireplaces, made by Minton of Stoke-on-Trent in 1847–8, incorporate the Myddelton Biddulph monogram. Pugin was responsible, in association with Herbert Minton, for the revival of the lost medieval art of encaustic tile-making. The seventeenth-century silver-plated candle sconces have the Myddelton arms on their back plates.

Perhaps the most characterful room at Chirk is the Servants' Hall, furnished with a complete set of Jacobean tables and benches. The Parliament clock on the wall, made in 1763 by John Jones of Chester, has the hand crest of the Myddeltons. On brackets on either side of the fireplace are sejant greyhounds holding cartouches, which form part of a set of carved figures made in 1673 by Nicholas Needham for the earlier Great Staircase. The greyhounds possibly sat on the newel posts, like the Sackville leopards on the Jacobean staircase at Knole (q.v.).

The most magnificent heraldic display at Chirk, however, and one of the finest of its type, is not inside the castle, but on the edge of the park; it is the famous wrought iron screen and gates made by the Davies Brothers between 1712 and 1719. It was originally in front of the castle but was transferred to the New Hall entrance to the park in 1770, and moved to its present location in 1888. It is one of the most accomplished achievements of baroque ironwork. The exuberant overthrow is emblazoned with the Myddelton arms and flanked by wolves made of lead sitting on the openwork cast iron gate piers.

Clandon Park

SURREY

ONSLOW

ARMS: Argent a Fess Gules between six Cornish Choughs proper

CREST: On a Wreath of the Colours (Argent and Gules) A Falcon Sable beaked legged and belled Or preying on a Partridge lying on its back Or

SUPPORTERS: On either side a Falcon proper with bells on the legs Gold the bewits Gules

MOTTO: *Festina Lente* [On slow!]

The Onslows are another family who rose to prominence in the sixteenth century through the law. They were Roundheads in the Civil War. Arthur Onslow (d.1688), who like his father, Sir Richard Onslow (d.1664) 'the red fox of Surrey', was a Member of Parliament, was created a baronet in 1674 in reversion after the death without male issue of his father-in-law, Sir Thomas Foote, Bt. (d.1687) sometime Lord Mayor of London.

The Onslow family have produced three Speakers of the House of Commons, beginning in the reign of Elizabeth I with Richard Onslow, the 'Black Speaker', so called because of his swarthy complexion. A later Richard Onslow, a supporter of William III and known as 'Stiff Dick' from his staunchness to the Whig cause, was Speaker of the House of Commons from 1708 to 1710. He was created 1st Lord Onslow in 1716. His son Thomas was a figure in the City, who presided in 1720 over the insurance company known at the time as 'Onslow's Bubble'. He married a rich Jamaican heiress, Elizabeth Knight, and used her fortune (derived from sugar and slaves) to build the present Clandon Park, which was designed by the Italian architect Giacomo Leoni. Legend has it that she was unhappy and 'her spirit still haunts the house that her riches built.' Their only son died childless, and the title then went to a cousin, George Onslow, who had already been created 1st Lord Cranley.

George was the son of the third and best-known family Speaker, Arthur Onslow. He was Speaker for thirty-three years through five successive Parliaments under the Hanoverians, and was responsible for much of the procedure still used in the House of Commons today. His son George lacked his father's integrity and consistency, and his long political career was one of calculated opportunism, ingratiating himself with whoever was in power at the time. As a result, he was raised to an earldom in 1801.

The house designed by Leoni is a distinguished example of the early eighteenth-century transition from baroque to Palladian style. Its strongly classical architecture gave little scope for heraldic display, which is mainly confined to later alterations, accoutrements and furnishings. The most prominent display of the family arms, with

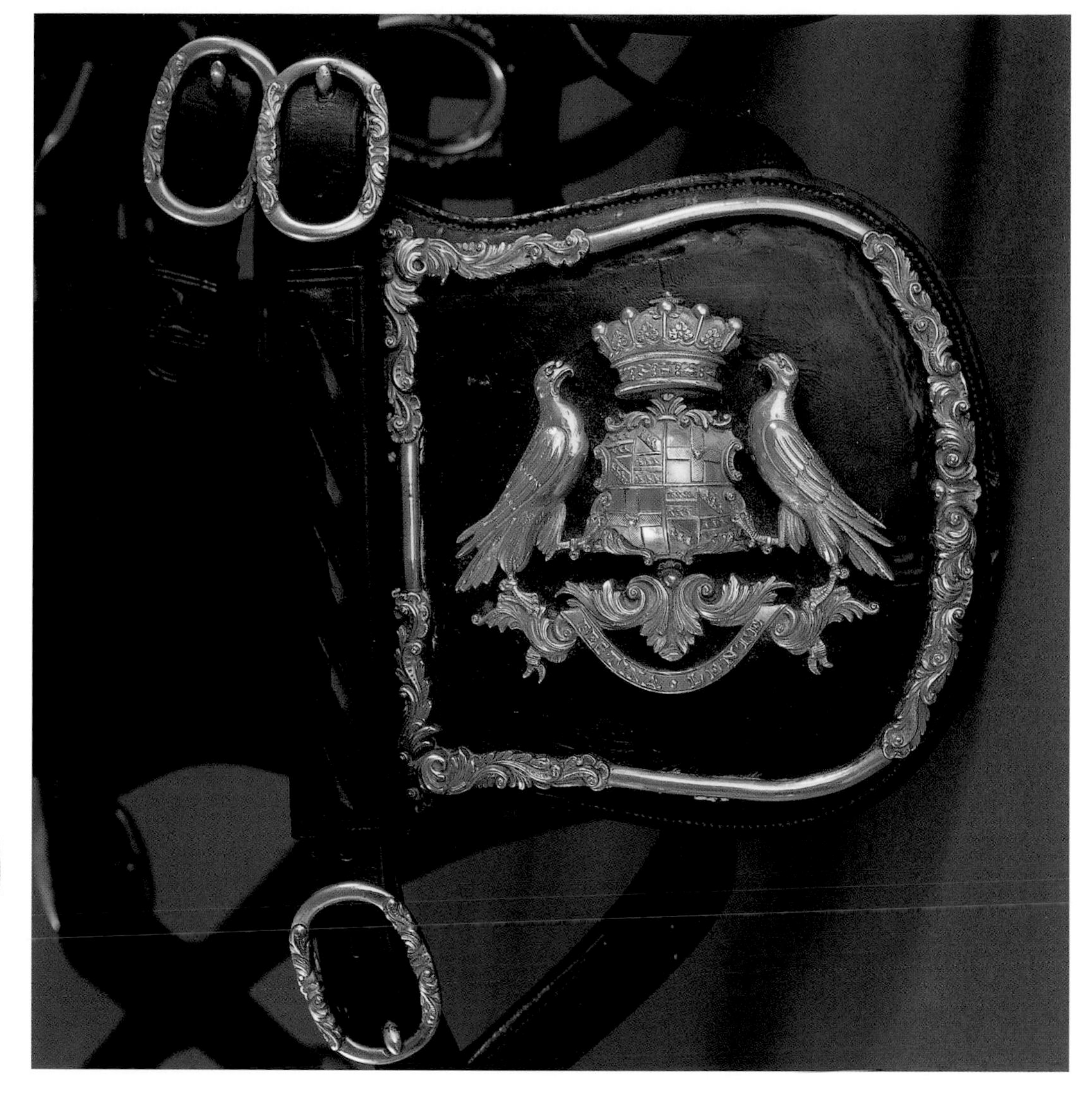

ABOVE LEFT: *An early nineteenth-century Worcester plate showing Lord Onslow's arms, crest, supporters and motto.*

ABOVE RIGHT: *A horse's harness showing the arms of 1&4 grand-quarters of Onslow and Harding 2&3 Bridges, with an earl's coronet, supporters and motto postdating the creation of the earldom in 1801.*

motto and coronet, is incorporated in the gilded ironwork of the lodge gates on the Guildford road, which were originally in front of the house. The 2nd Lord Onslow, who built the house, celebrated his rank in the plasterwork of the Hall, where a baron's coronet appears on all four sides. The hall chairs have the crest and an earl's coronet, which indicates their later date, and some heraldic banners hang above. The newels of the South Staircase's plain eighteenth-century balustrade were decorated with a Victorian carved crest of the Onslow family at the foot and a supporter holding a banner of arms on the first half-landing. These were commissioned in Florence by the 4th Earl in 1881, when he revived the house after a long period of neglect. Elsewhere in the house is a magnificent Worcester dinner service made for the 1st Earl of Onslow and painted with the arms, crest, supporters and motto. There are also some particularly fine heraldic horse trappings of about the same date. In the Onslow Room there is a fine pedigree roll drawn up for the Speaker Arthur Onslow.

Cotehele House

CORNWALL

Edgcumbe

Arms: Gules on a Bend Ermines cotised Or three Boars' Heads couped Argent

Crest: On a Wreath Or and Gules A Boar passant Argent a Chaplet about the neck of laurel and oak proper

Badge: A Boar's Head couped and erect Argent armed Or issuing from a Laurel Wreath Vert

Supporters: On either side a Greyhound Argent gutty de poix collared dovetail Gules

Motto: *Au Plaisir Fort de Dieu* [At the all-powerful disposal of God]

Cotehele is one of the most remarkable antiquarian houses in England. It belonged to the Edgcumbe family from 1353 to 1947, although after 1553, when the family moved to Mount Edgcumbe near Plymouth, it was a secondary residence, and from the seventeenth century was only occupied occasionally. During the eighteenth century a deliberate attempt to preserve and enhance the 'olden tyme' atmosphere seems to have been made; the Hall was hung with arms and antlers, and the rooms with tapestries.

George, 1st Earl of Mount Edgcumbe, was a Fellow of the Society of Antiquaries, and he in particular was responsible for the cult of the past at Cotehele, and the arrangement of the dimly-lit rooms with arms, polished oak furniture and old needlework. By the early nineteenth century Cotehele's romantic appearance attracted curious tourists, and was described by topographers and antiquarians as an untouched example of an ancient manor house.

The Edgcumbes, created Earls of Mount Edgcumbe in 1789, have a direct male-line descent from the remote Middle Ages and came originally from Devon. William de Edgcumbe married Hilaria, the daughter and heiress of William de Cotehele of Cotehele, in the mid-fourteenth century, a marriage commemorated by an impaled shield of Edgcumbe and Cotehele hanging in the central arch of the screens passage in the Hall. Perhaps the most distinguished members of the family were Sir Richard Edgcumbe (d.1489) and his son Piers. Richard fought on the winning side at Bosworth and was knighted and appointed Comptroller of the Household and a member of the Privy Council by Henry VII. His son, Sir Piers (d.1539), fought in the French Wars of Henry VIII and became a Knight of the Bath on the creation of Prince Henry as Duke of York in 1494. He built the Great Hall at Cotehele.

The house has a double courtyard plan and is part medieval and part Tudor, stoutly built of local granite. The latest addition is the north-west tower of 1620. The interior is all that could be expected in a venerable manor house. The barrel-vaulted Chapel, which dates from the fifteenth and early sixteenth centuries, retains most of its original furnishings, albeit titivated by historically conscious later owners and their clever craftsmen. Like other contemporary houses, for instance the Chapel at Ightham Mote (q.v.), there is a display of heraldic allegiance to the Tudors – the green and white glazed floor tiles are in the Tudor livery colours and the barrel ceiling has the Tudor rose badge carved on the bosses. The east window has restored stained glass of the Crucifixion with three excellent quartered shields of Edgcumbe arms. Hanging on the wall is an eighteenth-century painted panel of the tomb of Sir Richard Edgcumbe at Morlaix in France showing his arms and helm. He died in France fighting for Anne of Brittany in 1489.

Sir Piers Edgcumbe's Great Hall also has heraldic glass in the windows recording Edgcumbe marriages up to and including his first marriage to Joan Durnford, whose arms *Sable a Ram's Head affronty Argent armed Or* help to date the room to before

A painting of the tomb of Sir Richard Edgcumbe (d.1489) at Morlaix in Brittany with shields of the quartered arms of Edgcumbe and Holland (his mother) and impaled arms of Edgcumbe, and a coat for Tremayne (his wife) containing escallops rather than the usual arms of three human arms flexed at the elbow and conjoined at the shoulder.

her death in 1520. The other West Country families represented here are Holland, Tremayne, Cotterel, Raleigh, Travanion, Carew, St Maure, Courtenay and Fitzwalter. Each is shown on an impaled shield set in a Gothic quatrefoil. The bay window has the Tudor royal arms encircled by the Garter. This scheme must originally have been more extensive.

More seemingly early royal heraldry can be found in the top middle panel of the Cotehele tester from an early sixteenth-century oak bed which hangs on the staircase landing and has long been the puzzle and delight of antiquaries. Flanked by Tudor roses, the Tudor royal arms are shown with England and France (Modern) quartered, as was their form from about 1405 between the reigns of Henry IV and James I in 1603, when the Scottish and Irish arms were incorporated, but the quarterings on the shield are the wrong way round. The French arms, with the fleur de lys, should be in the first and fourth quarters and England, with three lions passant guardant should be in the second and third quarters. The supporters are a lion (dexter) and a greyhound (sinister). This raises a question. Until the reign of James I, who adopted the English lion and the Scottish unicorn still used today, the supporters of the royal arms changed, but no late medieval or Tudor monarch used the combination shown here. This may have been the product of the ignorance of the Welsh carpenter who made it.

On the landing next to the tester is another curiosity. It is a rectangular blue and white china dish. This is a replica of the Corbridge Lanx, a Roman silver tray found at Corbridge in Northumberland in 1735. At the top are the arms of the 6th Duke of Somerset (q.v. Petworth). He had married the Percy heiress and so, at the time, owned in right of his wife the area where the Lanx was found. Up the stairs, the oak door to the Old Drawing Room is carved with Tudor roses in lozenge panels, another sign of Sir Piers Edgcumbe's support for the Tudor dynasty. The Edgcumbe crest is a boar's head and it can be seen in the cut-up borders of the old tapestries which were used to decorate the Old Dining Room and adjoining Punch Room. The full family arms with supporters and baron's coronet are engraved on the Georgian pewter plates on the Hall table, and with coronet and supporters, but not the crest, on the back of the little

The 1531 Cornwall Visitation entry showing a coat of six quarters, including (1) Edgcumbe (2) Holland (3) Durnford and (5) Bigbery (College of Arms Ms: G.2/21). Sir Piers Edgcumbe (d.1539) married Joan Durnford whose paternal grandmother was a Bigbery heiress.

child's dog cart, also in the Hall. This is a charming infant version of the painting of arms on family carriages. The arms and crest also appear in the fine seventeenth-century woodcarving over the fireplace in the Hall.

The sixteenth-century manuscript volume displayed in the King Charles Room at the top of the tower is the 'Creations of Nobility' of the Kings of England from William the Conqueror to Elizabeth I, showing their arms and those of the peers they created. There are a number of similar late sixteenth- or early seventeenth-century manuscripts in other collections. The Cotehele volume belonged to John Holland in the eighteenth century and has his bookplate – designed by Hogarth – which incorporates a small heraldic shield.

Coughton Court

WARWICKSHIRE

THROCKMORTON

ARMS: Gules on a Chevron Argent three Bars gemel Sable

CRESTS: (1) On a Wreath of the Colours (Argent and Gules) A Falcon rising Argent beaked legged jessed and belled Or
(2) On a Wreath of the Colours (Argent and Gules) An Elephant's Head couped Sable eared and tusked Or

MOTTO: *Virtus Sola Nobilitas* [Virtue is the only nobility]

The heraldry at Coughton is among the most extensive displays in any English house and records the long residence here of the Throckmorton family from the Middle Ages onwards. The Throckmortons acquired Coughton by the marriage of John Throckmorton to the Spiney heiress in 1409. As well as the Spiney property they inherited the Spiney quartering through this marriage, and also (according to family tradition) adopted an elephant's head crest in addition to their own falcon crest. The Throckmorton shield has the impressive simplicity of medieval heraldry, consisting of geometrical charges only, a silver chevron with three black bars gemel.

Coughton bristles with heraldry and the architecture and decoration comprises two exceptional displays dating from the sixteenth and the early nineteenth centuries. The first includes a good series of armorial glass, recording fifteenth- and sixteenth-century Throckmorton marriages, in the Drawing Room and Saloon. This was executed *c.*1579 and was formerly at Weston Underwood in Buckinghamshire, another family house. It was brought to Coughton by Sir Charles Throckmorton (d.1840). He and his successor, Sir Robert George Throckmorton (d.1862) who married Elizabeth Acton, were both keenly interested in their family history and were largely responsible for the character of this ancient house as it is today. Lady Throckmorton and her mother, Lady Acton, were also active in the 1820s and 1830s executing the extensive heraldic needlework throughout the house, including cushions, chair covers, firescreens and curtain pelmets, which is a special feature of Coughton.

There is a particularly handsome illuminated pedigree roll at Coughton which is dated 16 May 1781. This is based on the work of Sir William Dugdale, Garter, in the seventeenth century, and traces the family back to John of Throckmorton in the thirteenth century. The Throckmortons became important in the fifteenth century. Sir John Throckmorton (who married Eleanor Spiney) was Under-Treasurer of England,

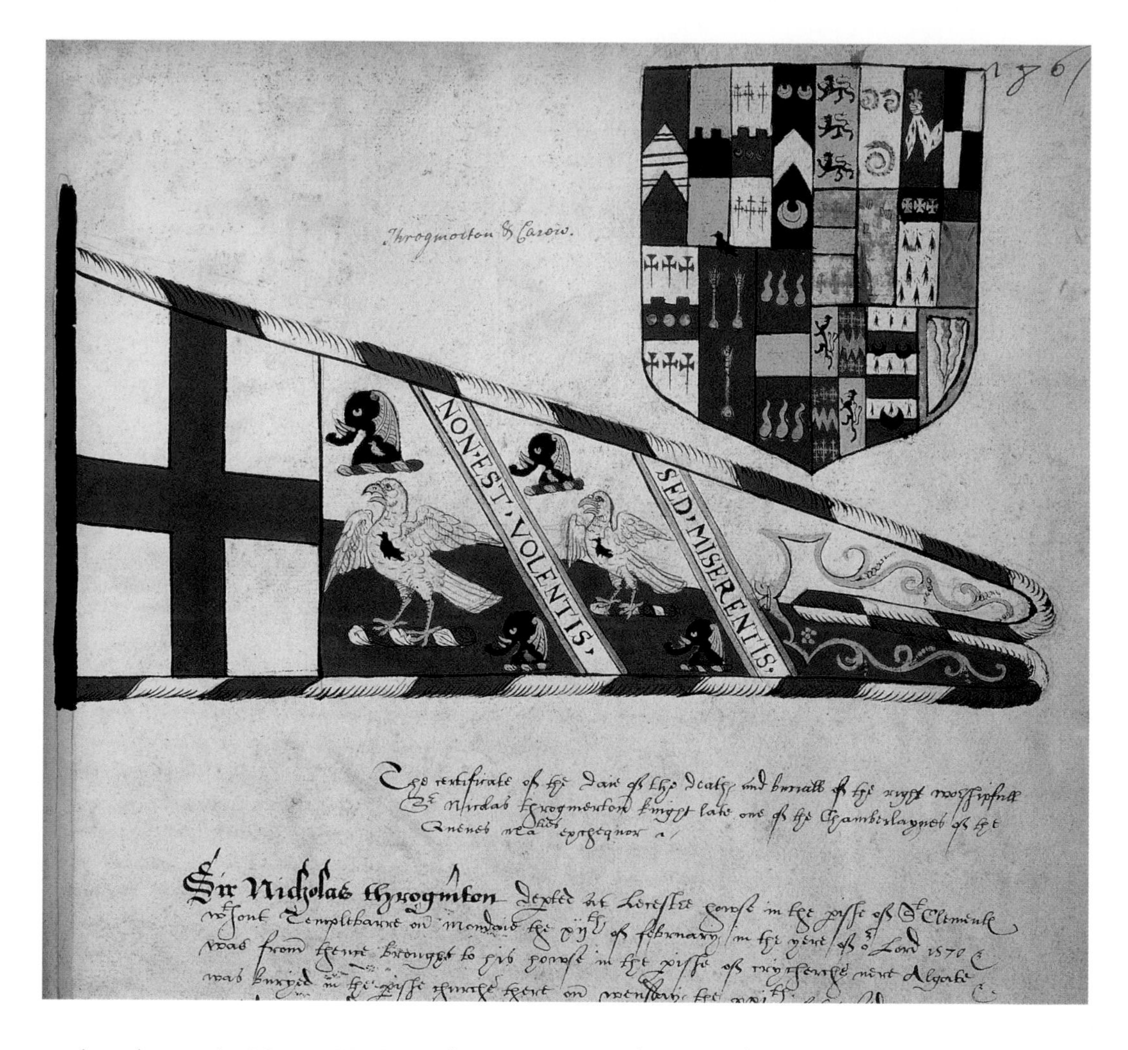

The funeral certificate of Sir Nicholas Throckmorton (d.12 Feb. 1570/1) showing the quartered and impaled arms of Throckmorton and Carew, the former differenced by a martlet, the cadency mark for a fourth son (College of Arms Ms: I.5/186).

and took part in Henry V's French campaign and it is said was present at the battle of Agincourt in 1415. His grandson was a supporter of the Tudors, fought for Henry VII and was created a member of Henry VIII's Privy Council. His son, Sir George, who died in 1553, built the great turreted Tudor gatehouse which remains the architectural centrepiece of the house today.

The Gatehouse is identical on the Entrance and Courtyard Fronts. Below the topmost window on both sides are panels of the royal arms of Henry VIII with his first supporters of a dragon and greyhound, flanked by the Beaufort portcullis and Tudor rose badges. Over the entrance arch were the quartered family arms with the elephant's head crest. Those on the entrance side fell down in 1916, but they still survive, much weathered, on the courtyard side with an array of the Throckmorton quarterings. In the spandrels of the entrance arch are impaled shields with Throckmorton quartering Spiney impaled with Vaux, and Throckmorton quartering Spiney impaled with Berkeley, for Sir George, the builder, who married Katherine (daughter of Lord Vaux of Harrowden), and his son Sir Robert, who married Muriel (daughter of Thomas, Lord Berkeley) as his first wife. As so often, the heraldic evidence helps to clarify the disputed date of a building, as the Gatehouse at Coughton must have been built before the death of Muriel Berkeley and Sir Robert's remarriage to Elizabeth Hussey.

Both Sir George and Sir Robert had a large number of children, many of whom married into other strongly Catholic Midlands families, Catesbys, Treshams, Digbys, Ardens. The Catholic sympathies of the Throckmortons were to land them in trouble; they or their relations were implicated in a series of Catholic plots against Elizabeth I and James I. Their house at Coughton was sacked in the Civil War and again at the time of the Revolution in 1688, when the Chapel was burnt down by a mob. Although they were created baronets by Charles I as a reward for their support for the Royalist cause, like most recusant families they were excluded by their religion from public life during the seventeenth and eighteenth centuries.

There is at Coughton a remarkable and unique heraldic testimony to the religious sufferings of the Throckmortons and their relations during the reign of Elizabeth I. This is a copy of the *Tabula Eliensis*, a medieval mural in the refectory at Ely Cathedral which bears the arms of the Kings and Queens of England, and those of the Abbots, Bishops and Deans of Ely. In addition to these notables, the Coughton version of the mural also has the arms of the Catholic recusants imprisoned in the Bishop's Palace at Ely, and at Banbury and Broughton Castle in Oxfordshire, during the Elizabethan persecution of Catholics. This forms a unique heraldic record of the late sixteenth-century Catholic gentry. It is dated 1596.

During the eighteenth century, Coughton fell into decay, and the family lived mainly at their other residences in Berkshire and Buckinghamshire. But a series of Acts of Parliament between 1788 and 1829 allowing Catholics and non-conformists to hold public office and attend university opened the way for a revival of the Throckmortons which is reflected in their restoration of Coughton at that time, and successive squires drew inspiration from their medieval ancestry.

Sir Charles, 7th Bt., who transferred the 1579 heraldic glass from Weston Underwood, had further panels made up in the same style to continue the family story. His successor Sir Robert George and his wife Elizabeth also added to the heraldic embellishment of the house, notably by the needlework which can be seen in almost every room. Much of this is to a consistent programme recording the descent and marriages of the Throckmortons. The Dining Room pelmet, for instance, has the arms of successive wives of Throckmortons from the fifteenth to the nineteenth century, from Abberbury to Acton. The screen in the Front Hall is an even more comprehensive record of family marriages and quarterings, and dates from about 1829.

As is so often the case with ancient manorial settlements, house and church sit side by side at Coughton, and the church, too, is redolent of family heraldry. There is a group of especially fine sixteenth-century tomb chests to successive Throckmortons: Sir George (d.1552), Sir Robert (d.1581) and Sir John (d.1580), all lavishly decorated with the quartered family arms, and those of their wives. The east window has the remains of stained glass of *c.*1533 installed under the terms of an earlier Sir Robert's will. Tudor badges can still be made out in the top lights. In the nave and chancel hangs an array of eighteenth- and nineteenth-century Throckmorton hatchments.

Cragside

NORTHUMBERLAND

Armstrong

Arms: Gules in fess a Tilting Spear Or headed Argent between two dexter Arms embowed in armour couped at the shoulder fesswise proper the hand extended also proper

Crest: On a Wreath of the Colours (Or and Gules) A dexter Arm embowed in armour fesswise couped at the shoulder and encircled at the elbow by a wreath of oak the hand grasping a Hammer all proper

Supporters: On either side a Figure habited as a Smith holding with the exterior hand a hammer resting on the shoulder all proper

Motto: *Fortis in Armis* [Strong in arms]

This Wagnerian house designed by Richard Norman Shaw between 1869 and 1884 set on a wooded Northumberland hillside is the brainchild of William George Armstrong, the Newcastle inventor and armaments manufacturer. Armstrong, the son of an Alderman of Newcastle, was one of the heroic figures of the second Industrial Revolution. Originally a solicitor, he was the inventor of the hydraulic crane and the celebrated Armstrong guns, and founder of the Elswick Works at Newcastle. He was born in 1810 and raised to the peerage as 1st Lord Armstrong of Cragside in 1887.

His pride in his industrial achievement is evident in the coat of arms which he chose: medieval canting heraldry – an arm strong. His crest is *A dexter Arm embowed in armour, the hand grasping a Hammer*, alluding to his business. The shield, too, comprises arms in armour – arms strong – and a spear. His supporters were two smiths holding hammers and his motto *Fortis in Armis*. The arms perfectly expressed Lord Armstrong's character, combining his pride in his work with a romantic medievalism – just like Cragside itself with its progressive technology, including the world's first hydro-electric domestic lighting, inside dramatic Tudor-Gothic architecture.

Lord Armstrong invested his industrial fortune in estates and two country houses in Northumberland, Cragside and Bamburgh Castle which remains with the family. He himself had no children and his property passed to his sister Ann's issue, his great-nephew William Watson-Armstrong becoming Lord Armstrong of the second creation in 1903. As well as his peerage, the original Lord Armstrong received many other honours and awards. One, of which he was particularly proud, was the Freedom of the City of Newcastle which was granted to him on 1 September 1896 in recognition of his substantial contribution to the economic life of the area. The presentation casket is on display at Cragside, emblazoned with the medieval arms of the city in enamel. The crest in the form of a castle and the charges on the shield symbolise the origins of Newcastle as a fortress at the east end of the Roman Wall, and the seahorse supporters allude to the city's role as a port, especially for the export of coal from the Durham and Northumberland coal fields. Castles appear on the seals of Newcastle from the thirteenth century onwards and these civic arms were confirmed by Norroy with the grant of the crest and supporters at the Visitation of Northumberland in 1575.

FORTIS IN ARMIS

To All and Singular to whom these Presents shall come Sir Albert William Woods, Knight, Garter Principal King of Arms, Sendeth Greeting:- Whereas Her Majesty by Letters Patent under the Great Seal of the United Kingdom of Great Britain and Ireland bearing date the sixth day of July last hath been graciously pleased to create Sir George William Armstrong, Knight Companion of the Most Honourable Order of the Bath a Peer of the said United Kingdom of Great Britain and Ireland by the name style and title of Baron Armstrong of Cragside in the County of Northumberland, to hold to him and the heirs male of his body lawfully begotten. And it being a privilege of the Peers of the Realm to bear Supporters to their Arms as well for their greater honour as to distinguish them from persons of inferior rank. Know Ye that I the said Garter by virtue of my Office and with the consent

LEFT: *The College of Arms record of the 1887 grant of supporters to the 1st Lord Armstrong (College of Arms Ms: Grants 64/84).*

BELOW: *The presentation casket, decorated on the side with the armorial bearings of the city of Newcastle upon Tyne, containing the Freedom of the City granted to the 1st Lord Armstrong in 1896.*

Dunham Massey

CHESHIRE

Booth

Arms: Argent three Boars' Heads erased and erect Sable

Crest: On a Wreath of the Colours (Argent and Sable) Upon a Garland of Leaves Vert a Lion passant Argent

Supporters: On either side a Boar Sable armed bristled and eyed Or

Motto: *Quod Ero Spero* [What I shall be, I hope]

Grey

Arms: Barry of six Argent and Azure

Crest: On a Wreath of the Colours (Argent and Azure) A Unicorn passant Ermine armed maned tufted and unguled Or in front of a Sun in Splendour Or

Supporters: On either side a Unicorn Ermine armed maned tufted and unguled Or

Motto: *A Ma Puissance* [To my power]

Dunham Massey is a great early eighteenth-century house built on an Elizabethan plan, which has successively been the seat of the holders of two different Earldoms, the Booths, Earls of Warrington, and the Greys, Earls of Stamford; the Greys acquiring the estate through the marriage of Lady Mary Booth, daughter and heiress of the 2nd Earl of Warrington, to the 4th Earl of Stamford in the eighteenth century.

The 2nd Lord Delamer of the Booth family was created Earl of Warrington in 1690 as a reward for his support for William III. He was a strong Protestant and an extreme Whig, as was his son, the 2nd Earl. The latter had a difficult character but was a distinguished patron who rebuilt his ancestral home in the 1730s.

In the Muniment Room is a beautiful illuminated pedigree drawn up in 1711 for the 2nd Earl of Warrington. The frontispiece makes a glorious show of forty-eight quarterings, which must have provided some consolation for this cantankerous man, who loathed his wife and had no son of his own, though he and his daughter Mary seem to have been fond of each other. As an heiress she carried all his possessions, including the house and these forty-eight heraldic quarterings, to her husband, the 4th Earl of Stamford. It is quite clear that as well as being a very difficult man, the Earl of Warrington was very proud of his lineage. This may have been one of the reasons why he rebuilt his house on a courtyard plan like the Leghs of Lyme (q.v.), rather than adopting a more up-to-date Palladian layout; such archaism demonstrated the grandeur and antiquity of his family. His interest in heraldry also seems to have extended beyond the contemporary norm, as is made clear by the survival of fragments of Spitalfields silk woven for him with his full arms and coronet – a rare extravagance.

The large stone carving of the Stamford arms at the top of the neo-Caroline centrepiece added to the Entrance Front by Compton Hall in 1905 commemorates the 9th Earl of Stamford's revival of the house as his principal seat after many years of neglect. The same achievement appears over the Dining Room fireplace. The courtyard rainwater heads have the gilded cypher and coronet of the 2nd Earl of Warrington which date from his rebuilding of the courtyard in 1732.

In the Great Hall the well-carved stone chimneypiece, designed by the little known Huguenot architect Monsieur Boujet, displays the arms of the 2nd Earl of Warrington with his distinctive boar supporters complete with sharp tusks and curly tails, and a very large coronet. The pier-glass frames in the Hall have his coroneted cypher. Some of the books in the Library have his cypher, too, while others have the bookplate of his daughter with the Grey arms impaled.

The heraldic glory of Dunham Massey is the Warrington plate, which is one of the most magnificent groups of early eighteenth-century silver by Huguenot craftsmen. It provides a feast of heraldry. Since the Middle Ages precious plate has been a vehicle for the display of corporate, ecclesiastical, noble and royal arms. By the seventeenth and eighteenth centuries, it had become conventional to show the crest or arms engraved with heraldic supporters, crests or coronets fully modelled and imaginatively used as plinths, handles or finials. This can be seen on the plate commissioned by the 2nd Earl of Warrington from a range of the Huguenot silversmiths. The wine cistern by Philip Rollos dated 1701 has wonderfully modelled wild boars (the Warrington supporters) as its handles. The chapel plate and dining plate is all engraved with the Warrington arms. The dressing service made by Magdalen Feline in 1754 for Lady Mary Booth shows her arms impaled with those of her husband, the 4th Earl of Stamford, thus uniting the heraldry of the two families responsible for Dunham Massey as it is today.

The silver wine cistern of 1701 at Dunham Massey with handles derived from the wild boar supporters of the Earls of Warrington.

Dunster Castle

SOMERSET

LUTTRELL

ARMS: Or a Bend between six Martlets Sable

CREST: Issuing from a Crest Coronet Or five Ostrich Feathers Argent

SUPPORTERS: On either side a Swan Argent ducally gorged and chained Or

MOTTO: *Quaesita Marte Tuenda Arte* [Gained by strength, held by skill]

The Luttrells owned Dunster for nearly six hundred years, from the fourteenth to the twentieth centuries. They were descended from a younger son of a junior branch of the baronial family of Luttrell of Irnham in Lincolnshire, and owed their position to the prestigious marriage in the fourteenth century of Sir Andrew Luttrell, the second son of Sir John Luttrell of Chilton in Devonshire, to Lady Elizabeth Courtenay, daughter of the Earl of Devon. She was a member of one of the greatest medieval noble families – her mother, Margaret (Bohun), Countess of Devon, was a granddaughter of King Edward I. Lady Elizabeth established the Luttrell dynasty at Dunster by buying the reversion of the property from Lady Bohun in 1376; Sir Andrew and Lady Elizabeth's son, Sir Hugh Luttrell, came into possession of the castle following Lady Bohun's death in 1404. The Luttrells at Dunster became extinct in the male line after the death of Alexander Luttrell in 1737, but his daughter Margaret married Henry Fownes, who changed his name to Luttrell, and their descendants lived in the castle for a further two hundred years.

Dunster is basically a late sixteenth- and early seventeeth-century L-shaped house, erected by George Luttrell (d.1629) on the site of the thirteenth-century living quarters, but a 'restoration' by Anthony Salvin in 1867-8 for George Fownes Luttrell made it look more like a castle, with the addition of turrets, towers and battlements. The heraldry, too, is a mixture of different dates. The oldest is the display of eight carved shields over the entrance arch of the fifteenth-century Gatehouse. Two of the shields are blank. The other six form an early family tree; from Sir Andrew (d.1378) – Luttrell impaling Courtenay – down to Sir Hugh (d.1521) – Luttrell impaling Hill.

Over the front door of the house is a large carved achievement designed by Salvin. It shows the arms of George Fownes Luttrell (d.1910), who was responsible for the Victorian restoration, impaled with those of his wife, Anne Elizabeth Periam Hood. The arms are supported by chained swans and surmounted by the Luttrell crest.

The swans and the panache crest were both derived by the Luttrells from the Courtenays. Their use of swans had come through Lady Elizabeth Luttrell's mother, Margaret, Countess of Devon and daughter of Humphrey de Bohun, Earl of Hereford and Essex. In *The Swan Badge and Swan Knight* Sir Anthony Wagner shows that a group of distantly related royal and noble families stretching across Europe all used swans in their heraldry because their ancestors claimed relationship to the Crusader Godfrey de Bouillon (d.1100) whom legend made the grandson of the mythical Swan Knight. The tomb effigy of Margaret, Countess of Devon in Exeter Cathedral has a pair of graceful mourning swans at her feet.

The Luttrell arms appear on an eighteenth-century lead rainwater head high up on the west wing, together with the date 1729. Inside the front porch there is a carved and painted achievement of the arms of Luttrell impaling Courtenay commemorating Sir Andrew and Lady Elizabeth who originally purchased the castle.

The arms of Luttrell quartering Fownes impaling Hood for George Fownes Luttrell and his wife, Anne Elizabeth Periam Hood (married 1852), with swan supporters, crest and motto carved and hatched in stone over the main entrance at Dunster.

The Luttrell arms are again displayed, with the swan supporters and the date 1589, in the Inner Hall. They are quartered with Hadley, and commemorate George Luttrell (d.1629) who built the late Elizabethan house at Dunster. There are some good hall chairs on which the panache crest is painted, and the Luttrell feathers also appear in marquetry on a side table in the Dining Room. The plasterwork frieze of the Dining Room, dating from 1681, has a fine impaled achievement of the arms of Luttrell and Tregonwell. The Tregonwell crest appears in the plasterwork. The room was remodelled by Col. Francis Luttrell (d.1690) who married Mary Tregonwell.

On the first floor, the Morning Room, which was decorated in the 1770s by Henry Fownes Luttrell, has a marble chimneypiece with the five-feather Luttrell crest. More interesting heraldically is the pedigree roll at the top of the Oak Staircase, and there are some fascinating small paintings of arms on the staircase of which the most unexpected is one of the arms granted by Royal Warrant in 1686 to Henry FitzJames, second illegitimate son of James II and Arabella Churchill, with the crest of a seahorse on a chapeau. Another small painting in the same group shows Luttrell impaling Baker for Narcissus Luttrell (d.1732), a cadet of the family who collated the muniments. His grandfather was Narcissus Mapowder, which explains the painting of the arms of Mapowder. There is also a wash drawing of Luttrell impaling Trevelyan with the swan supporters. These are the arms of the last of the male-line Luttrells, Alexander (d.1737) who married Margaret Trevelyan. In the Tenants Hall there are two firebacks of the royal arms; one shows the arms of Elizabeth I and the other the Stuart arms.

Erddig

DENBIGHSHIRE

MELLER

ARMS: Argent three Ouzells or Black Birds proper a Chief indented Sable

CREST: On a Wreath of the Colours (Argent and Sable) A Pied Bull's Head erased proper accolled with an Eastern Diadem crested and holding in his mouth the upper end of a broken Lance Or pointed proper

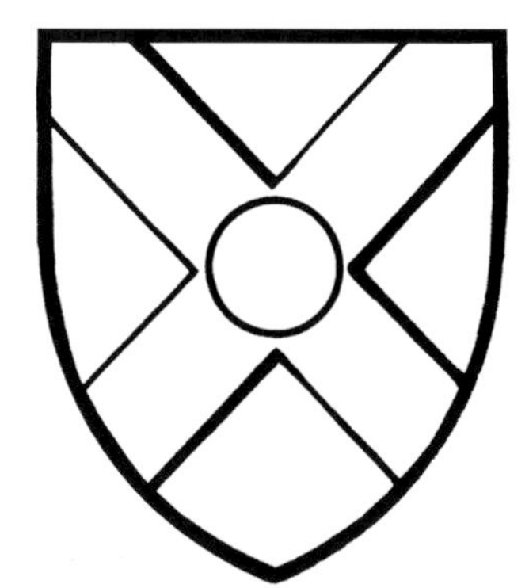

YORKE

ARMS: Argent on a Saltire Azure a Bezant

CREST: On a Wreath of the Colours (Argent and Azure) A Lion's Head erased proper collared Gules the collar charged with a Bezant

MOTTO: *Nec Cupias Nec Metuas* [Neither desire nor fear]

Erddig belonged to the Yorkes from 1733 when it was inherited by Simon Yorke from his uncle, John Meller, a London lawyer. The Meller arms appear in reverse on the glass-top table in the Tapestry Room, perhaps because they were copied from a seal. Successive Simon and Philip Yorkes were all of strong antiquarian bent – always a good augur for heraldry in country houses.

A painting certified by Sir John Vanbrugh (d.1726), Clarenceux King of Arms, of the arms and crest granted to John Meller in 1707.

Perhaps the most rare and spectacular piece of heraldry at Erddig is in the Tapestry Room. The large blue and white Delft vase, probably made by Adriaen Kochs (*c.*1690-1700) for Hampton Court, was traditionally a gift from Queen Anne to Mrs Wanley, a relation of Dorothy Hutton, the wife of Simon Yorke I. It is decorated with a shield of the arms of William and Mary, encircled by the Garter and topped by a large crown. William and Mary changed their arms three times in the early months of their reign, pending recognition by the Scottish Parliament. The arms on the Erddig vase show the form that they finally adopted.

Other glass and china in the house bears the family arms: the left-hand Boulle cabinet in the Saloon houses a glass beaker with the impaled arms of Yorke and Hutton, commemorating the marriage of Simon Yorke I and Dorothy Hutton in 1739. Perhaps rather surprisingly the gilt and silvered gesso furniture and pier glasses for which Erddig is famous are not crested – the tops of mirror frames were usually a favourite position for heraldic display. Some of the silver has arms engraved in the conventional fashion: in the Butler's Pantry is a splendid set of sauce boats, with the impaled arms of Philip Yorke I and his wife Elizabeth, the daughter of Sir John Cust, Speaker of the House of Commons (q.v. Belton).

Cut paperwork by Betty Ratcliffe showing the arms of Yorke quartering Hutton and Meller, impaling Cust, to commemorate the marriage in 1770 of Philip Yorke and Elizabeth Cust.

In the Chapel is a hatchment with the arms of Simon Yorke II impaled with that of his wife Margaret, daughter of John Holland of Teyrdan. He died in 1834, and this would have hung on the front of his house for a year afterwards to mark the event. His wife outlived him by fourteen years; that she survived her husband's death is indicated by the fact that the background on the hatchment behind his arms is black, while that behind hers is white.

Another charming heraldic allusion at Erddig are the cut paper silhouettes made by Betty Ratcliffe (d. *c.*1810), maid and companion to Dorothy Yorke. One shows the arms of Yorke quartering Meller and impaling Hutton, and the other Yorke quartering Hutton and Meller, impaling Cust, to commemorate the marriages of Simon Yorke and Dorothy Hutton in 1739 and Philip Yorke and Elizabeth Cust in 1770.

The most extensive display of heraldry at Erddig can be found in the Tribes Room, which has panel paintings of Welsh arms over the fireplace and round the walls. They are taken from the illustrations in Philip Yorke I's *Royal Tribes of Wales*, which was published in 1799; the book itself is in the Library at Erddig. Philip was the most distinguished of the Yorke antiquaries, and his researches into Welsh history, genealogy and heraldry were pioneering work in the late eighteenth century. Welsh heraldry is a complex subject, and has indeed been described as 'a retrospective fiction'. It was a late development, by English or European standards, and only evolved in the fourteenth and fifteenth centuries by means of attributing arms to ancestors who lived in a pre-heraldic period, in particular the founders of the Welsh Royal and Noble Tribes, whose existence is partly based on oral tradition. Philip Yorke's studies were an attempt to elucidate this fascinating historical phenomenon, and to record the various family arms which emerged from the Celtic mists and myths.

FELBRIGG HALL

NORFOLK

WINDHAM

ARMS: Azure a Chevron between three Lions' Heads erased Or

CREST: On a Wreath of the Colours (Or and Azure) On a Fetterlock Or within the chain thereof Or and Azure a Lion's Head erased Or

MOTTO: *Au Bon Droit* [With good right]

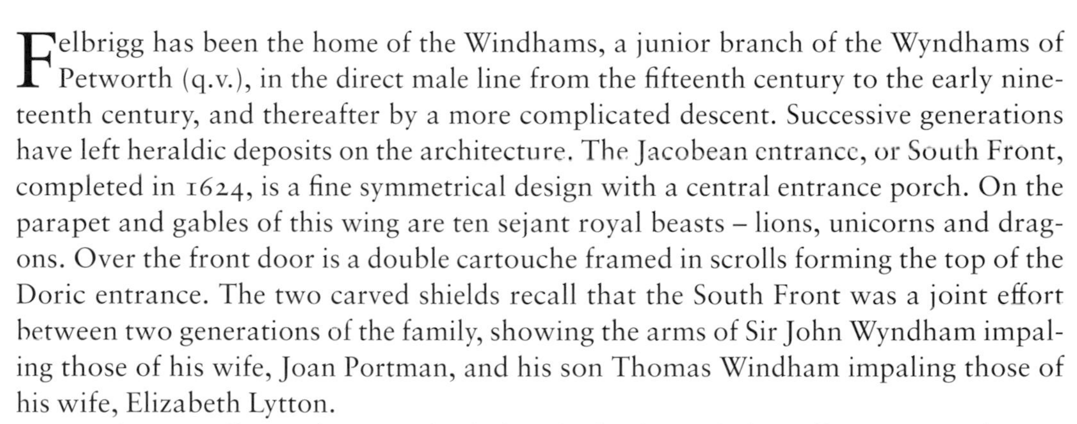

Felbrigg has been the home of the Windhams, a junior branch of the Wyndhams of Petworth (q.v.), in the direct male line from the fifteenth century to the early nineteenth century, and thereafter by a more complicated descent. Successive generations have left heraldic deposits on the architecture. The Jacobean entrance, or South Front, completed in 1624, is a fine symmetrical design with a central entrance porch. On the parapet and gables of this wing are ten sejant royal beasts – lions, unicorns and dragons. Over the front door is a double cartouche framed in scrolls forming the top of the Doric entrance. The two carved shields recall that the South Front was a joint effort between two generations of the family, showing the arms of Sir John Wyndham impaling those of his wife, Joan Portman, and his son Thomas Windham impaling those of his wife, Elizabeth Lytton.

Sir John Wyndham (d.1645), the father, had inherited the Felbrigg estate from a cousin. He paid for the building of the house, and his account books record 'divers great sums of money' spent on construction work in Norfolk. It was intended, however, that the new house would be the residence of his second surviving son, Thomas, who went to live there around 1615, while Sir John continued to live at Orchard Wyndham in Somerset, the ancient home of the Wyndhams, who eventually inherited Petworth.

The Windhams succeeded each other at Felbrigg through the seventeenth and eighteenth centuries, squires managing their estates, and Members of Parliament. In the 1680s William Windham I added a new wing to the design of William Samwell, with rich plaster ceilings by Edward Goudge. The interior of the house was remodelled in

the eighteenth century by James Paine in rococo taste, and a Gothic Library created in 1753 by William Windham II. It still houses his books, uniformly bound and containing his eighteenth-century heraldic bookplate. In the cove over the fireplace of the Cabinet is a cartouche with William Windham II's arms impaled with those of his wife. The Dining Room plasterwork incorporates chains which are thought to be an allusion to the Windham fetterlock crest. The Georgian hall chairs in the entrance passage also have the Windham crest.

The last of the male heirs, William Windham III, was a supporter of Pitt the Younger and pursued an active political career, but his intellectual scruples and changes of mind exasperated his contemporaries and earned him the nickname of 'Weathercock Windham'. On his death, childless, in 1810, he bequeathed the estate to William Lukin, the grandson of his mother by her first marriage and therefore not a Windham. Among others, Lady Holland, the famous Whig hostess, disapproved of William's leaving Felbrigg out of the family: 'a curious instance of weakness in Windham, and one that probably never would have been drawn forth, but for the feelings stirred up by the French Revolution ...' Despite the lack of a blood connection, William Lukin took the Windham name and arms and moved into Felbrigg on the death of William Windham's widow, Cecilia, in 1824. He immediately embarked on alterations, mainly the rebuilding of the stables using W. J. Donthorn, a pupil of Jeffry Wyatville.

His eldest son, William Howe Windham, succeeded to the estate in 1833 and soon after, he remodelled the Great Hall in a Jacobean revival taste under the direction of J. C. Buckler. Buckler was the second generation of a remarkable dynasty of Oxford antiquarian architects who played a considerable role in the nineteenth-century heraldic revival. His father, John, was an architect to Magdalen College, while his son, Charles Alban Buckler, was to become Surrey Herald Extraordinary and the architect of the massive late nineteenth-century reconstruction of Arundel Castle for the Duke of Norfolk. William Howe Windham built the lodges and several cottages on the estate, some designed by Buckler and decorated with carved armorial tablets. The principal lodges have the Windham arms and crest.

At Felbrigg, Buckler's reconstruction of the Hall involved filling the upper portions of the windows with a remarkable assemblage of Continental stained glass, Swiss, Dutch, German and Flemish, dating from the fifteenth and sixteenth centuries, as well as glass from the church of St Peter Mancroft in Norwich. These panels contain a quantity of armorial glass, as well as portraits of historical figures dressed in heraldic tabards of their arms. Buckler also added some modern heraldic glass to the collection. In the south bay window are two panels with the quartered Windham arms. In the west bay window, the six lower lights have the Windham motto *A Bon Droit*, the crest and arms. Buckler also incorporated an armorial stone panel of the 1620s over the fireplace, which complements that over the front door and shows the Windham arms. The crest is carved in the spandrels of the fireplace.

The (Lukin) Windhams' ownership of Felbrigg came to an end with William Frederick Windham – 'Mad Windham' – who spent his time pretending to be a policeman, consorting with prostitutes and acting as an amateur guard on the railway. His behavioural oddities caused his relations to institute an unsuccessful judicial inquiry

The Jacobean entrance of 1624 at Felbrigg with, over the front door, the impaled arms of Sir John Wyndham and his wife, Joan Portman, and of their son Thomas Windham and his wife, Elizabeth Lytton (married 1620).

The arms of Wyndham/ Windham from a page of Wrythe's Book of c.1480 painted for John Wrythe, Garter King of Arms (d.1504). The page also illustrates the arms of Luttrell (Dunster), Harington (quartered by Tresham of Lyveden New Bield) and Cornewall, descended from an illegitimate son of Richard, Earl of Cornwall, founder of Hailes Abbey (College of Arms Ms: M.10/58).

into his state of mind, a court case which was conducted 'at enormous length, and with the utmost scandal and publicity'. In 1863 the house and its contents with a substantial portion of the estate was purchased by John Ketton, a Norwich merchant. But it was not long before the Windhams returned with the marriage of his daughter Anna to Thomas Wyndham Cremer, a descendant of the Wyndhams through the female line. Their grandson, R.W. Ketton-Cremer, squire and man of letters, was a bachelor and bequeathed the property to the National Trust on his death in 1969.

Gawthorpe Hall

LANCASHIRE

Kay-Shuttleworth

Arms, Quarterly: (1&4 Shuttleworth) Argent three Weavers' Shuttles Sable tipped and furnished Or; (2&3 Kay) Argent three Ermine Spots in bend between two Bendlets Sable the whole between two Crescents Azure

Crests: (1 Shuttleworth) On a Wreath of the Colours (Argent and Sable) A cubit Arm in armour the hand in a gauntlet proper grasping a Shuttle Sable tipped and furnished Or
(2 Kay) On a Wreath of the Colours (Argent and Sable) On a Crescent Or a Goldfinch proper

Supporters (1902): (Dexter) A Man habited as a Weaver proper holding in the exterior hand a Shuttle Sable tipped furnished and thread pendent Or; (Sinister) A Sailor habited and holding in the exterior hand a Ship's Lantern proper

Motto: *Kynd Kynn Knawne Kepe* [Keep your own kin-kind]

The quartered arms of Sir James Phillips Kay-Shutleworth, 1st Bt., with the badge of the baronetage and two crests carved in stone in 1851 above the entrance door to the Library at Gawthorpe.

The Drawing Room at Gawthorpe with firedogs designed by A.W.N. Pugin, on which there are shields of arms, and supplied in the 1850s by J.G. Crace.

The Shuttleworths owned land hereabouts for over two hundred years before the present house was begun in 1600 by the Rev. Lawrence Shuttleworth. The family fortune was made by his elder brother Richard, a successful Elizabethan lawyer who became Chief Justice of Chester. In 1842, the heiress Janet Shuttleworth married Dr James Phillips Kay, doctor and educationalist, who assumed the additional name of Shuttleworth and was created a baronet for his distinguished public service. In 1849 they employed Sir Charles Barry to restore and modernise Gawthorpe Hall. As a result the house is both a late Elizabethan/Jacobean and a Victorian building with fine heraldry from both periods, but especially of the latter.

In the centre of the parapet at the top of the tower, which was heightened by Barry, is a large Victorian shield of the Kay-Shuttleworth arms. Like the Armstrong and Lucy arms (q.v. Cragside and Charlecote), the Shuttleworth arms comprising three shuttles, and the crest with a hand also holding a shuttle, fall into the group known as 'canting' arms, which are a pun on the family name. They are especially appropriate in Lancashire with its long weaving tradition.

All over the house, inside and out, is the archaic sounding Kay motto, adopted by the Kay-Shuttleworths in the nineteenth century, *Kynd Kynn Knawne Kepe*. It is carved over the front door, which is a remodelling by Barry, though most of the exterior of the house remained unchanged.

Inside the Entrance Hall a splendid stone panel, made in 1851, has the quartered arms of Kay-Shuttleworth with Shuttleworth quartering Barton in pretence and a baronet's badge, for Sir James and Lady Kay-Shuttleworth. The old Great Hall was remodelled by Barry as the Dining Room, and he was also responsible for the handsome chimneypiece with its heraldic overmantel. In the centre is a large cartouche with the quartered Kay-Shuttleworth arms, with crests above; this is flanked by (left) four shields of Shuttleworth and Kay arms, and (right) four shields of arms brought into the family by heiresses.

In the Drawing Room, which retains its original inlaid Elizabethan panelling, plaster frieze and ceiling, the fireplace was inserted by Barry and adorned by a pair of splendid Pugin firedogs with shields of arms. They are part of an extensive series of furnishings designed by A.W.N. Pugin, supplied in the 1850s by J.G. Crace, at the time of Barry's remodelling of the house.

Upstairs, the Long Gallery retains its original carved chimneypiece. It is dated 1603 and bears the arms of James I, dating the completion of the house to his reign. One of the bedrooms on this floor also has a Jacobean overmantel, this time in plaster, with the Shuttleworth arms, crest and motto of *Prudentia Justicia* [Prudence by Justice].

Sir James and Janet Kay-Shuttleworth's eldest son Ughtred held office in successive late nineteenth-century governments as Under-Secretary of State for India and Chancellor of the Duchy of Lancaster and was created a peer in 1902. On his elevation he continued the shuttle theme of the family arms by choosing a weaver holding a shuttle as one of his supporters.

HANBURY HALL

WORCESTERSHIRE

VERNON

ARMS: Or on a Fess Azure three Garbs Or and in centre chief a Cross Crosslet fitchy Gules

CREST: On a Wreath of the Colours (Or and Azure) A demi Woman proper habited Or and Purpure crined Or wreathed about the temples with wheat and holding in her arms a Garb Or

MOTTO: *Vernon Semper Viret* [Vernon always flourishes] *Ver Non Semper Viret* [The spring (season) does not always flourish]

The house was built *c.*1701 for Thomas Vernon, whose family had lived at Hanbury since 1580, when the Rev. Richard Vernon was appointed Rector there. His son Edward purchased the estate in 1631. Thomas Vernon (d.1721), a Whig M.P. for Worcestershire and a successful Chancery lawyer, added greatly to his family's property in Worcestershire. His cousin and successor, Bowater Vernon (d.1735), was also elected to Parliament but was unseated on petition, the elections committee finding that all but one of his fifty-two voters had been bribed at a total cost of nearly £700. Bowater Vernon's son, Thomas Vernon (d.1771), was also a Whig and M.P. for Worcester 1746-61. The family were created baronets in the nineteenth century.

Thomas Vernon 'signed' his new house in the conventional way with a carved relief of his arms over the front door, depicted on an oval with the initials T.V. and the date 1701. Inside, the finest feature is the scheme of paintings in the Hall by Thornhill. Unlike the wall paintings in the Chapel at Wimpole (q.v.) in which Thornhill included the Harley arms, the Thornhill murals in the Hall and Staircase at Hanbury do not incorporate heraldry, only cyphers of Thomas Vernon's initials in the ceiling above the staircase. There are, however, seven oval cartouches of arms with crests above the doors in the Hall, recording various marriages. The motto is carved on the alabaster slab of the chimneypiece.

Good heraldry can be seen elsewhere. The splendid parcel gilt pier glass in the Blue Bedroom has the Vernon arms carved in the pediment, and in the Smoking Room a pair of firescreens display the arms of Vernon impaling Foley for the 1st Baronet's parents, who married in 1831.

A Chamberlain's Worcester service, also of the 1830s, in the Dining Room, has the crest and motto. The best china at Hanbury, however, is the Chinese armorial service produced for Bowater Vernon *c.*1730. This has a large-scale depiction of the Vernon crest in the centre. It was transformed, however, by an oriental painter, from a woman with a wheatsheaf into a Chinaman with a sheaf of rice. Bowater Vernon's wife's arms – Cornwallis – are accurately depicted on the rim.

A Chinese armorial plate of c.1730 produced for Bowater Vernon with an oriental version of the crest of Vernon in the centre and the arms of his wife (Cornwallis) on the rim.

Hardwick Hall

DERBYSHIRE

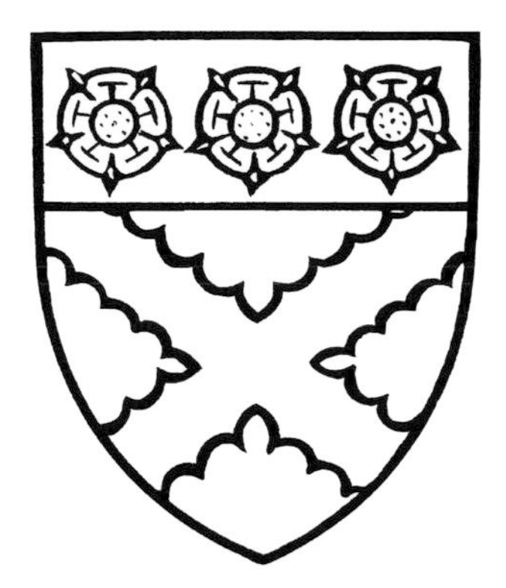

Hardwick

Arms: Argent a Saltire engrailed Azure on a Chief also Azure three Roses Argent barbed and seeded proper

Crest: On a Wreath of the Colours (Argent and Azure) On a Mount Vert a Stag passant proper gorged with a plain collar Azure charged with Roses Argent

Cavendish

Arms: Sable three Stags' Heads Argent attired Or

Crest: On a Wreath of the Colours (Argent and Sable) A Serpent nowed Vert

Supporters: On either side a Stag proper wreathed round the neck with a Chaplet of Roses alternately Argent and Azure

Motto: *Cavendo Tutus* [Safe by being cautious]

Some houses proclaim the occupancy of several generations of a family through the evolving heraldry of succeeding owners. This is not the case at Hardwick; everything proclaims the status of just one person – its builder, the redoubtable Bess of Hardwick.

Her mark is everywhere, from the coroneted cypher E.S. for Elizabeth Countess of Shrewsbury, larger than life in the strapwork cresting at the top of the towers, to her arms on the chimneypieces, plasterwork, marquetry, needlework, tapestries and other textiles that adorn the rooms. There is probably no other house in England which is so closely connected in the popular imagination with one person.

Bess was born at Hardwick in 1527. Her family were minor gentry who had been resident there for six generations. The story of her rise in the world, through four financially successful marriages is well known. In 1544 she wedded her cousin Robert Barley. He died a few months later leaving her the customary widow's jointure of about £66 a year. Her second marriage in 1547 to Sir William Cavendish greatly enhanced her status. As a commissioner for the dissolution of the monasteries he had made a large fortune. To please her he sold all his existing property and bought estates in Derbyshire and Nottinghamshire, and they built a large new house at Chatsworth. Six of their eight children survived, from whom three ducal dynasties are descended: the

Devonshires from William, the second son, and the Newcastles and Portlands from the third son, Charles. Sir William died in 1557, leaving Bess most of his property. Two years later she married Sir William St Loe, Captain of the Guard and Butler of the Royal Household under Elizabeth I – another social advance for Bess. He died five years later, leaving most of his property to her, rather than to his own family. In 1568 she made the most successful marital coup of all: she married George Talbot, 6th Earl of Shrewsbury, a widower and head of one of the grandest and richest families in England. It was a triple marriage, for at the same time his second son and eventual heir married her daughter Mary, and his daughter married her eldest son Henry. But Shrewsbury's marriage to Bess broke down in mutual dislike and disagreement during the 1580s, and when in 1583 Bess bought the family estate at Hardwick from the executors of her brother James, who had died bankrupt in 1581, she went back to live there in solitary splendour. She rebuilt the Old Hall, but when Lord Shrewsbury himself died in 1590 Bess received a huge widow's jointure which she promptly spent on building a completely new Hall at Hardwick.

Bess marked her completion of the shell of the house with two large stone carvings of her paternal arms on lozenges with supporters in the centre of the balustrades on both façades. They were erected in 1595; that on the west was carved by Thomas Accres, that on the east by Abraham Smith. Accres's arms have gone, but Smith's were restored from collapsed fragments and reinstated in 1911. Few houses have quite such prominent armorial display. At Hardwick we are left in no doubt that the local squire's daughter had made spectacularly good. However, the use of her paternal arms with supporters was incorrect and suggested, no doubt intentionally, that she was a peeress in her own right, rather than the estranged wife of an Earl.

The same ambitious heraldic theme continues in the Entrance Hall. Over the chimneypiece is the most enormous plaster representation of Bess's paternal arms on a lozenge. She did not impale her late husband's arms but surmounted the lozenge with a coronet and supported it with two life-size stags (their antlers are real). The eglantines (wild roses) which form part of Bess of Hardwick's arms (ironically a symbol of chastity) were much used by her in the decoration of Hardwick.

Hardwick was inherited by Bess's favourite son, William Cavendish. His descendants adopted the Hardwick stags as the supporters of their arms first as Earls, then as Dukes of Devonshire. The long Cavendish ownership of the house is commemorated by their crest, a snake, which is painted on roundels beneath the east windows of the Hall with their motto *Cavendo Tutus*.

In the Hall are some of the embroidered textiles, made for Bess to furnish the house and for which it has always been famous. The set showing the *Virtues*, embroidered at about the time of Bess's marriage to Lord Shrewsbury, have her arms impaled with those of her husband; his badge, a talbot (hunting dog), also appears.

Heraldic overmantels and spectacular needlework and tapestries can be found throughout the house, which was much enhanced in the early nineteenth century by the 6th Duke of Devonshire, who added furnishings from his other houses to play up the picturesque 'olden tyme' atmosphere of Hardwick. The tapestries on the staircase walls, for instance, came from the Leicester Apartment at Chatsworth – to mitigate the

The arms of Hardwick on a lozenge over the chimneypiece of the Great Hall at Hardwick with stag supporters derived from the crest of Hardwick. It is technically incorrect, as it suggests Bess of Hardwick was a peeress in her own right.

dreary whitewash. The Cavendish snake crest and ducal coronet can be seen woven into their borders.

The Drawing Room on the first floor, which was Bess's own 'Withdrawing Chamber', has another plasterwork armorial chimneypiece; here Bess's quartered arms are supported by stags and topped off with her coronet. Beneath is the Latin couplet: *Sanguine cornu corde oculo pede cervus et aure / Nobilis et claro pondere nobilior* [The stag, noble in blood, horn, heart, eye, foot and ear made more noble by the fame of its burden]. The burden is, of course, Bess of Hardwick's arms. Also in this room is a very rare *verre églomisé* mirror panel with two shields of Bess's arms impaled with Talbot in the corners, and a large shield of her arms and crest in the centre. Round the upper part of the Drawing Room walls are a set of Flemish tapestries, part of a lot bought by Bess from Sir William Hatton, the nephew and heir of Sir Christopher Hatton; there are others in the Long Gallery. 'My ladies Armes' painted on canvas were sewn over the Hatton arms, but in here, all except one of these have been removed. The superimposed arms survive on the Gallery set. Bess, who always had a sharp eye for a bargain, had £5 knocked off the price because of having to change the arms.

On the top landing, outside the High Great Chamber, is a table, the top inlaid with a shield of the impaled Talbot and Hardwick arms. This is thought to be the 'inlayde borde' which was recorded in Bess's Withdrawing Chamber in her inventory of 1601. In the High Great Chamber itself the plaster frieze over the fireplace depicts not Bess's own arms (as in her own Withdrawing Chamber) but the royal arms of Elizabeth I, encircled by the Garter and with the motto *Dieu et mon Droit*, supported by a lion and dragon, indicating the more formal, public purpose of the room where Bess would have received guests in state. The magnificent marquetry table in the centre of the room is inlaid with the arms of Talbot impaling Hardwick and Cavendish impaling Talbot, and mottoes. It was probably made to commemorate the marriages of Bess to Lord Shrewsbury and Henry Cavendish to Grace Talbot in 1568. The canopy in the High Great Chamber has the arms of Cavendish impaling Bruce for William Cavendish, 2nd Earl of Devonshire and his wife, Christian Bruce, whom he married in 1608.

In the Mary Queen of Scots Room, over the door, is a semi-circular panel with the Scottish royal arms and the initials M.R. The arms are very similar to Mary's own seal, and may be contemporary. It is thought that they were probably brought to Hardwick from the Mary Queen of Scots Apartment at Chatsworth in 1690 and moved to their present position in the eighteenth century when there was a considerable romantic cult of the tragic Queen. Although Lord Shrewsbury was her gaoler, Mary never stayed at Hardwick (she was executed before the New Hall was built), although she did spend some time at Chatsworth. Over the chimneypiece in the Mary Queen of Scots Room, the arms of Hardwick on a lozenge appear in plaster with supporters and a countess's coronet with, on either side, Hardwick impaling Leeke for Bess's parents, and Cavendish impaling Keighley for her son William. A generational arrangement of arms is often found in late Elizabethan and Jacobean heraldic decoration and is especially conspicuous here. The most elaborate chimneypiece of all is in the Cut Velvet Bedroom. It shows the arms of Hardwick flanked by six shields of the impaled arms of Bess of Hardwick's six surviving children – a splendid statement of her dynastic ambitions.

The High Great Chamber at Hardwick with, on the back cloth of the canopy, the arms of Cavendish impaling Bruce, for the marriage in 1608 of the 2nd Earl of Devonshire, with one Cavendish and one Bruce supporter and the crest of Cavendish.

HUGHENDEN MANOR

BUCKINGHAMSHIRE

DISRAELI

ARMS: Per saltire Gules and Argent a Tower triple towered in chief proper two Lions rampant in fesse Sable and an Eagle displayed in base Or

CREST: On a Wreath of the Colours (Argent and Gules) A Tower triple towered issuant from a Wreath of Oak all proper

SUPPORTERS: (Dexter) An Eagle Or (sinister) A Lion also Or each gorged with a Collar Gules and pendant therefrom an Escutcheon Gules charged with a Tower triple towered Argent

MOTTO: *Forti Nihil Difficile* [Nothing is difficult to the brave]

Disraeli bought Hughenden in 1848, with the financial assistance of the sons of the 4th Duke of Portland, for at the time it was considered that an ambitious and prominent member of the Conservative party needed a country seat of his own. Disraeli remodelled the simple Georgian house in 1862 to the design of the Victorian 'rogue architect' E. B. Lamb, whose obituary in *The Builder* commented that 'he constantly endeavoured, even at the expense sometimes of beauty, to exhibit originality'. The interior retains much of the atmosphere and appearance it had in Disraeli's lifetime, thanks partly to careful twentieth-century restoration. In the Library the books still have his heraldic bookplates, some of them showing the Garter which he was awarded in 1878, while the silk banner firescreen in the room was embroidered with the Beaconsfield arms by Hannah de Rothschild, Countess of Rosebery, who presented it to Disraeli. In Disraeli's day this was the Drawing Room, and what is now the Drawing Room was the Library, an arrangement which was reversed by Disraeli's nephew and heir, Major Coningsby Disraeli, who lived at Hughenden from 1888 till his death in 1936. In the Dining Room the carved wooden chimneypiece inserted by Coningsby Disraeli has the family motto *Forti Nihil Difficile*.

Upstairs in the Politicians' Room are two elaborately illuminated Victorian peerage patents, one to Disraeli's wife, Mary Anne, when she was made Viscountess Beaconsfield in her own right in 1868 and one to Disraeli when he was created Earl of Beaconsfield in 1876. Also on display in the room are enamelled presentation caskets with Disraeli's full achievement of arms as Earl of Beaconsfield, one containing the freedom of the City of London, the other an address from the British residents of California. The inkwell from Gregory XVI has the Pope's arms on it.

What is interesting about the heraldic decoration at Hughenden is that it pre-dates the formal grants of arms in 1869 and 1876 and uses the arms assumed by Disraeli's father. Impaled arms pre-dating the grants appear over the front door, in the centre boss of the Hall ceiling and the adjoining anteroom next to the Library. They also

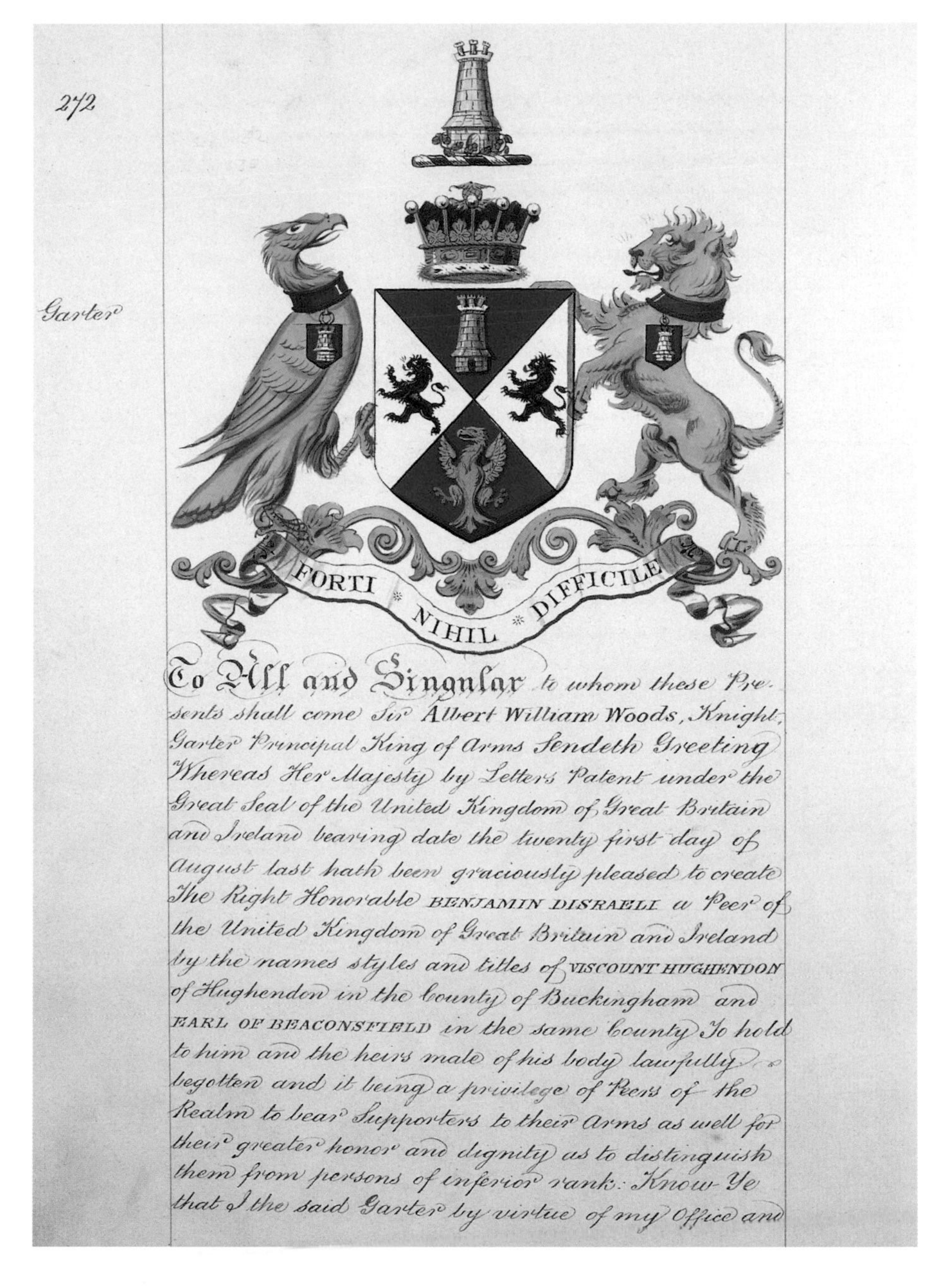

272

Garter

FORTI NIHIL DIFFICILE

To All and Singular to whom these Presents shall come Sir Albert William Woods, Knight, Garter Principal King of Arms Sendeth Greeting Whereas Her Majesty by Letters Patent under the Great Seal of the United Kingdom of Great Britain and Ireland bearing date the twenty first day of August last hath been graciously pleased to create The Right Honorable BENJAMIN DISRAELI a Peer of the United Kingdom of Great Britain and Ireland by the names styles and titles of VISCOUNT HUGHENDON of Hughenden in the County of Buckingham and EARL OF BEACONSFIELD in the same County To hold to him and the heirs male of his body lawfully begotten and it being a privilege of Peers of the Realm to bear Supporters to their Arms as well for their greater honor and dignity as to distinguish them from persons of inferior rank: Know Ye that I the said Garter by virtue of my Office and

A record of the 1876 grant of supporters to Benjamin Disraeli, 1st Earl of Beaconsfield (College of Arms Ms: Grants 59/272).

appear on the South (Garden) Front and on a carved oak Gothic armchair in the Garden Hall which was made by John Baldwin in 1863. Disraeli's actual arms have the same linear appearance but the colours are different; before the grant, the eagle in the base is black on a gold background; after the grant both the eagle and tower were on red backgrounds and the eagle is gold. Even greater is the change in his wife's arms which appear in the architectural detail just as a bunch of grapes and nothing more. The grapes are a canting reference to Lady Beaconsfield's uncle, General Sir James Viney, whose heir she became on the death of her brother in 1834.

Ickworth

SUFFOLK

Hervey

Arms: Gules on a Bend Argent three Trefoils slipped Vert

Crest: On a Wreath of the Colours (Argent and Gules) An Ounce passant Sable spotted ducally collared and chain reflexed over the back Or holding in the dexter paw a Trefoil slipped Vert

Supporters: On either side an Ounce Sable bezanty each ducally collared and chain reflexed over the back Or

Motto: *Je N'Oublieray Jamais* [I shall never forget]

The Herveys are among the most unconventional of English families, and their extraordinary house with its central rotunda, quadrant links and large flanking wings – one never completed, the other the private family residence – reflects their oddity. It was begun in 1796 and first inhabited in 1829, but the estate had been in the family since the mid-fifteenth century.

The oddness crept in through Elizabeth Felton, the heiress second wife of the 1st Earl of Bristol – a staunch Whig and supporter of the Glorious Revolution who was ennobled in 1703 and elevated to the earldom in 1714. She introduced a strain of mental instability which manifested itself in extreme eccentricity and disregard for convention so that contemporaries decided that when God created the world he made 'men, women and Herveys' (Lady Mary Wortley Montagu). Of Elizabeth Felton's sons the eldest was epileptic, another eloped with his godfather's wife, the third spent his youth in a series of extravagant misdemeanours but ended up in Holy Orders. Another Felton was sacked from Eton and dismissed from Court as one of the Princess of Wales's pages for 'misconduct' although subsequently cleared. William became a Captain in the Navy but was court-martialled for brutality. John, who predeceased his father, was *the* Lord Hervey, the mercurial and brilliant Vice-Chamberlain, Lord Privy Seal and chronicler of the Court of George II immortalized by Pope as Sporos: 'Amphibious thing! ... Now trips a lady, and now struts a lord'. His wife was the beautiful Molly Leppell, the Queen's Maid of Honour. But their children were hardly less eccentric than their 'wicked' uncles.

The three eldest sons in turn inherited the title as 2nd, 3rd and 4th Earls of Bristol. George, the 2nd Earl, was a man of inordinate pride, Minister at Turin and Ambassador to Madrid, and spent his life seeking the Garter and a dukedom – in vain. Augustus, the second son, was an Admiral and the English Casanova. He left a bevy of illegitimate children. His wife was even more notorious. She was Elizabeth Chudleigh, the bigamous Duchess of Kingston whose appearance at the Venetian Ambassador's Ball in 1749 as 'Iphigenia for the Sacrifice' caused a sensation; Mrs Montagu commented that she was so naked that the High Priest could have read her entrails. The 4th Earl, Frederick, was the notorious Earl-Bishop of Derry who spent his life travelling around Europe in plush breeches, purple slippers and a straw hat, which credulous foreigners assumed to be the canonicals of an Anglican Bishop.

The Earl-Bishop commissioned the designs for Ickworth from Mario Asprucci, architect to Prince Borghese in Rome, but never visited the site once work was begun under the direction of Francis Sandys, architect brother of one of his chaplains. The shell was left incomplete on the Bishop's death near Albano – in the outhouse of an Italian peasant who would not admit a heretic prelate to his cottage. The house was finished and furnished by his son, who was created the 1st Marquess of Bristol by his brother-in-law, the Prime Minister, Lord Liverpool.

A silver soup tureen by Frederick Kandler, 1752, with a quartered coat incorrectly rearranged after the paternal arms of Hervey in order of rank with (2) Thomas of Brotherton, son of King Edward I (3) a grand quarter of (i) Howard (ii) Warren (iii) Fitzalan (iv) Audley and (4) Felton and the crest of Hervey as the handle, with supporters and a coronet of rank.

Ickworth has the true aura of neo-classical megalomania: the façade extends for over 600 feet, and the main rooms are thirty feet high. By contrast the heraldry at Ickworth is sadly conventional. The hall chairs are painted in the usual way with crest and coronet. The portrait of John, Lord Hervey by Van Loo shows him holding the purse of office of the Lord Privy Seal, embroidered with the royal arms of George II, and the purse itself is displayed in a glass case underneath. A large eighteenth-century Chinese export dinner service is painted with the impaled arms of John Augustus, Lord Hervey and his wife, Elizabeth Drummond. Hanging on the walls of the staircase are some family pedigrees on vellum painted with arms. The 1st Earl of Bristol's arms appear on a cartouche over the door to his early eighteenth-century summer house in the grounds.

The greatest heraldic treasure at Ickworth, however, is the magnificent ambassadorial plate made for the 2nd Earl when he was Ambassador to Spain and earlier Minister at Turin. This fully reflects the pride of this arrogant man. The four superlative soup tureens were supplied for his diplomatic employment in Turin in 1752; two made in London by Frederick Kandler, and two more to match in Italy. They have the full achievement of his own arms with earl's coronet and supporters, while the Hervey crest serves as the handle on the lids. The ambassadorial plate is complemented by earlier and later silver and silver gilt services by de Lamerie, and candelabra by Paul

Victorian brass firedogs in the Pompeian Room at Ickworth incorporating ounces derived from the crest and supporters of Lord Bristol.

Storr which are also emblazoned with the Hervey arms. The rococo candelabra by Simon le Sage of 1758 bear George II's arms and were issued to the 2nd Earl of Bristol on his appointment to Spain in 1758.

The only quirkier bits of heraldry at Ickworth are the Victorian brass firedogs in the Pompeian Room of 1879; they are large brass animals representing the 'ounces sable', which support the Bristol arms, and were presumably designed by J. D. Crace as part of his scheme for this room.

Ightham Mote

KENT

SELBY

ARMS: Barry of eight Or and Sable

CREST: On a Wreath of the Colours (Or and Sable) A Saracen's Head couped at the shoulders proper vested Gules wreathed around the temples with a Torse Or and Sable the ends tied on the sinister side in a bow

MOTTO: *Fort et Loyal* [Bold and loyal]

Ightham Mote is the sort of ancient manor where you would expect to find a lot of heraldry, nor are you disappointed. It is a moated courtyard house dating from the fourteenth century where little seems to have changed though in fact the evolution of the house is very complicated. It was begun, and the moat dug, by Sir Thomas Cawne, who lived there from 1340 till his death in 1347. From him the property passed into the hands of the Haut family. Sir Richard Haut was Treasurer to the Household of Prince Edward (son of Edward IV and Elizabeth Woodville and one of the princes later murdered in the Tower) and High Sheriff of Kent in 1478. He added the gate tower and south and west wings.

During the sixteenth century, Ightham Mote was sold frequently, a sign of the fluid land market in the Tudor period, when apart from a vast dispersal of former church property, many of the estates of the Crown and medieval corporations also passed through the market. In 1521 Ightham was bought by Richard Clement, a loyal supporter of the Tudors, whose career began as a page in the household of Henry VII. In 1544 it was sold again, to Sir John Allen, Lord Mayor of London. In 1591 his son, in turn, sold the property to Sir William Selby. The Selbys were to own it for the next three hundred years. Their arms, crest and motto, *Fort et Loyal*, can be seen on a restored stone tablet over the first floor window of the Entrance Tower. The stained glass in the windows of the Entrance Tower also shows the Selby arms, and their crest,

The saracen's head crest of Selby carved as the newel post on the Jacobean staircase at Ightham Mote.

a saracen's head, can be found on the newel of the Jacobean staircase, inserted by Sir William Selby II *c.*1611. The saracen's head again makes its appearance in the frieze of the Drawing Room, and the chimneypiece in that room has the arms of Sir William Selby II impaled with the quartered arms of his wife, Dorothy Bonham.

In the Courtyard it is the Clements, with their strong Tudor allegiance, who are most prominent. The decorative oak bargeboards of the old solar next to the Great Hall built by Richard Clement *c.*1521 are carved with three royal badges, as if hanging from twining branches: the Tudor rose, the French fleur de lys and the pomegranate of Granada – the badge of Catherine of Aragon. The prominent use of Catherine of Aragon's pomegranate in Richard Clement's decoration at Ightham Mote dates his work to before 1529; it would not have been flaunted so boldly after Henry VIII began divorce proceedings against his wife.

The west window of the Great Hall also contains a well-designed scheme of heraldic glass inserted by Richard Clement in the 1520s. The central light contains the royal arms of Henry VIII. In the side lights are crowned badges. To the left is Catherine of Aragon's pomegranate and the Tudor rose with two little pomegranates beneath it. To the right is the red rose of Lancaster with two little white roses beneath it, and the Beaufort portcullis, another Tudor badge indicating their descent from John of Gaunt and their claim to the throne. Henry VII's lavish use of the Beaufort portcullis in the decoration of his eponymous chapel at Westminster Abbey was the inspiration for much of Pugin's decoration in the Houses of Parliament, with the result that it has become the badge of the Palace of Westminster, and is now to be found, for instance, on House of Commons sherry bottles, and House of Lords chocolate boxes. The Great Hall was restored in the 1890s for the then owner Sir Thomas Colyer-Fergusson, whose crest is carved on the doors. The series of arms of successive owners and their connections round the Hall panelling is also of that date.

The principal display of Tudor heraldry at Ightham Mote, and one of the most important in England, is on the wagon ceiling of the new Chapel built between 1521 and 1529 by Richard Clement originally as a gallery. Though reconstructed, during a general restoration of the house in the 1890s, considerable effort was made to retain as much of the old fabric as possible, including the rare painted wooden barrel vault.

The ribs are painted with chevrons in the Tudor livery colours of green and white (or silver). The panels alternate. One has the royal badges: the roses of Lancaster, Tudor, and York, the Beaufort portcullis, the pomegranate (dimidiated with a rose), and other Spanish badges of Catherine of Aragon – the castle of Castile and arrows of Aragon. The alternate panels are painted in lozenges of the green and white livery colours, with roses or fleurs de lys at the intersections. This whole scheme is a rare survival of the temporary heraldic decorations which formed part of the settings of festivities in the royal palaces in the reign of Henry VIII. There is a strong possibility that it was part of a pavilion at the Field of the Cloth of Gold where Henry VIII met Francis I of France, near Boulogne in 1520, in a specially constructed camp with extravagant heraldic pavilions, and fountains flowing with wine, and that Richard Clement, who was in the royal entourage on that occasion, acquired it afterwards from the Royal Wardrobe and reused it as a more permanent fixture in his new Gallery at Ightham Mote.

Kedleston Hall

DERBYSHIRE

Curzon

Arms: Argent on a Bend Sable three Popinjays Or plain collared beaked and legged Gules

Crest: On a Wreath of the Colours (Argent and Sable) A Popinjay rising wings expanded and inverted Or plain collared beaked and legged Gules

Badge: A Cockatrice wings elevated the tail nowed and terminating in a dragon's head Gules feet and wattles Azure

Supporters: (Dexter) The Figure of Prudence represented by a Woman habited Argent mantled Azure holding in her sinister hand a Javelin entwined with a Remora proper; (Sinister) The Figure of Liberality represented by a like Woman habited Argent mantled Purpure holding a Cornucopia proper

Motto: *Let Curzon holde what Curzon helde*
Recte et Suaviter
[Rightly and agreeably]

Kedleston is remarkable in that as the seat of one of the oldest established families in the country, it nevertheless indulges in only the most discreet heraldic display. In this it is typical of the extreme restraint of late eighteenth-century English neo-classical architecture which derived its decorative vocabulary from Greece and Rome, and eschewed heraldry because of its Gothic associations. There is heraldry at Kedleston, but it is so minute that it has to be looked for and is easily mistaken for run of the mill classical ornament, as in the case of the Curzon cockatrice badge which looks like Desgodetz's Roman griffin.

The Curzons have lived at Kedleston for over eight centuries, but the great palace built by Nathaniel Curzon, 1st Lord Scarsdale between 1758 and 1768 to the designs of Matthew Brettingham I, James Paine and Robert Adam conceals rather than discloses the long history of continuous family tenure. The name Curzon derives from Courson in Normandy. A Curzon came to England under William the Conqueror, in the train of his de Ferrers overlord. Their acquisition of Kedleston came through the process of sub-infeudation after the Norman Conquest, whereby land in England was divided up and held in return for military service or 'knights' fees'. The Conqueror granted land to tenants-in-chief, barons and bishops, who in turn let parts of it to sub-tenants in return for knights' service. In south Derbyshire Henry de Ferrers was one of the principal tenants-in-chief; it is not surprising therefore that he should have rewarded a loyal henchman with some of his new English fiefs. The Curzons were granted lands under de Ferrers at Croxall, Staffordshire, Kedleston in Derbyshire and at West Lockinge in Berkshire, amounting to three knights' fees. In 1198 this inheritance was divided between two sons; Thomas de Curzon took Kedleston for his share and his male-line

LEFT: The Curzon cockatrice badge with the tail terminating in a dragon's head appears in roundels four times on the ceiling of the Marble Hall at Kedleston: twice above the front door and twice above the Saloon door.

descendants have been there ever since. A knightly family in the Middle Ages, they were created Nova Scotia baronets by Charles I in 1636, and Lord Scarsdale in George III's coronation honours in 1761, but they produced their greatest figure in the twentieth century: George Nathaniel, 1st and last Marquess Curzon, Viceroy of India, Foreign Secretary and benefactor of the National Trust.

Bearing all of this in mind, it is nothing short of astonishing that the pediment of the portico on the North Front is blank; presumably an heraldic cartouche would have been considered too baroque in the 1750s and 1760s. The Marble Hall, resplendent with alabaster monoliths and classical statuary, and mythological grisailles, the nearest thing to an Imperial Roman temple interior in Britain, at first glance seems even more of a heraldry-free zone than the façade; but persist, for in the centre of the friezes of Adam's twin chimneypieces are tiny marble tablets of the arms of the 1st Lord Scarsdale impaling Colyear for his wife Lady Caroline. Even here full-blooded heraldry has been sacrificed to eighteenth-century elegance. Instead of the shield the arms appear in an oval cartouche, and the supporters have been reduced to languid maidens sitting – rather than standing – on either side. Even when not redesigned by Adam, the Scarsdale arms are, however, an interesting clash of heraldic conventions. There is a contrast between the masculine medieval coat with its bend of gold popinjays and the two somewhat effete 1761 supporters of women in white night-dresses (actually Liberality and Prudence).

The Imperial Roman magnificence of the entrance atrium at Kedleston has nothing so ordinary as conventional hall chairs – instead carved and painted copies of sarcophagi, with striated fluting, line the walls. But they do have little ovals of the family arms painted on their ends with the badge of a Nova Scotia baronet on an escutcheon of pretence. The stucco ceiling, designed by George Richardson in 1774 incorporates the Curzon cockatrice badge in classical roundels in the coving. The full achievement of the Curzon arms makes an appearance in the State Dressing Room on the top of the gilt palm-tree-framed pier glass. The scagliola tops of the side tables of 1761-2 in the Family Corridor have a more colourful depiction of the arms of Curzon

RIGHT: The scagliola table top of 1761-2 in the Family Corridor at Kedleston showing the impaled arms of Sir Nathaniel Curzon, 5th Bt., created 1st Lord Scarsdale in 1761, and his wife, Caroline Colyear.

impaling Colyear. The silver in the Dining Room also has a conventional display of heraldry with the 1st Lord Scarsdale's arms (impaling Colyear). The most impressive piece is the eighteenth-century-style cistern made for Lord Curzon out of the presentation caskets he received as Viceroy of India between 1898 and 1905, which is magnificently engraved with his quartered arms. Lord Curzon was also responsible for the plaster panels of 1923 on the staircase walls which are ornamented with the popinjay crest.

The adjoining medieval church, so close it almost seems part of the outbuildings, is a celebration of the family lineage and heraldry, with its series of family monuments from the Middle Ages to the twentieth century, culminating in the Memorial Chapel of Lord Curzon, designed by G. F. Bodley, with its white marble tomb, hanging banners and all the trappings of greatness.

Knightshayes Court

DEVON

HEATHCOAT-AMORY

ARMS, Quarterly: (1&4 Amory) Argent two Bars Gules on a Bend engrailed with plain Cottises Sable two Annulets Argent; (2&3 Heathcoat) Vert three Piles one reversed in base between the others issuant from the chief Or each charged with a Pomme thereon a Cross Or

CRESTS: (1 Amory) On a Wreath of the Colours (Argent and Gules) The Battlements of a Tower Or therefrom issuant a Talbot's Head Azure charged with two Annulets fesswise and interlaced Or
(2 Heathcoat) On a Wreath of the Colours (Or and Vert) Upon a Mount Vert between two Roses springing from the same Gules stalked and leaved proper a Pomme charged with a Cross Or

MOTTO: *Amore Non Vi*
[By love not force]

Knightshayes is one of the few full-blooded Victorian Gothic Revival houses in the ownership of the National Trust. It was designed for Sir John Heathcoat-Amory by the brilliant and very eccentric William Burges in the 1870s and the decoration of the rooms was carried out, in a modified form, by J.D. Crace. Crace was the fifth generation of a dynasty of decorators whose careers spanned the nineteenth century, and whose Gothic and heraldic work was strongly influenced by A.W.N. Pugin, many of whose schemes the Craces were called in to execute. Pugin was largely responsible, in the wake of earlier designers like Thomas Willement (q.v. Charlecote) and J.C. Buckler (q.v. Oxburgh), for the full-blown revival of the decorative conventions of

The arms of Heathcoat-Amory quarterly (1&4) Amory (2&3) Heathcoat with two crests, the motto and badge of the baronetage carved on bellows at Knightshayes.

medieval heraldry, and had enormous influence on all the Victorian architects and designers who came after him. Burges's version of Gothic, like that of many of his contemporaries, was muscular and much influenced by French examples but enlivened by his own particular 'Billy Bunter' character and wit, such as the frieze of carved stone billiard balls on the outside of the Billiard Room.

The Heathcoat-Amorys, who originally created all this revived medieval splendour, were characteristic Victorian industrial entrepreneurs. Their fortune was based on the machine-manufacture of lace by John Heathcoat who, after the destruction of his original factory in Nottingham by Luddites, moved to Tiverton and started afresh there. His daughter Anne married Samuel Amory, a London lawyer and banker, and he expanded the business to become the largest lace factory in the world, as well as double-barrelling his name. His son in turn established himself as a country gentleman, buying the Knightshayes estate in 1860 and becoming an M.P., Deputy Lieutenant of the County and Justice of the Peace. This was the classic path for successful industrialists in the nineteenth century, and, indeed, in the twentieth.

The architecture of his new house fully expressed his aspirations, which were realised when John Heathcoat-Amory was created a baronet in 1874. Like many Victorian Gothic houses, Knightshayes is rich in heraldic decoration, but here there is an interesting anomaly in the heraldry. Until their own grant of arms at the time of their baronetcy the Amorys used an 'ancient' coat which was a spurious variation of the arms of Amory of Devon recorded in 1620. The Amorys of Knightshayes were not descended from this particular family and their use of the arms was unauthorised. Their own grant is substantially differenced. Because of the lengthy building history of the house most of the external heraldry uses the unauthorised shield of Amory (ancient) while the interior makes much use of their own new grant of arms. Burges's unexecuted plans show Amory (ancient) but the Crace decorations were able to draw on the new arms.

The heraldic scheme begins with the Entrance Lodge which bears the shields of Heathcoat, Amory (ancient) and Unwin (for the 1st Baronet and his wife). On the gateposts are Amory (ancient), to the left, and Unwin, to the right. The same arms can be found on the exterior of the house. The gables and chimneystacks all have carved stone shields with the arms of Amory (ancient). On the bell turret a talbot holds a shield with the same arms, somewhat weathered in its exposed position, high up. The arms in the spandrels of the bay window to the Hall, however, are more protected and survive in mint condition with Amory (ancient) to the left and Unwin to the right. The talbot's head crest makes his appearance over the front door.

The Garden Front is no less redolent of the family heraldry. In the central gable a well carved stone angel holds two shields, held on *trompe* ropes, of the arms of Amory (ancient) and Heathcoat, and above the garden door are three shields of Heathcoat, Amory (ancient) and Heathcoat and Amory (ancient) quartered (with baronet's badge) for Sir John Heathcoat-Amory, the 1st Baronet and builder of the house. The family heraldry even extends into the garden where some of the topiary has been clipped into a resemblance of the Amory talbot's head crest.

The Great Hall at Knightshayes was partly dismantled in about 1914 (part of a

The octagonal Morning Room at Knightshayes with the arms of Unwin quartering Rowe and Unwin alone on the corbels above the window. The talbots' heads on the carpet are derived from the crest of Amory.

process carried out everywhere in the house in reaction to Victoriana), but like many of the original Crace and Burges interiors it has been substantially restored to its original form since the National Trust acquired the property in 1973. The *pièce de résistance* was a carved oak screen with outsize shields of the arms of Unwin, Amory (ancient), Heathcoat and Rowe on its gallery; this last heraldic feature has recently been restored, following the reinstatement of the main part of the screen in 1995. A scheme of heraldic stained glass for the windows was never executed.

A better preserved Victorian scheme, though not as it happens the work of Burges, survives on the staircase. The newels are topped with six heraldic talbots – a reference to the family crest – each holding a shield of arms representing the descent of the Heathcoat-Amory family and their marriages. The shield at the foot of the stairs has the impaled arms of the first Sir John Heathcoat-Amory (the builder of the house) and his wife, Henrietta Unwin, while at the top are those of Amory (ancient). These were all carved in oak by Harry Hems, the Exeter sculptor, and the scheme was devised by Charles Worthy, the author of *Practical Heraldry*. Hanging above the stairs are the banners of the arms of Derick, Viscount Amory as a Knight of the Garter and as a Knight Grand Cross of the Order of St Michael and St George.

In the Dining Room, Burges proposed a pair of large hooded chimneypieces of French thirteenth-century inspiration, decorated with four large coloured shields of the Heathcoat-Amory arms, but these were excised from the revised scheme executed by Crace. Burges's original coloured designs survive at Knightshayes in a specially bound volume and are evidence of his jolly approach to heraldry, and the Middle Ages in general. Heraldry in the Dining Room is today restricted to the firedogs which have the arms of Amory (ancient) and Unwin, and talbot's head finials.

In the octagonal Morning Room, the eight corbels supporting the ceiling beams have coloured shields of arms. The two over the Dining Room door and those over the door into the Hall Corridor show Heathcoat-Amory impaling Unwin and Heathcoat-Amory alone. The two over the window show Unwin quartering Rowe and Unwin alone, and finally over the fireplace and facing the window are the arms of Heathcoat and Amory. The National Trust played up to this heraldic decoration in the restoration of the room in 1975 by providing a specially woven heraldic carpet incorporating the family's talbot's head. Some of the collection of majolica displayed in here is decorated with the arms of Italian families.

Burges had intended the house to have a scheme of resplendent heraldic stained glass, in the Staircase Hall and elsewhere, but this was not executed. The top of the Garden Entrance, however, does have colourful glass with Heathcoat-Amory impaling Unwin quartering Rowe. The crests of Amory and Heathcoat are also shown. In the Library, Burges's elaborate ceiling with characteristic 'jelly mould' vaults was executed but later covered over. Restored by the National Trust in 1984, it contains a pair of splendid and unusual copper armorial roundels showing the full achievements of arms and crests of Heathcoat and Amory. The heraldic colours are indicated by a scheme of 'hatching', a technique usually encountered on the smaller scale of table silver. These no doubt were the work of S. J. Nichols, Burges's favourite sculptor. The intended heraldic Gothic chimneypiece in here was never executed.

Knole

KENT

Sackville

Arms: Quarterly Or and Gules a Bend Vair

Crest: Out of a Coronet composed of Fleurs de lys Or an Estoile Argent

Badge: A Leopard Argent spotted Sable

Supporters: On either side a Leopard Argent spotted Sable

Motto: *Aut Nunquam Tentes aut Perfice* [Either never attempt, or accomplish]

In the late Middle Ages Knole was one of the country houses of the Archbishop of Canterbury. It was bought in 1456 for £266 4d by Archbishop Bourchier. He built most of the present house with its spreading courtyard plan and turreted gatehouses, like a stone version of Hampton Court. His badge, the Bourchier knot (q.v. Beningbrough), is carved on the oriel of the Inner Wicket. In 1538, Knole was confiscated from Bourchier's successors by Henry VIII, who grabbed episcopal houses and other ecclesiastical property as well as all the monastic and chantry estates and goods. In 1566 Knole was granted by Elizabeth I to Thomas Sackville, Lord Buckhurst, later 1st Earl of Dorset, subject to an existing lease. It was only in 1603 that he bought out the lease and began to remodel the house in a fashionable Jacobean manner to celebrate the Earldom of Dorset received in that year from James I.

Though enormously enriched by the Tudors, the Sackville family had a long descent before that, and could trace their lineage to a Norman ancestor, Herbrand de Sackville, whose name came from Saqueville near Dieppe in Normandy, and came to England after the Conquest. The estate of Buckhurst in Sussex was acquired *c.*1200, and it still belongs to the senior line of the Sackville-West family. The 1st Earl of Dorset's father, Sir Richard Sackville, had made good use of his close relationship to his cousins, the Boleyns, and did well out of Henry VIII's despoliation of the Church. As Chancellor of the Court of Augmentations, the financial department set up by the King to administer the former monastic estates, Richard Sackville acquired so much land and property for himself that he was nicknamed 'Fillsack'. Thomas, 1st Earl, was Lord High Treasurer to Elizabeth I and held many other important offices and appointments; one of his less enviable tasks was announcing her death warrant to Mary Queen of Scots at Fotheringhay. He used his father's wealth to good effect in the adornment of Knole.

Thomas Sackville stamped his mark everywhere on his new house. On the outside, he added the decorative, shaped gables, each of them topped with the spotted Sackville leopard, clasping a shield of the Sackville arms. The lead rainwater pipes are also ornamented with his insignia: the rainwater heads have his coroneted cypher and the date 1605, and the pipes are secured to the wall by richly embossed lead plaques with the Sackville arms, encircled by the Garter and supported by the ubiquitous leopard. He filled the windows with heraldic glass showing his family's descent and connections as well as royal arms and badges.

Dorset remodelled and embellished the Great Hall, built by Archbishop Bourchier. The carved oak screen, by William Portington, Master Carpenter to Elizabeth I and James I, is a wonderful example of Jacobean joinery and heraldry. In the centre at the top is a huge achievement of the Sackville arms, with the Garter, and leopard supporters. Two leopards sit on the adjoining pinnacles, for all the world like two domestic cats who have climbed up to get out of reach of tiresome humans. The same spotted leopard, together with the ram's head crest, can also be seen on the plinths of both

The screen of 1605-8 in the Great Hall at Knole with, at the top in the centre, the arms of the 1st Earl of Dorset. Lower down the screen the arms of Sackville impale Baker of Sissinghurst for the 1st Earl and his wife.

stages of pilasters on the screen, and the central run of panels contains carvings of arms. The inner set of iron firedogs have the Sackville arms and ram's head crest; the tall steel show firedogs have the arms and initials of Henry VIII and Anne Boleyn – rare survivals of Tudor furnishings. They are recorded in the 1799 inventory of Knole as having been acquired at a sale at Hever Castle, the old Boleyn home.

The 7th Earl, Lionel, was created Duke of Dorset in 1720 by King George I. He was Lord Warden of Dover Castle, and the large painting by John Wootton of his arrival there to take the oath of office in 1721 hangs over the Hall fireplace. It has a magnificent eighteenth-century frame topped by a huge duke's coronet and the Sackville leopards. The heraldic stained glass in the windows was arranged by the antiquarian-minded 3rd Duke in the late eighteenth century. It is of different dates, ranging from a sixteenth-century achievement of the royal arms of Elizabeth I to eighteenth-century painted panels of the ducal Sackville arms with the estoile crest.

The Great Staircase leading to the Galleries and luxurious sets of State Apartments on the first floor was another of the 1st Earl's alterations. It is a *tour de force* of Jacobean decoration, the walls painted in grisaille after allegorical engravings of Martin de Vos, while the newels of the staircase itself sport carved and painted leopards holding cartouches of the Sackville arms. The windows are enriched with contemporary painted glass of Sackville heraldry, including the leopard.

The famous furnishings of the State Rooms contain much of rare heraldic interest. Some of the furniture was brought to Knole at the end of the seventeenth century by the 6th Earl of Dorset, who as Lord Chamberlain to William and Mary procured many pieces from the royal palaces as his perquisites after the death of the Queen. James II's bed in the Venetian Ambassador's Room has a lion and unicorn, the supporters of the royal arms, carved on the cornice, as well as his cypher, crown and Garter on the headboard.

In the Ballroom, the Sackville arms are engraved, sgraffito-like, on to the slab of black Bethersden marble which forms the fire-arch. The gilded wall-lights, in the manner of William Kent, have the Sackville arms or the estoile crest. The carved pilasters have the leopard which also appears on the stucco ceiling in here, as well as in the Reynolds Room next door.

The fabulous silver in the King's Bedroom is engraved with arms of different dates. The sconces (dated 1685) have the impaled arms of the 6th Earl of Dorset and his second wife, Lady Mary Compton, daughter of the Earl of Northampton. The silver table and mirror are embossed with the coronet and monogram of Frances Cranfield, wife of the 5th Earl. Also in the King's Room is an Elizabethan carpet with the impaled arms of Curzon (of Croxall in Staffordshire) and Leveson which probably came to Knole in the time of the 4th Earl of Dorset, as these are the arms of his wife's parents.

In the Cartoon Gallery, which leads to the King's Room, is a portrait of Henry Howard, Earl of Surrey, grandfather of Lady Margaret Howard who married the 2nd Earl of Dorset. Poet, soldier and victim of Henry VIII, who ordered him to be beheaded in the last weeks of his reign, Henry Howard has some significance here, for he is the only person to have been executed for treason on heraldic grounds. He was accused of using the arms of Edward the Confessor, a privilege granted to his Mowbray ancestor by Richard II, and although he was entitled to quarter the arms of Thomas of Brotherton (son of Edward I) his enemies successfully misrepresented this to the jealous, dying King as tantamount to a claim to the throne. The controversial royal quartering, with a label for difference, is held aloft by a cherub.

The early seventeenth-century copies of the Raphael cartoons which gave the room its name have on their frames the arms of Cranfield with an earl's coronet, for Lionel Cranfield, 1st Earl of Middlesex (d.1645), the rich London merchant who became

OPPOSITE: *One of the carved and painted leopards on the newel posts of the Great Staircase at Knole holding an Italianate cartouche of the Sackville arms.*

A detail of the Elizabethan carpet in the King's Room at Knole showing the impaled arms of Curzon of Croxall and Leveson for Sir George Curzon and his wife, whose daughter Mary married the 4th Earl of Dorset in 1612.

Lord High Treasurer. In the windows of the Cartoon Gallery are twenty-one shields depicting the arms of successive Sackvilles impaled with those of their wives.

There is also much later heraldry at Knole. Part of the fascination of the great house derives from the eighteenth-century attitude towards the medieval and Jacobean architecture, with gentle interventions here and there intended to heighten the 'olden tyme' effect. Thus, in the Outer Courtyard the lead statue of a gladiator has the Sackville arms, encircled by the Garter, embossed on his shield. On the parapet of the Great Hall is a huge cartouche brought from Copt Hall, Essex, in 1701, which depicts the quartered arms of Lionel Cranfield, Earl of Middlesex impaled with those of his second wife, Anne Brett, the maternal grandparents of the 6th Earl of Dorset. Their arms also appear in the spandrels of the outer gatehouse. The wooden balustrade of the colonnade below was restored in the mid-eighteenth century, as is attested by embossed lead panels with the Garter, duke's coronet, the estoile crest, the cypher 'L.D.' for Lionel (Duke of) Dorset, and the date 1748. The Jacobean Second Painted Staircase is decorated with early eighteenth-century grisaille paintings on the walls. These were also added by the 1st Duke and incorporate the insignia of the Garter, the estoile crest and the duke's coronet. Successive Earls and Dukes of Dorset were very proud of their Garter, as is shown by the unique framed engraved glass panel hanging on the wall of the little closet off the King's Room, showing the arms of Charles, 6th Earl of Dorset to commemorate his installation as a Knight of the Garter on 24 February 1692.

Lacock Abbey

WILTSHIRE

Sharington

Arms: Gules two Crosses paty in pale Or voided Sable between two Flaunches checky Argent and Azure

Crest: On a Wreath Argent and Azure A Scorpion Or its tail erect gobony Or and Argent between two Elephants' Tusks per fess the upper part checky Argent and Azure the lower part Gules charged with a Cross paty Or voided Sable

Badge: A Scorpion its tail erect Argent

Talbot

Arms: Gules a Lion rampant within a Bordure engrailed Or

Crest: On a Chapeau Gules turned up Ermine A Lion passant Or

The Augustinian nunnery was founded at Lacock in 1229 by Ela, Countess of Salisbury in memory of her husband, William Longespee, Earl of Salisbury, one of the founders of Salisbury Cathedral and a supporter of King John. Ela herself

ABOVE: *The scorpion badge of Sir William Sharington (d.1553) on the boss in the centre of the carved stone table of c.1550 in Sharington's Tower at Lacock.*

joined the community on Christmas Day 1238 and became its first Abbess. Her eldest son died on Crusade; two granddaughters became nuns; and a younger son a priest, later becoming Bishop of Salisbury.

It is perhaps an instructive illustration of the decline of English public life between the thirteenth and sixteenth centuries to compare this noble and pious family with William Sharington who purchased the Abbey a year after its dissolution by Henry VIII in 1539. Sharington was one of the more dishonest of the Tudor 'new men'. He made a fortune by embezzling the proceeds of his office as Vice-Treasurer of the Bristol Mint, clipping the coins and pocketing the extra silver or gold. Though prosecuted and imprisoned in the Tower, he was eventually pardoned and released, returning to Lacock. There he had demolished the church and converted the upper storey of the thirteenth-century conventual buildings into a Renaissance country house, retaining the old cloisters. His badge, appropriately enough, was a scorpion which appears with his initials 'W.S.' carved on the stonework of his additions to Lacock, especially in the new Strongroom Tower, the parapet of which is surmounted by heraldic beasts. The scorpion badge also appears three times on Sharington's tomb in Lacock church, which with its renaissance detail was one of the most important Elizabethan monuments in England. His arms are also carved there, and impaled with those of his three wives.

The coin-clipping scorpion had no children of his own, and his estates therefore passed to his niece, Olive, who married John Talbot, a member of a cadet branch of the family of the Earls of Shrewsbury. Successive Talbots (the name continued, despite three inheritances through the female line) were squires of Lacock down to the death of Matilda Talbot in 1958; she gave the Abbey to the National Trust in 1944. The best-known member of the Lacock family was, perhaps, William Fox Talbot, the Victorian inventor of photography. The seventeenth-century funerary helms in the Stone Gallery show the Talbot crest; and the Talbot arms appear on the rare seventeenth-century *sgabello* chairs, also in the Stone Gallery.

The chief display of heraldry at Lacock is to be found in the Hall. This delightful Gothick interior was created in 1754 for John Ivory Talbot by Sanderson Miller, the gentleman architect and expert in Gothic. John Ivory Talbot had inherited Lacock from his grandfather in 1714, when he took the Talbot surname. Sanderson Miller and John Ivory Talbot covered the new Hall ceiling with painted plaster coats of arms, not just of the family but also of Ivory Talbot's friends – a charming tribute to Georgian hospitality. In the windows they arranged sixteenth-century heraldic glass which was probably salvaged from the old Hall on the site and may possibly be of Scorpion Sharington's time. The lavish display of heraldry in a room like the Hall at Lacock, particularly when compared to the restraint of a neo-classical house like Kedleston, shows how in the eighteenth century overt armorial decoration was associated in most people's eyes with Gothic architecture. There are some surviving carved medieval shields in the cloisters. This is the earliest heraldry at Lacock and makes it one of the few English country houses with authentic medieval armorial decoration. It is possible that this inspired John Ivory Talbot in the decoration of his new Hall.

OPPOSITE: *The Gothick Entrance Hall at Lacock designed by Sanderson Miller and completed in 1755. Miller's arms above the doorway, and those of other friends of John Ivory Talbot, were painted in 1756.*

Lanhydrock

CORNWALL

Robartes

Arms: Azure three Estoiles Or a Chief wavy also Or

Crest: On a Wreath of the Colours (Or and Azure) A Lion rampant Or holding a flaming Sword erect proper pommel and hilt Or

Supporters: On either side a Goat Argent ducally gorged Azure armed and unguled Or

Motto: *Quae Supra* [Things which are above]

The seventeenth-century front door at Lanhydrock with the arms of Carminow quartering Lower in the top centre and in the four quarters the arms of Hender, Robartes with the badge of the baronetage impaling Hender, Robartes with the badge of the baronetage impaling a blank and Robartes with the badge of the baronetage. The arms of Robartes postdate 1621 when Sir Richard Robartes, who purchased Lanhydrock in 1620, was created a baronet. He married Frances Hender in 1598.

Although part gutted by fire in 1881 Lanhydrock, at least from the outside, is a seventeenth-century house. It was built between 1630 and 1642 by the Robartes family, merchants from Truro. The original front door has richly carved oak panels with fine shields. The carved stone panel above depicts the quartered arms, goat supporters and motto *Quae Supra* of John, 2nd Lord Robartes, subsequently 1st Earl of Radnor. There is a magnificent Jacobean pedigree of his descent on a vellum roll, signed and dated by Sir William Segar, Garter, 1620, displayed in the Corner Room with three later grants. The great surviving Jacobean interior at Lanhydrock is the Long Gallery with its barrel plaster ceiling decorated with biblical scenes and the impaled arms of the 2nd Lord Robartes and his first wife, Lady Lucy Rich, over the east window. This room was made into the Library in the 1880s. Lanhydrock possesses a fine collection of old books, and the Lanhydrock Atlas of 1694, displayed in this room, has a contemporary binding stamped with quartered arms.

The other principal rooms in the house were reconstructed after the fire by Richard Coad, a pupil of George Gilbert Scott. They are competent and comfortable and retain a suitably Jacobean aura. They have the usual Victorian display of heraldry, including needlework chair covers with impaled arms. The Morning Room has an elaborate plaster heraldic overmantel with the arms of Robartes impaling Dickinson. Her Ladyship's Bedroom has a similar overmantel with the impaled arms. The elaborate barrel ceiling in this room also depicts shields of Robartes impaled with Dickinson. These are the arms of Thomas, 2nd Baron Robartes (of the second creation) and 6th Viscount

The plaster overmantel in the Morning Room at Lanhydrock with a full achievement of the arms of the 2nd Baron Robartes (d.1930) impaled with those of his wife, Mary Dickinson.

Clifden, who restored Lanhydrock after the 1881 fire. His wife Mary was the daughter of Francis Dickinson of Kingweston, the Vanbrugh house near Bristol. Their eldest son Thomas was killed in the First World War and his school photographs in the Study make an evocative memorial to doomed Edwardian youth. Their mounts are embellished with the Eton arms.

A good deal of the special interest of Lanhydrock comes from the completeness of its domestic offices: kitchen, dairy, larders and so forth. They have been suitably furnished by the National Trust. Footmen's liveries can be seen hanging in their cupboards in a special Footmens' Livery Room on the top floor. They are blue and silver with silver crested buttons and belonged to the servants of the Tregonings of Landue. English servants' liveries of this type remained the same from the eighteenth to the twentieth centuries. On the whole, they have not been worn in private households since the Second World War (though they are still used on state occasions in the Royal Household), so are rarely seen. But like the engraved arms on silver plate, painted crests on hall chairs and carriage doors, armorial bookplates in the Library or hatchments hung after death, they were for centuries part of the standard heraldic paraphernalia of armigerous families. Footmen's coats were often made up in the family livery colours (red and silver in the case of the Dukes of Norfolk, for instance, or canary yellow for the Earls of Lonsdale), while the double rows of decorative silver buttons were embossed with the appropriate crest, coronet or full achievement of arms of the employer's family.

Lyme Park

CHESHIRE

LEGH

ARMS: Gules a Cross engrailed Argent with an augmentation of On an Inescutcheon Sable semy of Mullets Argent an Arm embowed in armour Argent the hand grasping a Standard Silver

CREST: Issuant out of a Crest Coronet Or a Ram's Head Argent armed Or in the mouth a sprig of Laurel Vert

SUPPORTERS (1892): On either side a Mastiff proper collared Sable

MOTTO: *En Dieu est Ma Foi* [In God is my faith]

A quadrangular gritstone palace, lying in a large romantic deerpark in the foothills of the Pennines, Lyme was for 548 years the seat of the Legh family. Originally granted to Piers I by Richard II in recognition of his father-in-law Sir Thomas Danyers' service at the Battle of Crécy where he rescued the standard of the Black Prince, it continued in their ownership till 1946 when it was given to the National Trust by the 3rd Lord Newton. The Leghs may have fought at Agincourt, certainly at Flodden, at Waterloo and at Inkerman; according to John Cornforth, 'one entertained Elizabeth's Essex, another went to the Tower for refusing to swear allegiance to William III, and a third was an Egyptologist in the age of Byron. And in almost every generation the pull of the past was strong ...'

The first record of a house on the present site was in 1465. It became the chief house of the Leghs during the reign of Elizabeth I. It was rebuilt as a quadrangle of stone by Sir Piers Legh VII *c.*1570, and was remodelled under Peter Legh X between *c.*1720 and 1730, to the design of Giacomo Leoni, keeping the quadrangular plan, and retaining substantial parts of the Elizabethan interior.

The Leghs are exceptional, but not unique, among English noble families in that whilst of ancient lineage, endowed with vast wealth from the Lancashire coal fields and frequently knighted in the Middle Ages, they had no hereditary title till the very end of the nineteenth century, when William John Legh was created 1st Lord Newton in 1892. They were proud to be Mr Legh of Lyme, in a house as big as the palace of many ruling Continental princes. This had something to do with being on the 'wrong side': they did not support William III; they were not Whigs; they had Jacobite sympathies.

Colonel Thomas Peter Legh did not marry the mother of his children. One of the peculiarities of the records at the College of Arms is the series of individual re-grants of the family arms to his sons and daughters in 1806, all suitably differenced with a wavy border. Successive generations of Leghs were extremely proud of these arms, and especially of the escutcheon of honour for Crécy with an arm holding a silver pennon, commemorating the English standard-bearer at that victory. So proud were they of this, that their footmen's livery had a spare sleeve, flapping at the back, to symbolise the flag-holding arm, and this escutcheon is to be found all over Lyme in addition, or in preference, to the ram's head crest or the full arms.

The Elizabethan North (Entrance) Front was part remodelled and regularised in 1676 by Richard Legh, and the lead rainwater heads record this with arms – surprisingly, in the form of Legh of Adlington – and monogram, impaling those of his wife, Elizabeth Chicheley. The classical centrepiece, inspired by Old Somerset House, survives from the Elizabethan house and displays the quartered arms of Sir Piers VII, with Coroun in the first quarter and Legh in the second, in the little pediment over the entrance arch.

In the Entrance Hall, the early eighteenth-century portrait of the Black Prince with the Prince of Wales feathers over the frame recalls the story of Sir Thomas Danyers' service in the Hundred Years War. The Edwardian gilt side tables have the Legh ram's head crest on their aprons. The adjoining Grand Staircase forms part of Leoni's work; the plaster ceiling by the Italian *stuccadore* Consiglio is embellished with the Crécy escutcheon, which also makes its proud appearance in the corners of the beautiful rococo ceiling of the Saloon. The famous carvings on the walls in here incorporate the Legh ram's head.

Upstairs, in the Long Gallery, some good Elizabethan heraldry survives in the chimneypiece, which is moulded with the royal arms of Elizabeth I. The Gallery ceiling,

LEFT: *The escutcheon of honour, granted in 1575 as an augmentation to the arms of Legh for the heroism of an ancestor at the Battle of Crécy in 1346, used as decoration in the plasterwork of the Library ceiling at Lyme.*

made by the house carpenter with a fretsaw in 1929, includes the Crécy escutcheon. The Mary Queen of Scots Room has an original sixteenth-century plaster ceiling, which provided the model for that in the Long Gallery. The Elizabethan overmantel incorporates the impaled arms of Gerard and Radcliffe surmounted by crests.

An achievement of the royal arms of James I appears in the overmantel of the Stag Parlour above a small carved version of the arms of Peter Legh IX, probably copied in the early nineteenth century from the overmantel in Paddock Cottage, a prospect tower in the park. The large Drawing Room next to it is the finest Elizabethan room at Lyme and has the most magnificent overmantel of all, with the coloured and gilded arms of Elizabeth I, encircled by the Garter.

In the early nineteenth century, when Lewis Wyatt designed some alterations and extensions at Lyme for Thomas Legh, a collection of old stained glass perhaps partly from Disley church was installed in the Drawing Room windows. Arranged like a brightly coloured patchwork quilt, it includes a quantity of heraldry alongside religious and allegorical subjects. In the bay window is sixteenth- and seventeenth-century glass. The arms of James I are prominent, at the top. The lower panes have the arms of the Leghs and successive heiress wives. The two side windows in the bay contain arms of the Knights of the Garter in the reign of Elizabeth I and of the Earls of Chester. Finally, the keystone of the arch of the 1863 Stable Block by Alfred Darbyshire is in the form of a handsome carved version of the ram's head crest.

LYVEDEN NEW BIELD

NORTHAMPTONSHIRE

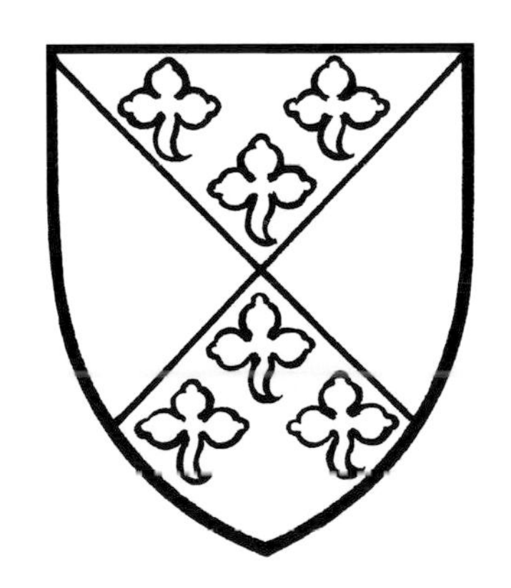

TRESHAM

ARMS: Per saltire Sable and Argent six Trefoils (2&1 and 1&2) Or

CREST: On a Wreath Or and Sable A Boar's Head erased at the neck Sable ducally gorged Or holding by the stalk in the mouth a Trefoil fessways slipped Vert

MOTTO: *Fecit mihi magna qui potens est* [He that is mighty hath done to me great things]

Sir Thomas Tresham (d.1605) was one of an interrelated group of Midlands Catholic families in the reign of Elizabeth I. His wife was a Throckmorton of Coughton (q.v.), his mother was a Catesby and his sister Mary married the 3rd Lord Vaux of Harrowden, while his children were married into the Stourton and Brudenell families, all of whom were strongly recusant at that date. Tresham was imprisoned on religious grounds in a variety of places, including the old Bishop's Palace at Ely in the Fens (which he hated), for a period of over twenty years. This did not stop him from pursuing his interests in theology, symbolism, heraldry and architecture, all of which found

The 1568 portrait of Sir Thomas Tresham (d.1605) with eighteen quarters. Quarters 3-7 came from his great-grandmother, Isabel Harrington, and 8-18 from his grandmother, Anne Parr.

expression, when he regained his liberty, in the great renaissance library which he collected, and in the buildings which he erected on his Northamptonshire estates at Rushton and Lyveden.

A substantial portion of his library passed to his Brudenell son-in-law, Lord Cardigan, and is still at Deene, but several of his buildings, which were architectural conceits expressing his theological interests, still stand, most notably the Triangular

Lodge at Rushton (now owned by English Heritage) and the New Bield at Lyveden.

Tresham had inherited an old manor house, the Old Bield, at Lyveden where he lived in alternation with his main house at Rushton. In the park, he began a lodge in 1594 which was never finished, but its shell survives in perfect order, and is a highly sophisticated design, part based on Serlio, whose *Book of Architecture* was in Tresham's library. This New Bield was designed for Tresham, by Robert Stickells, a royal clerk of works. It has a cruciform plan, and is carved with biblical inscriptions and emblems of the Passion, while the proportions were the product of symbolic numbers. Whereas the Triangular Lodge at Rushton celebrated the Trinity and Transubstantiation, the New Bield at Lyveden symbolized the Redemption and the Virgin Mary. Both buildings were also decorated with heraldry, which may sound incongruous, but was not to Tresham, for whom his heraldry had a religious significance.

Tresham all through his life had a passionate interest in heraldry, which was tangled up in his mind with his religious beliefs. He had a special personal devotion to the Trinity and had undergone an extraordinary experience while in prison at Ely where, during a debate on the Trinity, an unearthly power had knocked three times on the table in his room. Tresham's paternal arms were partly canting, being made up of threes like the *Tre* of his name, and like the Trinity. His shield was divided into triangles, and charged with trefoils. His motto, too, was Trinitarian. His wife's arms and

The 1585 bookplate of Sir Thomas Tresham of Lyveden and Rushton with twenty-five quarters. Quarters 3-7 came from Sir Thomas's great-grandmother, Isabel Harrington, and quarters 8-25 from his grandmother, Anne Parr.

those of his children's spouses symbolized a network of committed Catholic families.

In addition to the unusual, personal, religious meaning which his arms had for him, Tresham was also very proud of his family which had been gentry for a hundred years longer than many of his Northamptonshire neighbours such as the Hattons of Holdenby, the Spencers of Althorp or the Montagus of Boughton, who had all done well out of sheep and service to the Tudors. He could boast a whole series of quarterings brought in by early Tudor heiresses, including five from the Harringtons of Brixworth in Northamptonshire and more from the Parrs of Horton. He bore twenty-four quarterings on his bookplate, the second oldest printed English bookplate after Bacon's.

His buildings were intended as a vehicle for heraldic display in addition to their religious symbolism. At Rushton, there is a complete heraldic programme celebrating his descent, and the marriages of his children. At Lyveden New Bield, the arms are more personal with separate shields on the soffits of the arches in the bay window, depicting his own arms and those of his wife, Muriel Throckmorton.

Montacute House

SOMERSET

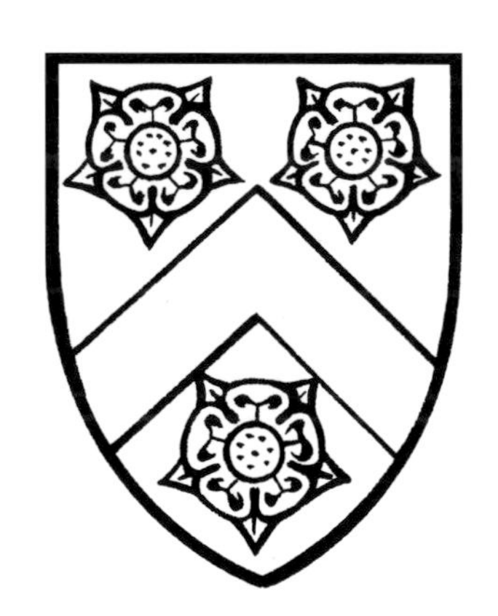

Phelips

Arms: Argent a Chevron between three Roses Gules barbed and seeded proper

Crest: On a Wreath of the Colours (Argent and Gules) A Square Fire Basket Or containing Flames proper

Motto: *Pro Aris et Focis* [For our altars and our homes]

An Elizabethan house, built like so many out of the profits of the law, in this case by Sir Edward Phelips, who became Speaker of the House of Commons and Master of the Rolls under James I. It was begun in 1588, the year of the Armada, and was finished by 1601. The date is carved beneath his arms on the East Front porch. Sir Edward's arms, impaled with those of his second wife, Elizabeth Pigott, also appear on the plaster overmantel of the Hall Chamber on the first floor. The master mason was probably William Arnold, builder of Wadham College, Oxford, who also worked at Cranborne Manor and Dunster (q.v.) in the West Country. The Phelips family lived here thereafter, but their fortunes declined precipitately in the nineteenth century, the house being let to a succession of tenants, including Lord Curzon; it was finally put up for sale in the 1920s. No buyer was forthcoming, and the house was eventually rescued, on the verge of demolition, by the Society for the Protection of Ancient Buildings and given by Ernest Cook (the travel agent) to the National Trust in the 1930s; it was one of the Trust's first country houses.

The house survives as a great Elizabethan mansion. The only major alterations and

The quartered full achievement of Phelips with an esquire's or gentleman's closed helm on a lozenge-shaped panel inserted in the Tudor façade from Clifton Maybank re-erected at Montacute in 1786-9.

The east bay window in the Library at Montacute with late sixteenth-century stained glass of arms including (top left) Phelips impaling Horsey.

additions were carried out in 1786-9 by Edward Phelips V, and are a remarkably early example of sympathy for old buildings and what is now called conservation. He added a new front on the west side, but re-used the frontage of an old Tudor house in the neighbourhood, Clifton Maybank, which was being partly demolished at the time. The purchase is recorded in his autobiography for 1786: 'On the 2nd of May, my wife and self attended the sale of materials of Clifton House, then pulling down. We bought the porch, arms, and pillars, and all the ornamental stone of the Front to be transferred to the intended Front at Montacute.' He 'signed' the reconstruction of the façade with his own coat of arms. Edward also bought a chimneypiece, some stained glass windows and oak panelling from Clifton for the embellishment of Montacute. The Horsey family of Clifton was in fact related to the Phelips family: Edith Phelips, who married Sir John Horsey, the builder of Clifton, was the aunt of Edward Phelips I.

Edward Phelips V also carried out some internal alterations in the 1780s, including the creation of the Common Parlour (now Dining Room) with its Elizabethan chimneypiece dated 1599 and showing the quartered Phelips arms impaling Malmaynes, which was inserted in 1787. This work too was remarkably sensitive to the Elizabethan architecture of Montacute.

In the Hall, the Elizabethan fireplace is a dignified Tuscan design in Ham Hill stone, and carries the arms of Phelips on its mantel. The Phelips arms are depicted, as a repeating motif, in the plaster frieze.

The most important contemporary heraldic feature of Montacute, however, is the sequence of armorial glass which fills the windows of the Hall, and the Great Chamber (now Library) upstairs. This is one of the best groups of late sixteenth-century glass in England, comparable with that in the Great Chamber at Gilling Castle, Yorkshire or in the Hall at Charlecote (q.v.). Interestingly, some of it, or something like it, is shown in the background of a portrait of Sir Edward Phelips, the builder, as Speaker which shows him standing in front of a window with panels of his quartered arms in the top light. It is thought that the stained glass was originally in the Long Gallery and was removed to its existing locations as part of the eighteenth-century alterations.

NOSTELL PRIORY

YORKSHIRE

WINN

ARMS: Ermine on a Fess Vert three Eagles displayed Or

CREST: On a Wreath of the Colours (Argent and Vert) A demi Eagle wings displayed Or plain collared Ermine

SUPPORTERS: On either side a Dragon reguardant Vert gorged with a Riband Or pendant therefrom an Escocheon Gules charged with a Rose Argent

MOTTO: *Tout Pour Dieu et ma Patrie* [All for God and my Country]

The present large but lop-sided eighteenth-century house was built for Sir Rowland Winn, 4th Bt. The original design by Col. James Moyser was executed by James Paine. But the chief distinction of the place is the interior that was begun by Paine and

The pediment over the Entrance Front at Nostell with a carved stone full achievement of c.1743 showing the arms of Sir Rowland Winn, 4th Bt. quartering Herbert with those of his wife, Susanna Henshaw, quartering Roper in pretence.

completed and decorated by Robert Adam in 1766-76 and the furniture supplied by Chippendale at the same time.

The priory was an Augustinian house dedicated to St Oswald, the martyr king of Northumbria. At the Dissolution it was acquired by Dr Thomas Leigh, the 'fattest and most pompous' of Henry VIII's commissioners. It changed hands several times until it was bought in 1650 by George and Rowland Winn, Aldermen of the City of London who had already acquired estates in Lincolnshire, where the family are still large landowners.

The founder of the family was the Aldermen's grandfather, George Winn, Draper to Elizabeth I. Rich merchants turned landowners, the elder Alderman, George Winn, was created a baronet at the Restoration as part of Charles II's wholesale bestowal of honours on those who had supported the Royalist cause. In 1885 his descendant, Rowland Winn (d.1893), became 1st Lord St Oswald in recognition of his political services as a Lord of the Treasury and Conservative Whip.

The pediment over the attached portico on the Entrance Front contains a large carved achievement of the Winn arms quartering Herbert, with Henshaw quartering

The architectural bookcases in the Library at Nostell designed by Adam in 1766 with the Winn demi eagle crest painted in grisaille in the pediments.

Roper in pretence, for Sir Rowland Winn, 4th Bt., who married Susanna Henshaw in 1729. The arms are the only carved ornament on this otherwise plain Palladian design.

The arms or crest are used discreetly but frequently in much of the interior decoration and furniture, reflecting Sir Rowland's sense of family. The crest is a demi eagle with its wings displayed, which – fortunately – was suited to Roman-inspired architecture. The eagle appears painted on the oval backs of the hall chairs in the Top Hall, which were designed for the room by Adam and executed by Chippendale. Perhaps more unexpected is its appearance, painted in grisaille, in the pediments of Adam's handsome architectural bookcases in the Library. It is also to be seen carved and gilded on the central roundels of Chippendale's semi-circular pier tables in the Saloon, as if it were a classical cameo, and appears again, in a more florid rococo mode, at the top of the broken pediments of James Paine's splendidly architectural plaster frames to the full-length portraits of the 4th Baronet and his brother, Col. Edmund Harbord Winn (d.1763), at either end of the Dining Room. As well as the crest, these frames also contain a decorative cartouche of the Winn arms. Sir Rowland's are quartered with Henshaw in pretence. Also to be seen in the Dining Room is part of an extensive Chinese export porcelain service of *c.*1808 showing the arms of Hannay impaling White.

The ubiquity of the Winn eagle inside Nostell is completed by its appearance on the famous dolls' house which dates from about 1740 and is complete in every detail. The Winn arms in its pediment are the same as those in the pediment of the main house.

Nunnington Hall

YORKSHIRE

Graham

Arms, Quarterly: (1&4 Graham) On a Chief Sable three Escallops Or; (2&3 Stuart) Or a Fess checky Argent and Azure in chief a Chevron Gules over all in the centre point a Crescent Gules

Crest: On a Wreath Or and Sable A Demi-Vol Or

Supporters: (Dexter) An Eagle (sinister) A Lion both Ermine armed Gules crowned Or

Motto: *Reason contents me*

The house was built in the sixteenth century by Dr Robert Huickes, physician to Elizabeth I, and reconstructed after damage in the Civil War by Richard Graham, 1st Viscount Preston when he inherited in 1685. It is the latter, with his Jacobite and Catholic sympathies, who is responsible for the special character of the house. Graham was a keen servant of the Stuarts and had served as Charles II's ambassador to France in 1682, a post he held till the death of the King in 1685.

His peerage in 1681 was a reward for his services. After the 1688 Revolution, however, he was imprisoned in the Tower and heavily fined for his overt Catholicism and support for the deposed James II for whom he was Master of the Wardrobe. Lord Preston's arms (re-carved in 1962 by John Bunting to replace the weathered originals) appear in a cartouche in the broken pediment of the central first floor window on the Entrance Front. His arms with supporters, motto and viscount's coronet also appear in the elaborately carved cartouche over the chimneypiece in the Oak Hall, the design for which is derived from an engraving in Jean Barbet's *Livre d'Architecture*. The Preston arms are quartered and impaled with those of his wife, Lady Anne Howard, daughter of the 1st Earl of Carlisle.

The Preston and Howard arms appear again in the unique painted ceiling of Lord Preston's Room. This comprises two large canvas panels with the full arms of Viscount Preston and the Earl of Carlisle (father of Lady Anne), and two smaller panels painted with the Graham and Howard crests, respectively. It is thought that these were painted by the Flemish-born artist Jacob Huysmans whom Preston had paid £25

The arms of the 1st Viscount Preston and those of his father-in-law, the 1st Earl of Carlisle, on the ceiling at Nunnington. The latter wrongly show the royal arms of Scotland on the bend rather than the Flodden augmentation.

for painting the ceiling of the Great Staircase at Nunnington in 1686 and may have supplied these panels at the same time. As a foreigner, Huysmans may have been responsible for the mistake in the Flodden augmentation on the arms of Howard, which is shown as the royal arms of Scotland rather than a *demi Lion with an Arrow through its mouth within a double Tressure*. There is nothing like them in any other English country house.

From 1839 to 1952 Nunnington belonged to the Rutsons. There is an eighteenth-century watercolour of the impaled arms of William Rutson (d.1793) and Elizabeth Carlton, the grandparents of the William Rutson who purchased Nunnington. The Rutson arms, used without authority until the formal grant in 1850, are those of the Rudston family of Yorkshire, baronets.

Osterley Park

MIDDLESEX

Child-Villiers

Arms, Quarterly: (1&4 Villiers) Argent on a Cross Gules five Escallops Or; (2&3 Child) Gules a Chevron engrailed Ermine between three Eagles close Argent each gorged with a ducal Coronet Or

Crests: (1 Villiers) On a Wreath of the Colours (Argent and Gules) A Lion rampant Argent ducally crowned Or
(2 Child) On a Wreath of the Colours (Argent and Gules) On a Rock proper an Eagle rising Argent gorged with a ducal Coronet Or and holding in the beak an Adder proper

Supporters: On either side a Lion rampant Argent ducally crowned Or plain gorged Gules the collar charged with three Escallops Or

Motto: *Fidei Coticula Crux* [The cross is the touchstone of faith]

This quadrangular brick house was built *c.*1576 by Sir Thomas Gresham, the Elizabethan banker and Lord Mayor of London. It was acquired by Sir Francis Child, the Elder, M.P. for Devizes, in 1713. He was banker-goldsmith to William III and Lord Mayor of London, as was his son, Sir Francis 'the Younger'. The latter's nephew, Robert Child (d.1782), remodelled Osterley completely between 1763 and 1780, creating the unparalleled Adam interior which is the house's chief claim to fame. He was much distressed by the elopement to Gretna Green of his only child Sarah Anne with the 10th Earl of Westmorland. To prevent the main line of the Westmorlands benefiting from this scandalous behaviour, he left Osterley to her second child whether male or female. This was a daughter, Sarah Sophia (d.1867), who married George Villiers, the 5th Earl of Jersey. Osterley belonged to the Earls of Jersey down to 1949, when the 9th Earl gave it to the National Trust.

There is no Gresham heraldry at Osterley, but the later owners have left their mark.

Like the Winns of Nostell (q.v.), the Childs had an eagle for their crest, and also an eagle as the charge on their shield, so managed to bypass Adam's distaste for heraldry in decoration by using their family emblem as a classical ornament. Thus the Entrance Front of Osterley has a pair of magnificent carved stone eagles with collars in the form of ducal coronets, mounting guard on either side of the great flight of steps to the portico. The unwary may assume that these are copies of the Aldobrandini eagle or some other Roman sculpture. They are, in fact, the Child crest without the adder in its beak. In the Entrance Hall, the marble chimneypieces, designed by Adam in 1768, are also embellished with the Child crest.

The full Child arms and crest are painted on the Chinese armorial dinner service, the only one known with a powder blue border. It was made in the 1720s for Sir Francis Child, the Younger, who also commissioned a large set of armorial lacquer hall furniture at the same time. The arms were comparatively new, the grant having been made in 1701. The china and the furniture were then at the Child house in Lincoln's Inn Fields but were brought to Osterley when Robert Child decided to sell the Lincoln's Inn Fields house in 1767. The Jerseys had the Chinese service enlarged to match in the 1820s. The black and gold lacquer hall chairs with the arms are now in the South Passage, as are the similarly decorated pair of lacquer chests and a lacquer screen.

The Long Gallery has a plaster frieze which pre-dates Adam's remodelling and probably dates from the 1740s; it is decorated with marigolds – not strictly heraldry, but the symbol of Child's Bank, which was situated at the Marygold by Temple Bar, and was the source of the riches which paid for Osterley. The marigold with the sun shining down on it all within a circlet inscribed *Ainsi Mon Arne* also appears embroidered in the centre of one of the long settees. At the other end of the Long Gallery in the centre of another long settee is an embroidered full achievement of Child-Villiers impaling Leigh for the 7th Earl of Jersey, who married in 1872 the Hon. Margaret Elizabeth Leigh.

A plate from the Chinese armorial dinner service of the 1720s made for Sir Francis Child, the Younger, of Osterley.

Adam's 1776 design for the state bed at Osterley with the Child eagle and adder crest alternating with marigolds on the valance.

The Child eagle crest is one of the principal motifs in the decoration of the state bed in the State Bedchamber, designed by Adam in 1776. It appears on the embroidered valance, alternating with the marigolds which refer to the bank. The crest is also incorporated, carved and gilded this time, in a roundel on the headboard of the bed. This whole theatrical composition embellished with heraldry, and classical symbols of sleep and fertility, was an optimistic celebration of the posterity of the Child dynasty. In the adjoining Etruscan Dressing Room the needlework panel for the firescreen, designed by Adam in 1776 and worked by Robert Child's wife, also contains an oval of the crest in the centre.

Oxburgh Hall

NORFOLK

Paston-Bedingfeld

Arms, Quarterly: (1&4 Bedingfeld) Ermine an Eagle displayed Gules; (2&3 Paston) Argent six Fleurs de Lys 3,2&1 Azure a Chief indented Or

Crests: (1 Bedingfeld) On a Wreath of the Colours (Argent and Gules) An Eagle displayed Or
(2 Paston) On a Wreath of the Colours (Or and Azure) A Griffin sejant wings elevated Or gorged with a Collar Gules therefrom a line held in the beak and terminating in a ring also Gules

Badge: A Fetter the thong Gules edged and studded and with buckles at both ends chained together Or

Motto: (Bedingfeld) *Despico Terrena Solem Contemplor* [I despise earthly things and contemplate the sun]
(Paston) *De mieulx je pense en mieulx* [From better I think to better]

There are few English country houses with as much heraldry as Oxburgh; every room contains illuminated pedigrees and escutcheons of arms, carved oak work or armorial china. This reflects the long history of the Bedingfelds, Catholic baronets. They built the house between 1476 and 1482, and still live there today. The present incumbent, Henry Paston-Bedingfeld, is himself a herald: York Herald of Arms. The

RIGHT: *A record of Bedingfeld quartering Tuddenham, the arms of Sir Edmund Bedingfeld (d.1496), the builder of Oxburgh (College of Arms Ms: L.10/26[b]).*

FAR RIGHT: *The Lambeth pottery dinner service of c.1719 showing the impaled arms of Sir Henry Arundell Bedingfeld, 3rd Bt. and his wife, Lady Elizabeth Boyle, whom he married in that year.*

OPPOSITE: *Detail of the heraldic ceiling in the Old Drawing Room, painted by J. D. Crace after 1870, showing the arms of Bedingfeld with Clavering in pretence for the 7th Baronet and his wife, who married in 1859.*

Bedingfelds trace their descent through the male line to sub-infeudation after the Norman Conquest. Their earliest ancestor, Ogier (a Viking name), held land at Bedingfeld near Eye in Suffolk of William Malet, who was one of the Conqueror's known companions at Hastings, suggesting that he came over from Normandy immediately after the Conquest.

In the Middle Ages the Bedingfelds were a knightly family, and fought at Crécy. They acquired Oxburgh by marriage in the fifteenth century, by which time they had already been established in England for 400 years. They were Yorkist supporters in the Wars of the Roses, and the Yorkist symbol of a falcon and fetterlock badge can be seen prominently displayed at Oxburgh, for instance on the bedcover in the King's Room. Later they supported the Tudors and were rewarded with some of the lands of Lambert Simnel's followers after his failed revolt; Henry VII and his Queen, Elizabeth of York, visited Oxburgh in 1497. Like many of the old gentry and nobility, the Bedingfelds remained Catholic in the sixteenth century and were Royalists in the Civil War. And, like many Royalist supporters, they were created baronets by Charles II after the Restoration.

In the eighteenth century the Bedingfeld boys, like most English Catholics, were educated on the Continent. They married well. Sir Henry, 3rd Bt.'s wife was the sister of Lord Burlington, the architect Earl, and a dinner service made at Lambeth in 1719, with the impaled arms of Bedingfeld and Boyle, commemorates the marriage. His son, Sir Richard, 4th Bt. (nicknamed Hooknose), married Mary Browne, the daughter of Viscount Montagu of Cowdray in Sussex. She brought to Oxburgh as her dowry the set of needlework hangings thought to be by Mary Queen of Scots which incorporate her cypher and crown.

Sir Henry, 6th Bt. married Margaret Paston, an heiress and the last of that famous medieval family. The family subsequently double-barrelled their name to Paston-Bedingfeld by a Royal Licence obtained in 1830 and thereafter quartered the beautiful Paston arms with their blue fleurs de lys.

Oxburgh had by that date fallen into decay, and Henry put 'The Ruin' as his address on top of his letters when writing to his brother. But Margaret inherited £50,000, so the young couple had the means to restore the house, which they did in full antiquarian spirit with the assistance of J. C. Buckler, J. G. Crace and possibly even Pugin himself, creating the present Library, Drawing Room and Dining Room. Old panelling and wood carvings were imported from the Continent, and the family heraldry was displayed everywhere. The Library fireplace, possibly by Pugin, has five shields of arms carved in its frieze. J. D. Crace later painted the ceiling of the Drawing Room with arms and heraldic badges.

Following the Catholic Emancipation Act in 1829, Henry and Margaret built a private Catholic Chapel in the grounds, which contains a feast of heraldry. The richly coloured armorial glass was designed by Thomas Willement in 1838. It is a superb example of nineteenth-century heraldic work, the coloured shields set into clear glass to great effect. The central light has the Bedingfeld red eagles holding a banner with the fetterlock and falcon badge, and shields of Bedingfeld arms. The side lights have the arms of heraldic heiresses, and the top lights have Yorkist royal badges.

Petworth House

SUSSEX

Percy

Arms, Quarterly: (1&4) (i&iv Percy often wrongly called Louvain) Or a Lion rampant Azure; (ii&iii Lucy) Gules three Lucies haurient 2&1 Argent; (2&3 old Percy) Azure five Fusils conjoined in fess Or

Crest: On a Chapeau Gules turned up Ermine A Lion statant the tail extended Azure

Badge: A Crescent Argent

Supporters: (Dexter) A Lion rampant Azure; (Sinister) A Lion rampant guardant Or ducally crowned Argent gorged with a Collar gobony Argent and Azure

Motto: *Esperaunce en Dieu* [Hope in God]

Seymour

Arms, Quarterly: (1&4 Augmentation) Or on a Pile Gules between six Fleurs de lys Azure three Lions passant guardant Or; (2&3 Seymour) Gules a pair of Wings inverted conjoined in lure Or

Crest: Issuing from a Crest Coronet Or a Phoenix in flames proper

Supporters: (Dexter) A Unicorn Argent armed maned tufted and unguled Or gorged with a ducal Coronet per pale Or and Azure a Line attached thereto gobony Or and Azure; (Sinister) A Bull Azure armed unguled and ducally gorged Or a Line Or attached to the collar

Motto: *Foy pour Devoir* [Faith for duty]

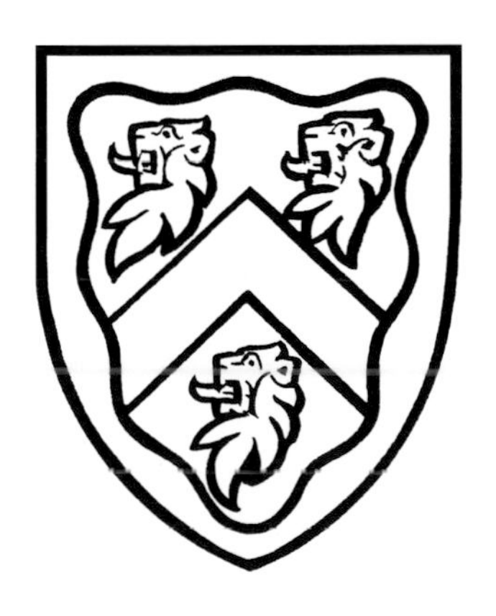

Wyndham
(1856 onwards)

Arms: Azure a Chevron between three Lions' Heads erased within a Bordure wavy Or

Crest: On a Wreath of the Colours (Or and Azure) A Lion's Head erased Or within a Fetterlock the lock Gold and the bow countercompony Or and Azure the head charged with a Saltire wavy Gules

Supporters: (Dexter) A Lion Azure winged invertedly and plain collared Or; (Sinister) A Griffin Argent gutty de sang plain collared Gules

Motto: *Au Bon Droit* [With good right]

The 'Proud Duke', Charles Seymour, 6th Duke of Somerset (d.1748), has left the most decisive mark on the ancient house of Petworth, which had been the seat of three creations of the Earldom of Northumberland. He rebuilt it as a baroque palace in 1688-96 and it is his arms which dominate the architecture. He married Elizabeth Percy, only surviving child of the 10th Earl of Northumberland (d.1670), who brought the house which had belonged to the Percys since the reign of King Stephen as her

ABOVE: *A seventeenth-century Italianate hall chair at Petworth with the Percy crescent badge beneath an earl's coronet.*

dowry. Evidence of the long Percy past is provided by the seventeenth-century Italianate hall chairs in the Grand Staircase Hall, which have the crescent badge of the Northumberlands, as do many of the seventeenth-century book bindings in the Library. The 3rd Earl of Northumberland's arms can also be seen on the fifteenth-century illuminated manuscript of Chaucer's *Canterbury Tales* displayed in the Somerset Room.

The 'Proud Duke' – even by the standards of seventeenth-century Dukes – was considered by contemporaries to be extraordinarily obsessed with his lineage and grandeur. Stories of his arrogance are legion. Outriders cleared the roads before his carriage so that he should not be subjected to the vulgar gaze; he partially disinherited one of his daughters for ignoring his instructions and daring to sit down in his presence, when he had dozed off; and according to Jeremiah Milles he treated all his 'country neighbours and indeed everybody else with such uncommon pride, and distance, that none of them visit Him'.

The Duke's crest was a phoenix rising from flames, and this together with the Seymour paired wings – the charge on his shield – is carved on the stone panels between the ground and first floor windows, and on the keystones of the great West Front, a wonderfully patrician effect. The Marble Hall, originally the main entrance to the house, has a pair of baroque achievements of the Duke's arms with Percy in pretence over the chimneypieces at either end with the Somerset supporters, a unicorn and a bull lying full length on either side of the segmental pediments, the whole topped with a huge duke's coronet. These two chimneypieces are among the best examples of integrated heraldry and architecture in any country house. The chased brass lockplates in the Marble Hall, and throughout the rooms, were made by the locksmith John Draper of Birmingham and are engraved with the Duke's crest.

The Grand Staircase, which was painted by Louis Laguerre after 1714 with scenes from the story of Prometheus, muses and gods, also includes in its decorative scheme a large shield of the quartered Somerset arms with Percy in pretence over the door from the Beauty Room. The 6th Duke's heraldry can also be found prominently displayed in the virtuoso limewood carvings by Grinling Gibbons, and his school, in the famous Carved Room. The full-length portraits of the Duke and his wife are surmounted by an immense pair of Seymour wings from which is suspended the George badge of the Order of the Garter. These are all the work of Gibbons himself. High up over the mirror between the central windows is an elaborate trophy of the Duke's arms and coronet, originally made in 1696 for the Hall of State.

The climax of the 'Proud Duke's' heraldry at Petworth, however, is the Chapel, which also contains numerous coats of arms documenting the Percys' medieval alliances in the windows, partly in heraldic glass and partly painted in the blocked side windows. The Duke copied the original heraldic glass in *trompe-l'oeil* paintwork. The glass, made about 1600, survives in the large window over the altar with the arms of successive Percys and their wives. The family pew at the west end is treated as a proscenium arch with carved and painted drapery and flying gilt angels holding a huge escutcheon of the Somerset arms encircled by the Garter, and with the largest coronet to be found in any English house. The Chapel arms are a remarkable testimony to the

OPPOSITE: *One of the two baroque achievements of the arms of the 6th Duke of Somerset, with Percy in pretence within the Garter, above the chimneypieces at either end of the Marble Hall at Petworth.*

The carved trophy by Grinling Gibbons of the 6th Duke of Somerset's arms with Percy in pretence within the Garter in the Carved Room at Petworth.

great pride the Duke took in his status – after the Duke of Norfolk he was the senior English Duke – and also in his family heraldry, which in addition to the Seymour quartering with wings also had a quartering with the fleurs de lys and three lions of the English royal arms. This was a coat of augmentation granted by King Henry VIII to the Seymour family to mark his marriage with Lady Jane Seymour. It would be difficult to have anything grander than that. But in addition to his ancestral arms the Duke was also able to display the arms of his heiress wife on an escutcheon of pretence. So in the centre of his shield, as it is depicted at Petworth, can be seen the medieval Percy arms with the azure lion and golden fusils, representing a family whose first recorded male line ancestor married a great-granddaughter of Charlemagne in 846.

On the death of the 7th Duke of Somerset in 1750, Petworth and the Earldom of Egremont (created in 1749) was inherited by his nephew, Sir Charles Wyndham,

4th Bt. His son in turn, George, 3rd Earl, was famous as the patron of Turner and other artists but did not marry the mother of his children till long after they were born. He was succeeded at Petworth by his eldest son George, created Lord Leconfield in 1859.

There is a good display of Wyndham heraldry in the Audit Room. Here hang the hatchments of the 3rd Earl of Egremont and 1st Lord Leconfield; and wheel-shaped displays of the bayonets of the local militia have the Wyndham crest, and the Wyndham arms on their central bosses. Also in the Audit Room is a seventeenth-century wood carving of the Stuart royal arms (incorrectly sporting the date 1791) which probably comes from the parish church.

Plas Newydd

ANGLESEY

PAGET

ARMS: Sable on a Cross engrailed between four Eagles displayed Argent five Lions passant Sable

CREST: On a Wreath of the Colours (Argent and Sable) A demi heraldic Tyger rampant Sable ducally gorged tufted and maned Argent

SUPPORTERS: On either side a heraldic Tyger Sable ducally gorged tufted and maned Argent

MOTTO: *Per il suo contrario* [By its opposite]

Plas Newydd has passed by descent from the fifteenth to the twentieth centuries from the Griffiths (belonging to one of the fifteen noble tribes of North Wales) by marriage to the Baylys, who as the result of a later marriage changed their name to Paget. In 1737 Sir Nicholas Bayly, 2nd Bt. of Plas Newydd married Caroline, great-niece and eventual heiress of the 7th Lord Paget. Their son, Henry, succeeded as 10th Lord Paget of Beaudesert, a barony created by writ of summons which could pass through a female heiress in the absence of males. Two years later, in 1784, Henry was made 1st Earl of Uxbridge, of the second creation. He assumed the surname and arms of Paget only by Royal Licence. His son, also Henry, was the famous General of the Waterloo period who was created Marquess of Anglesey for his military services. He lost a leg at Waterloo, hence his nickname 'One leg' or sometimes, less affectionately, 'Kill 'em'.

The Pagets were classic Tudor new men. William, 1st Lord Paget, was one of Henry VIII's principal advisers, a diplomat and Chancellor of the Duchy of Lancaster. He was one of the executors of the King's will and a governor of the young King Edward VI. His origins were obscure, and his opponents among the old nobility called him 'Catch-pole', as his father was thought to have been a manorial official. Beaudesert, his principal estate in Staffordshire, was granted to him by Henry VIII, together with all the lands of the suppressed Abbey of Burton which formed the basis of the family's wealth. Paget, according to his enemies, also made a fortune out of the corrupt conduct of his various offices, including that of the Chancellor of the Duchy of Lancaster. Whatever the truth, he survived and served Mary I as he had done her father and brother. His descendants were supporters of the Hanoverians, and were created Earls of Uxbridge in the eighteenth century for their public services, which were of a respectably conventional sort.

The Bayly/Pagets were extraordinary among English families for their accidental

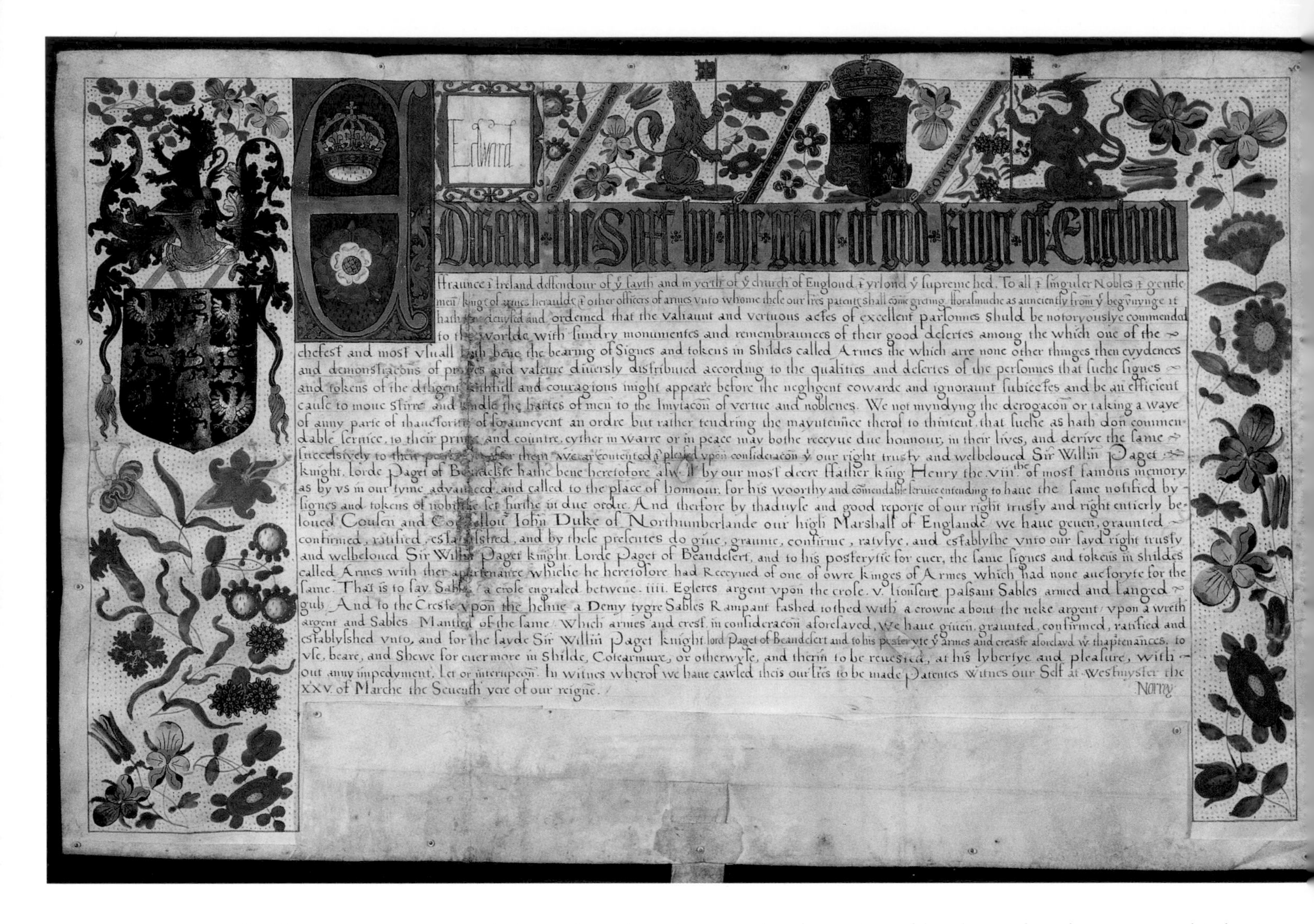

EDWARD the Sixt by the grace of god kinge of England
ffraunce & Ireland deffendour of ye fayth and in yerth of ye church of England & yrlond ye supreme hed. To all & singuler Nobles & gentlemen kinges of armes heraulde & other officers of armes vnto whome these our lres patentes shall come greting. fforasmuche as auncientlye from ye begynynge it hath [illegible] deuysed and ordeined that the valiaunt and vertuous actes of excellent parsonnes shuld be notoryouslye commended to the worlde with sundry monumentes and remembraunces of their good desertes among the which one of the chefest and most vsuall hath bene the bearing of Signes and tokens in Shildes called Armes the which arre none other thinges then evydences and demonstracons of prowes and valeure diuersly distributed according to the qualities and desertes of the personnes that suche signes and tokens of the diligent faithfull and couragious might appeare before the neghgent cowarde and ignoraunt subiectes and be an efficient cause to moue stirre and kindle the hartes of men to the Imytacon of vertue and noblenes. We not myndyng the derogacon or taking a waye of anny parte of thauctoritie of so auncyent an ordre but rather tendring the mayntennce therof to thintent. that suche as hath don commendable seruice. to their prince and countre. eyther in warre or in peace may bothe receyue due honour, in their lives, and derive the same successively to their posterite after them we ar contented & pleased vpon consideracon ye our right trusty and welbeloued Sir Willm Paget knight. lorde Paget of Beaudesert hathe bene heretofore alwell by our most deere ffather king Henry the viii[the] of most famous memory as by vs in our tyme advaunced. and called to the place of honnour. for his woorthy and comendable seruice entending to haue the same notified by signes and tokens of nobilitie set furthe in due ordre. And therfore by thaduyse and good reporte of our right trusty and right entierly beloued Cousen and Counsellor Iohn Duke of Northumberlande our high Marshall of Englande we haue geuen, graunted confirmed, ratified, establisshed, and by these presentes do giue, graunte, confirme, ratyfye, and establyshe vnto our sayd right trusty and welbeloued Sir Willm Paget knight. Lorde Paget of Beaudesert, and to his posterytie for euer, the same signes and tokens in shildes called Armes with ther appertenaunce whiche he heretofore had Receyued of one of owre kinges of Armes which had none auctoryte for the same. That is to say Sables a crose engraled betwene. iiii. Egletes argent vpon the crose. v. lionseux passant Sables armed and langed gules And to the Creste vpon the helme a Demy tygre Sables Rampant fashed tothed with a crowne a bout the neke argent vpon a wreth argent and Sables Mantled of the same Which armes and crest. in consideracon aforesayed, We haue giuen. graunted, confirmed, ratified and establyshed vnto, and for the sayde Sir Willm Paget knight. lord Paget of Beaudesert and to his posterytie ye armes and creaste aforsayd wt thapertenances. to vse, beare, and Shewe for euermore in Shilde, Cotearmure, or otherwyse, and therin to be reuested, at his lybertye and pleasure, without anny impedyment. let or interrupcon. In witnes wherof we haue cawsed theis our lres to be made Patentes Witnes our Self at Westmynster the XXV. of Marche the Seuenth yere of our reigne.

Norroy

The 1553 grant by King Edward VI confirming arms and a crest to William, 1st Lord Paget.

accumulation of wealth. As a result of a series of haphazard and unexpected inheritances, the family became extraordinarily rich in the late eighteenth century, with extensive lands in Ireland and the West Country, as well as their old estates in Wales and Staffordshire, and substantial mineral royalties from copper on Anglesey and coal on Cannock Chase. This provided the money for the Gothick reconstruction of Plas Newydd by James Wyatt and Potter of Lichfield, though some of the Gothick effect was toned down by the 6th Marquess in the twentieth century, when the house was remodelled by the architect Hal Goodhart-Rendel and the furnishings augmented with the contents of Beaudesert, the old Paget seat in Staffordshire which was demolished in 1933.

In the Entrance Hall is an unusually large set of twenty Georgian mahogany hall chairs with quartered Paget arms and a baron's coronet. They date from the early 1770s when Henry, 10th Lord Paget was remodelling Beaudesert, also to Wyatt's design. From the gallery of the Hall hang two Royal Horse Guards banners relating to

A detail of the mural at Plas Newydd painted in 1937-40 by Rex Whistler with the arms of Paget in grisaille as if carved in stone on the pillar at the end of the parapet wall.

the 1st Marquess's involvement in the Peninsular and Waterloo campaigns. At the foot of the staircase hangs the very rare Royal Patent from Edward VI of 1553 granting arms to William, 1st Lord Paget, the founder of the family.

The principal later addition to Plas Newydd is the Rex Whistler Room, painted for the 6th Marquess in 1937-40 and marking the twentieth-century revival of Plas Newydd after the depredations of the late Victorian 'Dancing Marquess' who squandered a fortune on jewels. It is the last and most extensive of Whistler's murals. Apart from all the imaginary architecture, and romantic seascape, in the centre of the long main wall is a *trompe l'oeil* of the 6th Marquess of Anglesey's arms and those of his wife, Lady Marjorie Manners, daughter of the 8th Duke of Rutland; they are treated as cartouches, carved out of stone on the two plinths at the ends of the parapet wall. Their heraldic symbols are also included in the simulated coffering of the ceiling. Rex Whistler also designed the heraldic bookplate of the present and 7th Marquess, a distinguished military historian.

Powis Castle

MONTGOMERYSHIRE

Herbert

Arms: Per pale Azure and Gules three Lions rampant Argent

Crest: On a Wreath of the Colours (Argent and Azure) A Wyvern with wings elevated and addorsed Vert gorged with a ducal Coronet Or and holding in its mouth a dexter Human Hand couped at the wrist Gules

Supporters (borne by Earls and Marquesses of Powis of the 1st creation): (Dexter) A Panther guardant Argent spotted with various colours with Fire issuing out of its mouth and ears proper and gorged with a ducal Coronet Azure; (Sinister) A Lion guardant Argent gorged with a ducal Coronet Gules

Motto: *Ung Je Serviray* [One will I serve]

The Herberts of Powis are descended from Edward, the younger son of William, 1st Earl of Pembroke, who purchased the castle in 1587. The property has passed twice through the female line by the marriage of Barbara Herbert in 1751 to Lord Herbert of Chirbury (a distant cousin), and her daughter Henrietta to Edward Clive, son of Clive of India. The Earldom of Powis has been created three times. The border castle is therefore not only the seat of a line of one of the great Welsh late medieval dynasties, but also of the descendants of a founder of the British Empire in India. The male line of the Herberts were ardent Royalists, Catholic recusants and Jacobites. The 1st Lord Powis unsuccessfully defended the castle against the Parliamentarians in the Civil War, while his grandson, the 3rd Lord Powis, who was advanced to a short-lived marquessate, accompanied James II into exile. Lady Powis was a Lady of the Bedchamber to Mary of Modena, and was given charge of the Prince of Wales (James, the Old Pretender) in exile, smuggling him to France. William III bestowed the castle on his relation, William van Zuylesteyn, created Earl of Rochford, but in 1722 George I reinstated the Herberts in their ancestral home, and the marquessate was revived till the death without heirs of William Herbert, the 1st and last Marquess, in 1748.

Clive of India is commemorated at Powis, not just by his Order of the Bath, which is displayed in the Gateway Room, but also by his silver seal with baron's coronet and supporters in the Clive Museum. The State Bedroom, decorated à la Versailles by the 1st Marquess, commemorates several royal visits to Powis. The chased doorplates record the visit of the future George V and Queen Mary in 1909, and the casement latches that of Edward VII as Prince of Wales. The C.R. cyphers in the decoration could be interpreted as a memorial to Charles I or to celebrate the restoration of Charles II, but could also be associated with the Duke of Beaufort's visit in 1684.

The Long Gallery created by Sir Edward Herbert in 1592-3 is full of heraldry. Over the chimneypiece are his arms, which have no fewer than eighteen quarterings. The

The seal matrix with the arms, supporters, motto and baron's coronet of the 1st Lord Clive (d.1774).

The heraldic plaster frieze in the Oak Drawing Room at Powis designed in 1902 by G.F. Bodley with coloured arms of Herbert and the wyvern crest uncoloured.

deep plaster frieze also contains a series of coloured shields of Sir Edward's ancestors set in strapwork cartouches. The firebacks feature the arms of William, later 1st Marquess of Powis, but here still with an earl's coronet, impaled with Somerset, as his wife was the sister of the 1st Duke of Beaufort.

A later variation of this theme can be found in the Oak Drawing Room on the first floor, where the architect G. F. Bodley designed an heraldic plaster frieze in 1902 which is instructively more elaborate than the sixteenth-century work in the Long Gallery. The heraldic fireplaces in the Dining Room on the ground floor were also designed by Bodley *c.*1904. They are of special interest as one shows the arms of the Earl of Powis, and the other those of his wife who was a peeress in her own right – the Baroness Darcy de Knayth, a medieval barony by writ which could descend to females in the absence of a male heir. As a peeress in her own right, her paternal arms are shown on a lozenge, with supporters.

Rufford Old Hall

LANCASHIRE

Hesketh

Arms: Argent on a Bend Sable three Garbs Or

Crest: On a Wreath of the Colours (Argent and Sable) A Garb Or banded Azure

Badge: A double-headed Eagle displayed Purpure armed Gules enfiled with a Circlet Or charged with four Pearls proper

Supporters: On either side a Griffin Or gorged with a Collar Gules thereon a Fleur de lys Gold and charged on the shoulder with a Rose Gules barbed and seeded proper

Motto: *Hora è Sempre* [Now and always]

The Tudor timber-framed Great Hall contains much ancient heraldic decoration. Rufford Old Hall is now L-shaped, one of the original sixteenth-century wings having been demolished and the office wing extended in brick in the seventeenth century by the trustees of Thomas Hesketh who was then a minor. The brick wing has the present entrance. Over it is a date stone of 1662 with the initials of Thomas Hesketh and a double-headed eagle, with a wheatsheaf superimposed, on a crest wreath.

The Hesketh acquired Rufford by marriage to the Fitton heiress in the thirteenth century. They also adopted the Fitton arms, with its *Bend Sable* and three gold wheatsheaves and used it as an intermittent alternative to their supposed ancient coat of a double-headed eagle. In the Middle Ages they were a knightly family. Sir William Hesketh of Rufford fought at Crécy in 1346. In the late fifteenth century they supported the Stanleys of Lathom and the Tudors, allegiances indicated by the heraldry in the Great Hall. Thomas Hesketh, in the early sixteenth century, had no surviving legitimate children, and so left the estate to his natural son Robert, who served with Henry VIII in France and was knighted. This second Robert built the Great Hall *c.*1530. The fact that he was illegitimate perhaps explains why he put so much ancestral heraldry into the decoration of his fine new Hall.

Inside the Great Hall, the bay window has early heraldic glass thought to date from 1495. It shows the quartered arms of Thomas Stanley encircled by the Garter. He was made a Knight of the Garter in 1483 and created 1st Earl of Derby by Henry VII for his support at the Battle of Bosworth in 1485. The Stanley eagle and child crest is in a separate pane above. The carved joinery is also embellished with heraldry. The most elaborate feature is the open timber roof. The hammerbeams have carved angels holding shields which are now plain but no doubt were originally painted with arms.

The carved bosses also have heraldry. Over the screen the first boss is carved with the arms of Ward of Sharples, and moving westwards towards the dais end can be found Hesketh, the quartered arms of Hesketh, Banastre, Ward of Sharples, and Dodingselles, Stanley and the Tudor rose. The arms of Ward of Sharples also reappear carved in the spandrels of the bay window together with the three legs conjoined or triskeles of the Isle of Man borne as a quartering by the Earls of Derby. The amazing movable screen, with its barbaric carved pinnacles, has the arms of Hesketh on one side and Banastre on the other. Thomas Hesketh, who died in 1413, married Margaret Banastre.

At the Reformation, the Hesketh, like many old Lancashire families, remained Catholic. A third Robert Hesketh, the head of the family, was an octogenarian during the Commonwealth and his estates were not sequestrated. He was succeeded by his grandson Thomas, a minor, who was brought up an Anglican. In the eighteenth century the Hesketh were created baronets, and built a new house further from the village. The Old Hall was repaired for occasional occupation in the early nineteenth century, a restoration commemorated by heraldic rainwater heads and the date 1821.

The early fifteenth-century movable screen in the Great Hall at Rufford carved in the centre with the arms of Hesketh.

St Michael's Mount

CORNWALL

St Aubyn

Arms: Ermine on a Cross Gules five Bezants

Crest: On a Wreath of the Colours (Argent and Gules) A Rock therefrom a Cornish Chough rising all proper

Motto: *In Se Teres* [Polished and rounded in himself]

This little fortified Benedictine monastery on a rock off the coast of Cornwall was granted, soon after the Norman Conquest, to the monks of Mont St Michel in Normandy. At the Dissolution it passed to the Crown and, because of its strategic location, remained in their hands to the end of the sixteenth century. During the Civil War Sir Francis Bassett defended it for the Royalist cause, but surrendered to the Parliamentarians in 1646. The following year Col. John St Aubyn, the Parliamentarian leader in Cornwall, was nominated military governor of the Mount. In 1659 he bought it and his descendants have lived there ever since, converting the buildings over the centuries into a charming but unusual house. The church with its tower is still the dominant element in the architectural ensemble and the heart of St Michael's Mount. It contains family memorial tablets, some with St Aubyn heraldry, and also banners of the Order of St John and the Grenadier Guards. The organ gallery at the west end has fifteen shields of arms of families connected with the monastery or who married the St Aubyns.

The St Aubyns were created baronets by Charles II. Sir John St Aubyn, 5th Bt. in the late eighteenth century had no legitimate offspring but fifteen illegitimate children. The baronetcy therefore became extinct, but Sir John's eldest son James eventually inherited the Mount and the estates. The baronetcy was recreated for Edward St Aubyn in 1866, and his son, John, became 1st Lord St Levan in 1887. The arms were re-granted with a wavy border for difference to Sir John's illegitimate offspring, as was also the case with the Leghs of Lyme (q.v.) and the Wyndhams of Petworth (q.v.).

The monks' refectory has been converted into the Great Hall, known as the Chevy Chase Room from the lively plaster frieze depicting hunting scenes. Over the fireplace is a large coloured plaster cartouche of the Stuart royal arms, probably created to celebrate the Restoration although it is dated 1641. At the other end of the room is a large shield of the St Aubyn arms impaled with Godolphin, erected by Col. John St Aubyn to mark his purchase of the property in the mid-seventeenth century. A long series of small coloured shields, with the arms of the St Aubyns and other families runs along the base of the roof, on the ends of the beams and beneath the frieze. There are also shields with the arms of St Michael's Mount (three towers), Mont St Michel (three escallops) and Edward the Confessor. The hanging military banners were brought here by the 2nd Lord St Levan. They are company banners of the Grenadier Guards, whom he commanded in 1904-8.

The Chevy Chase Room at St Michael's Mount with the royal arms dated 1641 over the fireplace and a series of small coloured shields.

The St Aubyn boatmen with the arms of St Aubyn on their left sleeves and the crest on their caps.

The Entrance Hall also contains a fine late seventeenth-century plaster cartouche of the impaled arms of the 1st Baronet St Aubyn and Dickinson over the chimneypiece. This, with the frieze, was moved from an upstairs bedroom. In the Armoury is the banner of Major-General Sir John Kennedy as a Knight of the Order of St Michael and St George. He was the father-in-law of the present Lord St Levan.

In the vestibule of the Blue Drawing Room is an unusual set of four eighteenth-century Gothick armchairs, their backs with shields of the St Aubyn arms impaled with Wingfield commemorating a marriage in 1760, which is also the date of the transformation of the Old Lady Chapel into this delightful suite of three rooms.

At high tide the Mount is only accessible by boat, and the eighteenth-century family barge used on special occasions is preserved in the boat house. The boatmen dressed in family livery: a long red coat with a large brass badge of the St Aubyn arms on the left sleeve and crested buttons, and a black leather cap with the family crest of a Cornish chough on a rock, also in brass, on the front. One of the boatmen's liveries dating from the mid-eighteenth century is on display in the castle, and is among the most curious heraldic artefacts in any English house.

A changing display of family silver in the Museum also includes pieces with the crest and arms. In the passage outside the Museum is a good copy of Thomas Martyn's 1748 Map of Cornwall decorated with shields of arms of the original subscribers, including the St Aubyns of St Michael's Mount.

SALTRAM

DEVON

PARKER

ARMS: Sable a Stag's Head cabossed between two Flaunches Argent

CREST: On a Wreath of the Colours (Argent and Sable) A Cubit Arm vested Azure cuffed and slashed Argent the Hand proper holding a Stag's attire Gules

SUPPORTERS: (Dexter) A Stag Argent Collar Or suspending a Shield Vert charged with a Horse's Head couped Argent bridled Or; (Sinister) A Greyhound Sable Collar Or suspending a Shield Gules thereon a ducal Coronet Or

MOTTO: *Fideli Certa Merces* [Reward is certain to the faithful]

The eighteenth-century approach to Saltram made a heraldic show. The Merafield Lodge to the park, designed by Robert Adam but executed in a modified form, proclaimed the ownership of the seat within, with a pair of life-size figures of stags on plinths, representing one of the Parker supporters. The stags were moved in the early

The Coade stone arms, supporters, motto and earl's coronet in the pediment over the Entrance Front at Saltram. The earl's coronet dates this heraldry to after the creation of the earldom of Morley in 1815.

nineteenth century to the Stag Lodge, a new entrance created in 1810 by the 1st Earl of Morley, and have since been moved again. (They have currently been removed for conservation.)

These stags at the gate formed an overture. The main fanfare is the full heraldic achievement with earl's coronet, motto and supporters in the pediment of the Entrance Front, a *tour de force* of Coade stone (the stag has real antlers). Further heraldry is to be found on the lead rainwater heads of the Chapel dated 1748. These have the Parker stag's head, impaled with the three swords of the Pouletts whose arms are *Sable three Swords in pile points downward Argent pommels and hilts Or*. They are the arms of John Parker and his wife, Lady Catherine, who was the daughter of the 1st Earl Poulett, Queen Anne's Secretary of State. Lady Catherine was the dominant partner in this marriage and it was she who began the remodelling of the attractively sited Saltram, which was bought by John Parker's father in 1712 in preference to the older Parker seats at North Molton and Boringdon.

Their son John was created 1st Lord Boringdon in 1784. He continued his mother's work, remodelling the house and planting the park, employing Robert Adam to create the beautifully decorated rooms for which Saltram is famous. His son, also John, was raised to an earldom in recognition of his intellectual and political abilities and consistent support for William Pitt the Younger. Although not ennobled until the reign of George III, the Parkers were an ancient Devon family recorded at North Molton since the fifteenth century, and at Boringdon from the early seventeenth. Their rise into the aristocracy came in the eighteenth century through marriage and political service.

Like many eighteenth-century houses, Saltram makes sparing use of heraldry in the interior. There are some good mahogany hall chairs with the arms and earl's coronet on their backs in the Entrance Hall, and in the Morning Room can be seen a pair of silver salvers with the arms and a baron's coronet made for Lord Boringdon. The Marseilles faience dinner service in the Dining Room, of *c.*1760, has the Parker crest, an interesting example of English heraldry on French eighteenth-century pottery.

The oldest piece of heraldry at Saltram is hidden away in the Inner Courtyard. There, on the sixteenth-century tower, can be seen a shield of the impaled and quartered arms of Parker, now much weathered, with the wife's arms being indecipherable. This was probably brought by the Parkers from one of their ancient houses. The fourth and last quarter on the Parker side is Ellicott, so must relate to a descendant of John Parker of North Molton to whom the arms were granted in 1547 and his wife, Elizabeth Ellicott, and possibly to their son, Edmund Parker, who married *c.*1560.

A hall chair at Saltram with the arms of Parker displayed on a peer's robe of estate beneath an earl's coronet for the 1st Earl of Morley.

Sizergh Castle

CUMBRIA

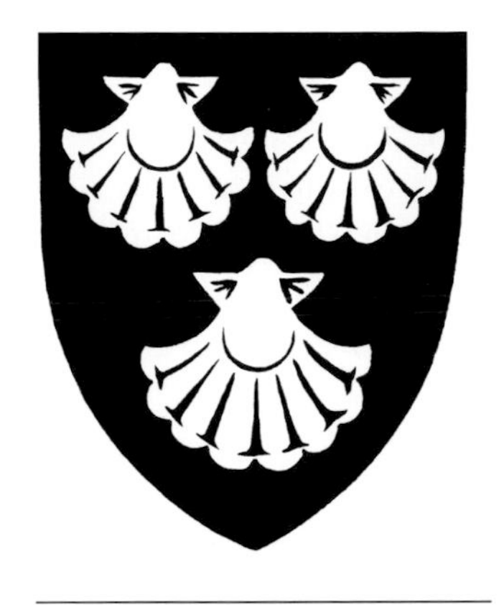

Strickland

Arms: Sable three Escallops Argent

Crest: On a Wreath of the Colours (Argent and Sable) a Holly Tree fructed proper

Motto: *Sans Mal* [Without evil]

The Stricklands have lived at Sizergh since 1239, when Sir William Strickland married Elizabeth, the heiress of the Deincourts, who had been granted the lands by Henry II in the 1170s. In the Middle Ages they were a knightly family fighting for the Crown on the Scottish borders, in Ireland and France. Sir Thomas Strickland was the English banner bearer at Agincourt in 1415.

They were mainly Lancastrian supporters in the Wars of the Roses and rode out the religious storms of the sixteenth century. Sir Thomas Strickland had in the late fifteenth century married Agnes Parr of Kendal – aunt of Henry VIII's last Queen – which may have helped, and Walter Strickland's (d.1569) mother and grandmother were both heiresses who had increased the family fortune. In the later sixteenth century they were thus able to remodel and convert the old fortified pele tower at Sizergh into an Elizabethan mansion.

As Royalists they were fined over £1000 in the Civil War. Thomas Strickland (d.1694) seriously mismanaged his finances and was forced to sell his Yorkshire estates. At the 1688 Revolution, the Stricklands, who had become strong Catholics in the seventeenth century, remained loyal to James II, joining him in exile at St Germain, where Lady Strickland was governess to the young Prince James. The eighteenth and nineteenth centuries, as a result, were mainly spent in an impoverished recusant twilight, though the marriage to the heiress Cecilia Towneley in 1762 introduced a welcome injection of capital and enabled the house to be repaired. There was a further revival in the late nineteenth and early twentieth centuries, when Sir Gerald Strickland, M.P., Colonial Governor and Prime Minister of Malta was created 1st Lord Strickland, and salvaged Sizergh. His daughter and her husband, Henry Hornyold (who added the Strickland name), with their son Thomas gave the house and estate to the National Trust in 1950.

The core of Sizergh is the tall, sturdy pele tower which was built in about 1350. It is dated by the carved heraldic escutcheon beneath the top window on the courtyard side. This displays the quartered arms of Deincourt and Strickland with the original Strickland crest – a 'fagotte of holly'. This cannot be earlier than the mid-fourteenth century when crests first came into general use in English heraldry. The holly tree crest appears on the heads of the eighteenth-century lead rainwater pipes of the central block and in a little niche over the central Gothick window of the first floor on the Entrance Front.

The interior of Sizergh is famed for its Elizabethan plaster ceilings, oak panelling and carved heraldic chimneypieces. These form part of the remodelling of the house by Walter Strickland (d.1569) and his redoubtable wife Alice, the daughter of Nicholas Tempest of Lanchester, Co. Durham. She continued the work in her widowhood, and the minority of the son and heir. The visitor is immediately introduced to the works of Walter and Alice Strickland in the Entrance Hall, where the carved oak screen, which

ABOVE: *The carved overmantel of 1563 in the Old Dining Room at Sizergh with the quartered arms of Strickland, Deincourt, Neville and Ward arranged in an unusual form, as the four quarters each appear four times.*

LEFT: *The 1558 screen in the Entrance Hall at Sizergh with, in the pediment, the quartered arms, the supporters and crest.*

was originally in the Great Hall on the first floor, is dated 1558 and has the family arms in the pediment and the holly crest.

The woodcarving at Sizergh is one of the most extensive sequences of Elizabethan heraldic decoration. There are five magnificently carved heraldic chimneypieces, all dated, in the main rooms at Sizergh. That in the Old Dining Room (1563) has the quartered arms of Strickland, Deincourt, Neville and Ward, (arranged in an unusual form as the four coats each appear four times) with supporters and crest. In the Dining Room (1564) there are three large achievements marking a more elaborate celebration of Walter's heraldry. The central shield displays the quartered arms of Strickland, Deincourt, Neville and Ward, again with supporters of the Ward stag and the Neville bull, and the Strickland holly crest on top. The side shields show Strickland quartered with Deincourt impaling Neville and Ward, and, the other, Strickland quartered with Neville and Ward impaling Tempest quartered with Umfraville, and celebrate his father's marriage to the heiress Katherine Neville as well as his own to Alice Tempest. The Georgian firescreens contain twentieth-century needlework with the quartered family arms, for Gerald Strickland and his wife, Lady Edeline Sackville.

In the adjoining Queen's Room, the overmantel is dated 1569 and has the arms of Elizabeth I with lion and dragon supporters, set in scrollwork containing the Tudor rose, all very finely carved.

In the Boynton Room the chimneypiece (dated 1575) celebrates Alice Tempest herself and her third marriage. In the centre are the quartered arms of Sir Thomas Boynton of Barmston in Yorkshire impaling those of Alice (Tempest quartering Umfraville). After Walter Strickland's death she was married to Thomas Boynton, but continued to live at Sizergh. She had three husbands in all. Like Bess of Hardwick, she was industrious, strong-willed and had a fine taste for architecture, as these beautifully carved fireplaces and the other Elizabethan work at Sizergh demonstrate.

The panelling from the Inlaid Chamber was sold to the Victoria and Albert Museum in 1891, but reinstated in 1999. The plaster ceiling is decorated with goats (the Boynton crest) and collared and chained stags (a Strickland supporter), and ovals of arms showing Strickland quartering Deincourt, Neville and Ward; Tempest quartering Umfraville; and Boynton quartering Boynton ancient, Delsee and Monceaux. The inclusion of her last husband's arms proves that the Inlaid Chamber at Sizergh, one of the finest Elizabethan interiors in England, was very much Alice's brainchild and that she continued the work at Sizergh regardless of which husband she was married to at the time. The top lights of the windows in the Inlaid Chamber also have shields of the family arms in stained glass.

In addition to the chimneypieces made for the house, in the Bindloss Room is a fine overmantel dated 1629 which was brought in the nineteenth century from Borwick Hall, near Carnforth. It is carved with the arms of Sir Francis Bindloss impaled with those of his wife, Cecilia West, daughter of Thomas Lord De La Warr, Governor of Virginia. The bed in the Bindloss Room is a mid-nineteenth-century antiquarian creation made out of woodwork from the old Strickland family pew in Kendal church: it is carved with a large holly tree crest at the foot.

On the main staircase half landing is an eighteenth-century table with an Italian scagliola top dated 1708, showing the impaled arms of Strickland and Trentham for Winifred (d.1725), widow of Sir Thomas Strickland, which must have been made for her during her exile abroad as a Jacobite. The same arms appear on the pewter service in the top room of the pele tower. Hanging over the main landing is the armorial banner of Lord Strickland as a Knight Grand Cross of St Michael and St George. The two High Sheriff's banners in the Entrance Hall have the quartered arms of Strickland and Hornyold. The late Lt-Commander Thomas Hornyold-Strickland was the last High Sheriff of Westmorland before the old county became part of Cumbria.

The ironwork balustrade of the lower flight of stairs from the Hall to the main floor uses the cockle shell of the Strickland arms as a finial and the shell also appears on top of the forecourt gateposts.

Snowshill Manor

GLOUCESTERSHIRE

Wade

Arms, Quarterly: (1 Wade) Azure a Saltire between four Escallops Or; (2 Wade) Or a Chevron between three Falcons' Heads erased Sable; (3 Comyn) Gules three Garbs of Cummin Or; (4 Fleming) Barry of six Argent and Azure in chief three Maunches Gules

Crest: On a Wreath Or and Sable A Rhinoceros Argent

This extraordinary magpie's nest is the creation of one man – Charles Paget Wade – who bought the manor, then a derelict farm, in 1917. He restored the house and laid out the hillside gardens, but the point of Snowshill is not the architecture but the crammed and atmospheric interiors, rather like a series of stage sets all with appropriately romantic names: Meridian, Zenith, Mermaid, Top Royal, Dragon, Nadir. The contents are amazingly eclectic with a range of objects, from carpentry tools, bicycles, musical instruments, toys and reliquaries to Japanese armour, all crammed into every space. Heraldry plays a strong role in this assemblage redolent of Merrie England.

Charles Wade was a characteristic romantic of his generation. Brought up in Suffolk and educated at Uppingham, he had trained as an architect, working for a time with Parker and Unwin on the design of Hampstead Garden Suburb. The death of his father in 1911, however, had left him financially independent with an assured income from the family sugar estates at St Kitts in the Caribbean. After the First World War he settled at Snowshill in the Cotswolds which was then the centre of the English Arts & Crafts Movement, C. R. Ashbee, Ernest Gimson and the Barnsleys all then being active in the area and promoting revived craftsmanship, design and architecture, and maintaining vernacular traditions.

Wade shared their principles and vision, as is demonstrated in his sensitive, understated restoration of this house, and his love of old craft tools. All this was part of a general romanticism which was reflected in Wade's self-consciously archaic way of life and his love of dressing up in historic costumes. It was also demonstrated in his invention of a fanciful personal genealogy from Armagil Wade of Belseys, Hampstead, a member of the Privy Council in the sixteenth century; a cadet descendant of whom – he claimed – had settled in the West Indies and founded his own branch of the Wade family. He assumed and used the arms of Armagil Wade *Azure a Saltire between four Escallops Or*, but without authority. He never registered his pedigree at the College of Arms, or proved his right to the Wade heraldry. It is not clear how seriously Wade intended this heraldic fantasy. It may have been an elaborate personal joke, as one suspects was much of his display at Snowshill.

Joke or not, the Wade heraldry is elaborately presented in the Entrance Hall of the house where the panels he painted depict the quartered and impaled arms of Wade 'ancestors', each with a Latin biographical inscription underneath. Painted Wade arms can also be found in Zenith and other rooms. An accomplished heraldic painter, Wade also painted a long series of wooden shields with the arms of persons and families connected with the history and manor of Snowshill, including King Henry VIII and John Dudley, Duke of Northumberland. This series begins in the Entrance Hall and can be found throughout the house hanging on the walls of staircases and rooms. As well as his own family arms, Wade had a general interest in heraldry and collected many fine heraldic objects. They include a number of historic hatchments, banners and royal

A tous ceulx qui ces presentes lres verront ou oyront Gylbert Dethyk als Norrey principal herault et Roy darmes des parties du north en ceste roiaulme dangleterre dalariuere du trent vers le Northe salut Equite veult et rasori ordonne que les hommes verteux et du noble courage soyent par leurs merites et bonne renomme remuneres non seulement leurs propers psones en ceste vie mortelle sy brieue et transitoire mais apres eulx ceulx qui de leurs corps seront procrees soyent en toutes places dhonneut aueq autres renomees par certaines ensignes et demonstrances dhonneur et noblesse a celle fin qui par leures exemples aultrs plus sefforcent duser leurs iours en faitz darmes et oeures verteulx pour aquerer le renoum dauceenne noblesse en leurs lignees et posterites Et pource le Norrey Roy darmes Come auant dict non seulement par commune renommee mais aussy par le raport et testmoniage de plieusieurs dignes de foy et credit suis pour certayn aduerty et informe que Armigill Wade natyf des parties du north dauant dit sest tousiours sy saigement deporte en tous ses affaires tellement quil a bien deserui en toutes places dhonneur destr admis recen compte et nombre au nombre et Compaignie dautres nobles psonaiges Et po la remembrance du telle sy grande vertu et noblesse par lauctorite et puoir annexe attribue a moy et a mon dit office du Roy darmes par le Roy nre souuerayn seigneur par expresses parollez sur son grand seau Iay ordonne et assigne au dit Armigill Wade et a son dit posterite blason heaulme et tymbre en maniere que sensuyt Cest ascauoir dor sur ung cheueron sable troys gerbes de commin dargent entre troys testes de faulco rasy sable langue geules sur une Torse dor et sable ung demy grifon verre dargent et sable membre geules tenant entre ses ungles une gerbe Commin mantele geules doble dargent cy plus plainement est depecte en la marge A auoir et tenir au dit Armigill et a sa posterite a tousiourmais En tesmoignie de ce le Norrey Roy darmes come dessus ay signe ces presentes aueq mon propre main et mys mon seau aueq le seau de mon dit office du Roy darmes Donne en Londres le primier iour du moys de nouembre lan du nre salueur mil cinque Cens quarant e Sept et le priemier an du regne du nre sire le Roy Edward le Syxesme par la grace de dieu Roy dangleterre france et dirlande defenseur de la foy et apres dieu de lesglise dangletere et dirlande Suprem chief

Armigell Wade

Armigell wade

LEFT: *A record of the grant of arms and crest to Armagil Wade in 1547 (College of Arms Ms: Vincent 163/11).*

arms. The hatchments begin with a Continental bishop in the Entrance Hall and include a rare one for George III in Meridian.

The series of royal arms are a special feature of Snowshill; they include a fine carved wood panel of Charles II's arms in Admiral, George III's, painted on board on the stairs to the attic floor, and Charles I's (on an arched panel) and Charles II's (painted on canvas) on the top landing. Originally these would all have hung in churches to emphasise the monarch's role as Supreme Governor of the Church of England.

It would be difficult to list everything of heraldic interest at Snowshill, but other particularly eye-catching objects are the side of a nineteenth-century coach with the arms and coronet of Earl Cowper in the Corridor, and a set of leather fire buckets with the two crests and baron's coronet of Lord Henniker. The heraldic banners in Meridian came originally from St George's Chapel, Windsor, where they hung over the stalls of the Garter knights. They date from the nineteenth century and include those of the Duke of Kent and the Duke of Cambridge.

The climax of Snowshill's heraldic decoration is to be found in Dragon, the medieval hall of the house. All round this room are shields, again painted by Wade, of the owners and occupiers of the manor beginning with the Abbots of Winchcombe in the Middle Ages down to Charles Wade, each identified by name. Between the windows, by contrast, hang the carved and painted Russian imperial arms with their distinctive eagle displaying the shields of constituent territories on its wings.

In the midst of all this brought-in exoticism and romantic Arts & Crafts genealogy it comes as a shock to find that the arms in the semi-circular pediment over the front door were placed there by William Sambach who built this part of the house in *c.*1720.

RIGHT: *A detail from the record of confirmation of the quartered arms and the grant of the rhinoceros crest to William Wade in 1574 (College of Arms Ms: Vincent 162/158).*

Speke Hall

LANCASHIRE

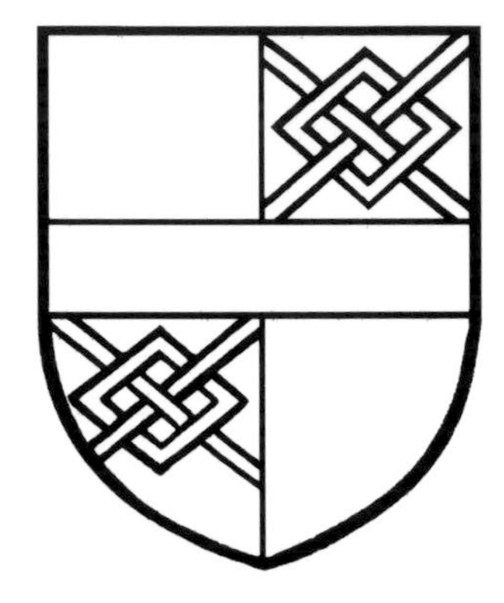

Norris

Arms: Quarterly Argent and Gules in the second and third quarters a Fret Or over all a Fess Azure

Crest: On a Wreath Argent and Azure An Eagle rising Sable beaked and legged Or

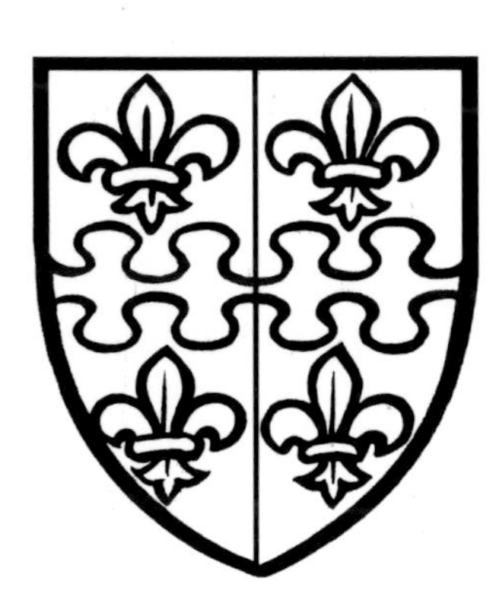

Watt

Arms: Per pale Or and Azure a Fess nebuly between four Fleurs de Lys two in chief and two in base all counter-changed

Crest: On a Wreath of the Colours (Or and Azure) A Greyhound sejant Argent semy de Lys Azure supporting with the dexter paw two Arrows saltireways points downwards proper

Motto: *Vigueur de Dessus* [Strength is from above]

Speke Hall is a prime example of Joseph Nash's *Mansions of Olden Time*, and his romantic lithographs of 1849 still give the best impression of the house. Though encircled by the twentieth-century industrial suburbs of Liverpool, it is a remarkably well-preserved Tudor black and white half-timbered building. It was built and owned for several centuries by the Norris family, but after a period of neglect it was bought in 1795 by Richard Watt, a Liverpool merchant who had made his fortune in the West Indies and the shipping business.

Richard Watt (d.1796) is an excellent example of eighteenth-century social mobility. He started off as the driver of a Hackney carriage in Liverpool, but studied at evening classes and went to Jamaica where he acquired a sugar plantation. On his return, he developed a lucrative shipping business in Liverpool, and invested his profits in two landed estates. His grandson, Francis, received a grant of arms in 1856.

The Watt family carried out a full restoration of Speke in the nineteenth century, refurnishing the empty rooms with 'antiques' from Wardour Street, and eventually bequeathing Speke to the National Trust in 1943. Their work is an interesting reflection of Victorian attitudes to ancient buildings and the self-conscious gentrification of the Watt family. The Watt arms and crest, both those assumed without authority and their own Victorian grant, can still be seen in different places at Speke, for instance on

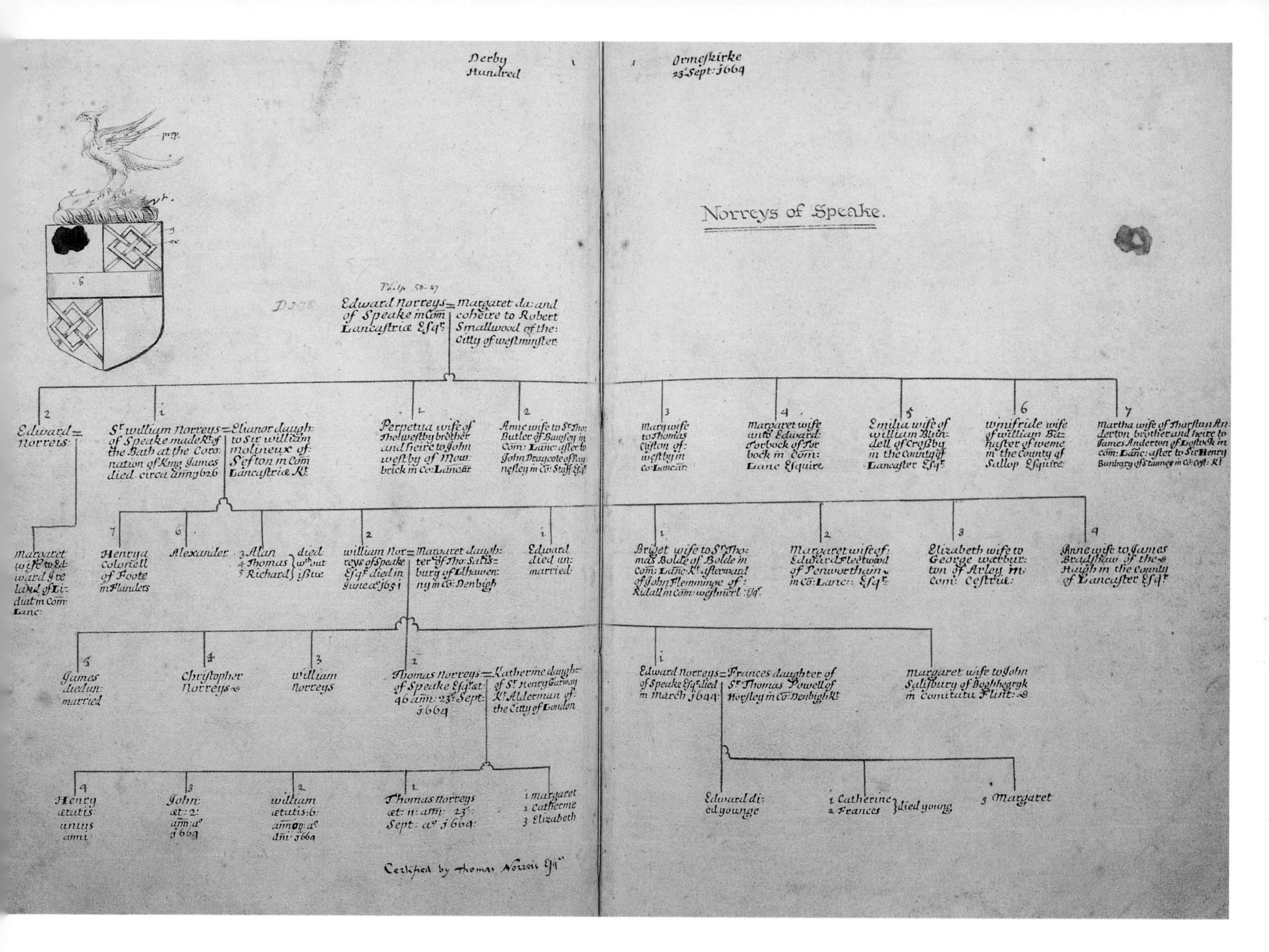

A 1664 Visitation entry of the arms, crest and pedigree of Thomas Norris of Speke, the arms and crest tricked, i.e. in pen and ink with the tinctures indicated (College of Arms Ms: C.37/82ᵇ-83).

the blue and white Copeland dinner service in the Small Dining Room, and in stained glass panels in the windows.

The original Norris heraldry is also still to be found at Speke. The Great Hall, with its dark oak panelling, contains several coats of arms on shields high above the fireplace. An old inscription records that the wainscot was installed here in 1564 by Sir William Norris IV, but his son Edward probably added more in the 1570s, as the heraldry attests. The 'Great Wainscot', fine carved Renaissance work, at the dais end, is said by tradition to have been looted from the Palace of Holyroodhouse in Edinburgh, but it was probably introduced by Edward Norris.

The windows in the Great Hall have interesting stained glass. It was rearranged in an antiquarian spirit by the Watt family in the nineteenth century but incorporates old work including fragments of medieval glass brought from Garston church when it was rebuilt in 1876. There is some good seventeenth-century heraldic glass with the Norris arms, and those of their connections.

In the Great Parlour, the finest of the 'olden tyme' rooms at Speke with its moulded plaster ceiling and carved wainscot, the great chimneypiece includes little carved portraits of the family of Sir William Norris II, as well as the Norris crest, an erne or eagle. This was recorded in the 1567 Visitation, and may give an approximate date for the chimneypiece. The erne itself is canting heraldry: it is a pun on the name of Alice Erneys who married Sir Henry Norris (d.1431) *c.*1390, uniting the ownership of the manor of Speke, which had been divided between the Norris and Erneys families since the early fourteenth century. This whole chimneypiece reflects the interest of William Norris II in his family, which also led him to compile a long 'genealogical declaration' or family tree in 1563.

STOURHEAD

WILTSHIRE

HOARE

ARMS: Sable within a Bordure engrailed an Eagle displayed with two heads Argent on the breast an Ermine Spot

CREST: On a Wreath of the Colours (Argent and Sable) An Eagle's Head erased Argent charged with an Ermine Spot

MOTTO: *In Ardua* [On high]

The Stourton estates were bought in 1717 by the trustees of Richard Hoare, a London banker whose father, Sir Richard, had founded the family bank and served as Lord Mayor of London. In 1720 Richard's younger brother, Henry, acquired the estate from the trustees, demolished the old house of the Stourtons and built a Palladian villa designed by Colen Campbell on a new site, rechristening the property Stourhead. The famous grounds were laid out by his son, Henry, known as 'The Magnificent', and great-grandson, Sir Richard Colt Hoare, who also extended the house.

The Hoare arms, like those of several London bankers, comprised an eagle (e.g. the Childs of Osterley, q.v.), in the Hoares' case, a double-headed eagle. It gave its name to the Spread Eagle in the little model hamlet at the entrance to the garden, with its handsomely painted signboard. Heraldic signboards on English pubs date back to the middle ages and became widespread in the eighteenth century. They tend to be taken for granted, but they are often attractive examples of the heraldic painter's craft.

The portico on the Entrance Front of the house was added as late as 1838-9. It is approached by flights of steps with four large stone vases – with eagle handles – on the piers. Although copies of a classical original, the choice of the eagle pattern is not coincidental and the reference to the family bird would have been quietly relished. The pediment of the portico is now blank but in Colen Campbell's *Vitruvius Britannicus* an engraving shows it carved with the Hoare double-headed eagle.

The eagle head crest appears conventionally in the Hall, in the centre of the late eighteenth-century wheel-back hall chairs. More imaginative use is made of the family heraldry in the Music Room, where the fine overmantel has an inset painting in a Palladian frame with a broken scrolling pediment and gilded double-headed eagle on top. Anybody not aware of the Hoare heraldry would just assume this was based on some recherché classical source. The gilt gesso table in the alcove has the Colt arms on top,

ABOVE LEFT: *A plate from the Chinese armorial dinner service made for Henry Hoare (d.1785) with the arms of his wife, Susanna Colt, in pretence.*

ABOVE RIGHT: *A seventeenth-century German silver gilt double-headed eagle presented to Sir Richard Hoare when he was Lord Mayor of London in 1712 and reminiscent of the double-headed eagle in the arms of Hoare.*

and no doubt came to Stourhead as the result of the marriage in 1728 of the heiress Susanna Colt to Henry Hoare (d.1785). Their marriage is also commemorated by the fine Chinese armorial porcelain with the arms of Hoare with Colt in pretence.

The family emblem makes its most spectacular appearance in the Little Dining Room as a seventeenth-century silver gilt double-headed eagle set with semi-precious stones and a body carved out of a single piece of agate, made in Germany. It was presented to Sir Richard Hoare when he was Lord Mayor of London. The silver displayed in the same room is engraved with the arms of Hoare impaling Acland.

Apart from some medieval effigies in the church, the Stourtons of Stourton who owned the estate from before the Norman Conquest down to 1714 are now merely a memory at Stourhead. The tomb of the 6th Lord Stourton is particularly handsome. Their principal estates have been in Yorkshire since the late eighteenth century and the current head of the family, Lord Mowbray, Segrave and Stourton, lives in Scotland when Parliament is not sitting. However, their Wiltshire origins are not forgotten, for their medieval arms show six fountains representing the six springs in the park at Stourhead, which form the source of the River Stour and provided the water for Henry Hoare's lake.

Stowe

BUCKINGHAMSHIRE

Temple
(1688 onwards)

Arms, Quarterly: (1&4) Or an Eagle displayed Sable; (2&3) Argent two Bars Sable each charged with three Martlets Or

Crest: On a ducal Coronet A Martlet Or

Supporters (1714/15): (Dexter) A Lion per fess embattled Or and Gules; (Sinister) A Horse Argent powdered with Eagles displayed Sable

Motto: *Templa quam dilecta* [How beloved are the temples]

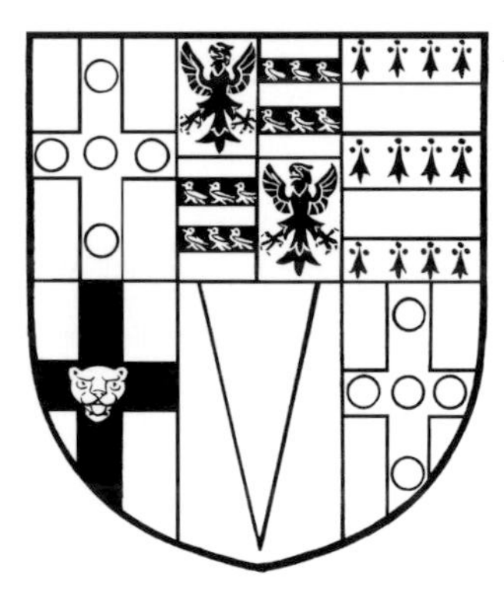

Temple-Nugent-Brydges-Chandos-Grenville
(1800 onwards)

Arms, Quarterly: (1&6 Grenville) Vert on a Cross Argent five Roundels Gules; (2) (i&iv Leofric) Or an Eagle displayed Sable; (ii&iii Temple) Argent two Bars Sable each charged with three Martlets Or; (3 Nugent) Ermine two Bars Gules; (4 Brydges) Argent on a Cross Sable a Leopard's Face Or; (5 Chandos) Or a Pile Gules

Crests: (1 Grenville) On a Wreath of the Colours (Argent and Vert) A Garb Vert (2 Brydges) On a Wreath of the Colours (Argent and Sable) The Bust of a Man's Head in profile couped below the shoulders proper vested paly Argent and Gules semy of Roundels counterchanged round the temples a Wreath Argent and Azure (3 Chandos) On a Wreath of the Colours (Or and Gules) A Saracen's Head affronty proper couped at the shoulders wreathed round the temples Argent and Purpure

Supporters: (Dexter) A Lion per fess embattled Or and Gules; (Sinister) A Horse Argent powdered with Eagles displayed Sable

In the eighteenth century, the United Kingdom was partly ruled from Stowe, then the principal seat of Grand Whiggery, the geographical and artistic centre of the cult of humane and political liberty which had its basis in the Revolution of 1688. The owners of Stowe and a formidable network of their cousins and nephews were a dominant force in government for over a century: the Grenville-Temples and their relations provided three Prime Ministers, Field Marshals, Viceroys of Ireland, Foreign Secretaries and other Ministers, ambassadors and colonial governors. They were also the model for the Viponts in Bulwer-Lytton's novel *What Will He Do With It?* The great domain was begun by Richard Temple, Viscount Cobham, continued by his nephew, the 2nd Earl Temple, and completed by his nephew, the 1st Marquess of Buckingham.

The princely scale of their seat with its incomparable landscape garden represents their overwhelming aspirations. Considering their dynastic pride and ambition it is rather odd that neither Viscount Cobham nor the 2nd Earl Temple, the chief creators of Stowe, produced a son, and both were succeeded by nephews. This, and numerous inheritances through heiresses, explain the much hyphenated family name which expanded from Grenville-Temple in the mid-eighteenth century to Temple-Nugent-Brydges-Chandos-Grenville in the early nineteenth century – an English record.

In the same way they ascended the staircase of the peerage, from Viscount to Earl, to Marquess and finally Duke of Buckingham in 1822; but by then the days of glory were over and by 1848 the 2nd Duke of Buckingham had gone spectacularly bankrupt. 'An ancient family ruined, their palace marked for destruction, and its contents scattered ... Stowe is no more ...' as Lord Macaulay put it in a *Times* obituary/editorial. He was a trifle pessimistic, for a denuded Stowe limped on till 1921 when it was finally sold, the house becoming the well known public school. The landscape garden was transferred by the school to the National Trust in 1989.

The Temples of Stowe chose an apt line derived from the Bible as their motto *Templa Quam Dilecta*. They then developed the pun further by filling their garden with more classical temples than any other in England. The resonances of the place are classical and political, and much of the symbolism in the garden reflects the political beliefs of its creators. The Stowe landscape evokes the world of Ancient Rome which the new Augustan age of Georgian England confidently sought to outdo. It also reflects the ambitions of its owners. The development and aggrandisement of Stowe was intimately connected with their political fortunes and aspirations, and their hereditary pursuit of a duke's coronet.

Although they believed themselves to be descended from Saxon Earls, the Temples of Stowe were Tudor 'new men' and their fortune was founded in sheep. They were supporters of Cromwell in the Civil War and were created baronets in the seventeenth century. The Grenvilles of Wotton who succeeded them were a medieval knightly family, descended from a genuine Norman ancestor. Each generation in the eighteenth century married an heiress, most notably the daughter of the last Duke of Chandos. It was these successive inheritances together with the enormous profits of eighteenth-century, pre-Reform, political office which paid for Stowe: the huge house, the plantations and lakes, the far-spreading avenues and the myriad temples and garden buildings.

Richard Grenville-Temple, 2nd Earl Temple, was closely associated in politics with his brother-in-law, William Pitt the Elder. Despite the fact that George II detested him, he used his all-powerful position in 1759 to press for the Garter. The King had to yield, but could not disguise his anger and at the formal investiture in 1760 threw the insignia at the importunate Earl and 'turned his back at the same instant in the rudest manner'. Despite the snub, Lord Temple was satisfied and splashed his Garter insignia all over Stowe, including the plasterwork of the State Bedroom. The gatepiers at the Oxford Lodge have his much quartered arms encircled by the Garter, with supporters and coronet, on the front panels, together with the Garter star on the side panels. Giant Garter stars also adorn the centre of the parapets of the two flanking pavilions on the South Front; these were carved by James Lovell and are flanked by statues of Religion

The quartered arms and supporters of Richard Temple, Viscount Cobham (d.1749), in mosaic in the Pebble Alcove at Stowe.

and Liberty, Peace and Plenty and surmount the immodest inscription 'Richardus Com. Temple. F. [ecit]'. Many other heraldic ornaments at Stowe disappeared in the sales of 1848 and 1921, but one of the most attractive survives in the Pebble Alcove in the garden. A delightful mosaic depicts the arms of Richard Temple, Viscount Cobham, the original creator of the garden.

The ceiling of the Gothic Temple at Stowe designed by James Gibbs and begun in 1744. Impaled arms of Temple are visible as are the arms of Grenville impaling Temple.

The most extraordinary flight of heraldic fancy at Stowe, however, is on the painted ceiling of the Gothic Temple designed by James Gibbs and begun in 1744. This large triangular Gothic edifice was the ideological climax of Lord Cobham's garden and a 'trumpet-call of Liberty, Enlightenment and the Constitution', all of which the Georgians thought derived from the Saxons, to whom they also credited Gothic architecture. The inner vault is decorated with shields of arms of notable ancestors of the Temple family, showing their descent and marriages, and emphasising the connection in eighteenth-century minds between the heraldic and the Gothic; and in the Temple's minds, the link between their Saxon ancestors and English liberty.

There are fifty-four heraldic shields culminating in a lozenge with the arms of Countess Temple, Lord Cobham's sister, with her brand new comital coronet, which she received in 1749, dating this painted decoration to *c.*1750. The other shields illustrate the marriages of all the heads of the Temple family, as well as twenty-nine marriages of younger children of the Stowe family. They are a striking demonstration of the family's passionate interest in their own genealogy, believing in their descent from Leofric, Earl of Mercia (d.1057), hence Sir Richard Temple's adoption of the *Eagle displayed Sable*, which he thought to be the Mercian eagle. The Stowe family and estate papers, now in the Huntington Library, California, are rich in genealogical and heraldic information and include the seventeenth-century *Pedigree of the Temples of Stowe*, a folio depicting 476 shields of the Temple arms and their quarterings, the source of the arms in the Gothic Temple.

Tattershall Castle

LINCOLNSHIRE

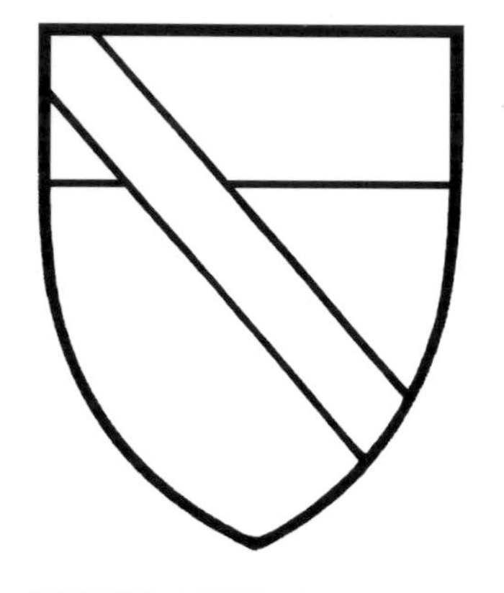

CROMWELL

ARMS: Argent a Chief Gules and over all a Bend Azure

CREST: On a Chapeau Gules turned up Ermine A Panache of Ostrich Feathers Argent

BADGE: A Purse Argent tasselled and buttoned Or

SUPPORTERS: On either side a Wild Man proper each with a Club over his shoulder

MOTTO: *Nay Je Droit* [Have I not the right]

Tattershall, with its castle, little dependent market town, great collegiate church, and almshouses is a textbook example of the *caput* or headquarters of a great feudal estate in the late Middle Ages. This was largely the development in the 1440s of an early medieval castle by Ralph, 3rd Lord Cromwell, Lord High Treasurer of England in 1433-43. He made a large fortune out of his various public offices – so large that in his will he instructed his executors to reimburse certain sums of money which were nagging at his conscience.

Lord Cromwell had no children, and on his death his estates were divided. All subsequently fell into decay, but the great brick tower, which formed Cromwell's private apartments, was rescued in 1911 and restored by Lord Curzon, who left the property to the National Trust in 1925. Stepping in at the eleventh hour, Curzon bought and reinstated the stone chimneypieces which had been removed for export to America.

Tattershall was one of a number of brick-built, moated, castellated mansions built by the English nobility in the fifteenth century on the model of the *wasserburgs* of Flanders, which they had seen during the Hundred Years War. As a young man Cromwell had fought in France and may have been present at Agincourt. The castellated architecture of the Tattershall tower was adopted as much for aesthetic and associational reasons as for any practical need for fortification and demonstrated Cromwell's lordship, wealth and rank. The frequent use of the Treasurer's purse, the Cromwell motto *Nay je Droit* and his arms and those of his wife and ancestors in the decoration further underlines this. They are found carved on the bosses of the brick vaults of the four corner turrets, and are prominently displayed on the chimneypieces, the principal architectural feature of the four main rooms – one on top of the other – in the body of the tower.

Though Cromwell owed his great wealth to his own exertions and career, his family was an old and distinguished one. The Cromwells had acquired Tattershall by the marriage of his grandfather, Ralph, 1st Lord Cromwell (d.1398), to the Bernack heiress of the Tattershalls. Previous generations of Cromwells, Bernacks and Tattershalls had also married heiresses, so Ralph Cromwell was entitled to quarter the arms of several great Anglo-Norman dynasties, including the d'Aubignys (Albini) and Marmions, while his wife was a Deyncourt whose mother was the coheiress of Lord Grey of Rotherfield. All these distinguished connections are represented in the heraldry carved on the Tattershall chimneypieces.

That in the Parlour is the most elaborate. In the centre, in the cusp of the ogee arch, is a shield of the Cromwell arms and above is an elaborate frieze of two rows of shields, alternating with the Treasurer's purse, representing his and his wife's heraldic alliances: Vipont, Albini, Marmion, Bernack, Cromwell quartering Tattershall impaling Deyncourt, and Cromwell quartering Tattershall with in the bottom row Clifton, Deyncourt, Driby and Grey of Rotherfield.

The Parlour chimneypiece at Tattershall carved with the Lord High Treasurer's purse and Common Gromwell for Ralph, 3rd Lord Cromwell, Lord High Treasurer 1433-43, interspersed with arms of related families. The first two shields in the top row are Vipont and d'Aubigny and the arms of Cromwell are in the centre.

The chimneypiece on the first floor is simpler, but better preserved, and of a design much copied in the nineteenth century with a frieze of shields and the Treasurer's purse in roundels: the larger shields are Tattershall; Cromwell quartering Tattershall impaling Deyncourt; and Albini. In the spaces above the roundels are seven smaller shields of Bernack; Driby; Cromwell; a broken shield; a second Cromwell; Tattershall; and Deyncourt.

The second floor chimneypiece has a frieze of Perpendicular blank tracery, the central panels containing little shields of the same arms, alternating with the Treasurer's purse. The third floor chimneypiece is a further variation on the theme, with cusped arched blank tracery framing eleven panels with the arms and purse alternating. In the spandrels is the purse hanging from a carved plant, identified as the

Common Gromwell, a rebus on the family name. Altogether the chimneypieces at Tattershall are among the best surviving examples of heraldic decoration in secular medieval architecture. The variety of the designs, with different arrangements of shields and tracery, is delightful.

As part of his exemplary restoration of the building, Lord Curzon continued the heraldic theme by inserting a carefully designed scheme of armorial glass in the windows to record the subsequent owners of Tattershall, which include several generations of the Fortescue family as well as his own.

Tatton Park

CHESHIRE

EGERTON

ARMS: Argent a Lion rampant Gules between three Pheons Sable

CREST: On a Wreath of the Colours (Argent and Gules) A Lion rampant supporting an Arrow palewise point downwards Or pheoned and flighted Argent

SUPPORTERS: (Dexter) A Griffin Argent gorged with a ducal Coronet Azure and pendant therefrom a Pheon Sable; (Sinister) A Lion Gules gorged with a plain collar Argent and pendant therefrom a Pheon Sable

MOTTO: *Sic Donec* [Thus until]

At first sight the crisp neo-classical Wyatt architecture of Tatton may not seem a happy hunting ground for heraldry. However, though the exterior of the house is Graeco-Roman at its most chaste, the long building history involving three generations of the Egertons, and two generations of Wyatt architects, Samuel and Lewis, means that the decoration of the house in the 1820s coincided with the stirrings of the Romantic revival and the more overt use of heraldry. Also in the case of the Egertons, situated close to vibrantly prosperous industrial development, there was a certain incentive to emphasise that theirs was an old race and that they were not new rich 'cottontots', even though much of their wealth derived from Stockport ground rents and the mercantile fortune inherited from the Hill family of Shenstone. So, though Repton's suggestion in his Red Book that the family arms be carved on milestones all over the estate to indicate the extent of Egerton ownership fell on deaf ears, more subtle heraldic demonstrations are present.

The Egertons of Tatton are descended from Thomas Egerton, Viscount Brackley, James I's Lord Chancellor. He was illegitimate, the son of Sir Richard Egerton of Ridley by Alice Sparke, 'a serving maid', but made his own fortune through the law.

The crest of Egerton in its post-1859 form on a cap of maintenance painted with the motto and an ill-defined coronet of rank on a salt box at Tatton.

The Lord Chancellor's direct descendants became the Earls and later Dukes of Bridgwater, and the Egertons of Tatton are descended from the third son of the 2nd Earl, Thomas, who inherited the Tatton estate in the late seventeenth century.

The Egerton crest is a lion holding an arrow. It can be seen on the weather vane of the Stables and on the book bindings in the Library. It also adorns the gilt brass door handles of all the principal rooms on the ground floor of the house, and can even be found enamelled on the salt containers and other provision jars in the Kitchen, and on the Servants' Hall plates. The arrow itself is used to decorate the flutes of the plaster beams supported by porphyry scagliola columns in Lewis Wyatt's Entrance Hall. Also in the Hall is a firescreen painted with numerous Egerton and Tatton quarterings.

In the Dining Room is a splendid display of Regency silver gilt plate by Paul Storr and Benjamin Smith. Much of this has the arms of Egerton impaled with Sykes for Wilbraham Egerton and his wife, Elizabeth Sykes, who married in 1806, and many of the items were made at that time. Some of it also had the royal arms, having been bought at the sale of the Duke of York (second son of George III) after his death in 1827.

Some Victorian heraldry can also be found at Tatton. There are a number of instances of Egerton impaling Amherst, *Gules three Tilting Spears erect Or*, for the 1st Earl Egerton and his first wife, Mary Amherst, whom he married in 1857. Their impaled arms appear on the metal gates in front of the house, on the archway dated 1884 to the right of the entrance and in stained glass in the family Entrance Hall.

The state coach of 1840 is very fine. Carriage doors were repainted for successive generations and this is demonstrated here as the arms on the carriage door are Egerton impaling Watson-Taylor of Urchfont for the 3rd Baron Egerton who succeeded in 1909 and died in 1920.

Uppark

SUSSEX

FETHERSTONHAUGH

ARMS: Gules on a Chevron between three Ostrich Feathers Argent a Roundel Sable

CREST: On a Wreath of the Colours (Argent and Gules) An Antelope statant Argent armed Or

Uppark was built *c.*1690 for Ford Grey, 3rd Lord Grey of Warke, who was created Earl of Tankerville in 1695, but was bought in 1747 for £19,000 by Sir Matthew Fetherstonhaugh who remodelled and refurnished the interior over the next twenty or so years. The dignified, sober architecture of the Uppark façades give little hint of the unprincipled but colourful character of Lord Tankerville who having been condemned to the Tower for plotting against James II got his gaoler drunk and escaped in disguise. He also took part in the Duke of Monmouth's rebellion but was captured after Sedgemoor. Though Monmouth was executed, Grey got off by testifying against his former adherents. His support for William III earned him an earldom. Having married Mary, daughter of the 1st Earl of Berkeley, he eloped with her sister Henrietta and was prosecuted by the outraged father; though convicted, he got off on a technicality. Dryden dismissed him as being 'Below the dignity of verse', and Bishop Burnet as a 'cowardly, perfidious person'.

Rather appropriately in the circumstances, as if by some posthumous court martial, the Tankerville arms have been degraded. They were removed from the great south pediment by the new owner, Sir Matthew Fetherstonhaugh, to make way for his own, and banished to a distant corner of the estate where they can still be seen built into the front of an old farmhouse. There is now no Tankerville heraldry at Uppark, but plenty of Fetherstonhaugh's. The achievement in the south pediment is a splendid rococo design, with the arms in a cartouche flanked by ostrich supporters. This carving survived the 1989 fire, although its stone base had to be replaced.

Sir Matthew Fetherstonhaugh was the beneficiary of an amazing stroke of luck. His father, Matthew Fetherstonhaugh, who was twice Mayor of Newcastle and had made money in the coal and wine trades, had purchased Fetherstonhaugh Castle – the ancient seat of the family – in Northumberland. In 1746, aged thirty-two, the younger Matthew inherited a gigantic fortune of £400,000 from the unrelated Sir Henry Fetherston, 2nd and last baronet of Hassingbrook Hall in Essex. Sir Henry had no children of his own or any other immediate heirs so chose the Northumberland Fetherstonhaughs as his beneficiaries. There were two conditions: Matthew had to buy an estate in the south of England and petition the Crown for a baronetcy, and he complied with both.

As well as marking his purchase of Uppark by placing the Fetherstonhaugh arms in the pediment, Sir Matthew totally remodelled the interior to create the wonderful rooms which have been so long admired, and restored by the National Trust after the devastating fire in 1989. All the elaborate plaster ceilings of the main rooms, which were brought down and smashed by falling debris from above have been re-made. Many fragments were, however, rescued and fitted into the new work, and one of these was a cartouche from the corner of the Little Drawing Room ceiling of *c.*1750 which incorporates the antelope crest of the Fetherstonhaughs. Sir Matthew also commissioned a Chinese dinner service *c.*1765 with his own arms impaled with those of his wife, Sarah Lethieullier, which is still in the Dining Room.

Sarah Lethieullier came from a cultivated Huguenot family, prominent merchants in the City of London. She brought to Uppark the famous doll's house, which is one of the two finest surviving English doll's houses; the other is at Nostell Priory (q.v.). The Uppark doll's house has the Lethieullier arms in the pediment.

Sir Matthew was succeeded at Uppark by his only son, Sir Harry Fetherstonhaugh. Sir Harry was a friend of the Prince Regent, and a man of taste who added fine French furniture and china to his father's creation. He is best remembered today for his liaison

The hatchment of Sir Harry Featherstonhaugh (d.1846) with his arms impaling those granted to his widow in 1848.

with the beautiful Emma Hart, the future Lady Hamilton, who supposedly danced naked on the dining room table at Uppark. When he was over seventy, Sir Harry eventually married his twenty-year-old dairy maid in 1825, to whom he left Uppark on his death aged ninety-one in 1846.

Sir Harry carried out further alterations to the design of Humphry Repton, including the transfer of the main entrance to the north side, where Repton designed an octagonal lobby and new entrance passage. These are furnished with benches and mahogany hall chairs painted, in the usual manner, with the Fetherstonhaugh arms and crest. Sir Harry also added to his father's collection of silver plate, some of which is still at Uppark, engraved with the family arms.

In the restaurant the hatchment of Sir Harry Fetherstonhaugh is displayed. It shows his arms impaled with those of his wife, Mary Ann Bullock (the former dairy maid), and the legend '*Non Omnis Moriar*' (We shall not wholly die). His widow lived on till 1874, so the background behind her arms is painted white, not black. Her own hatchment, a late example illustrating the conservatism with which she kept Uppark and its traditions throughout the nineteenth century, hangs in South Harting church.

The Vyne

HAMPSHIRE

Sandys

Arms: Argent a Cross raguly Sable

Crest: On a Wreath of the Colours (Argent and Sable) A Goat's Head couped at the neck Argent armed and between two Wings Or

Badge: A Goat Argent tufted armed unguled and winged Or

Supporters: On either side a Goat Argent tufted armed unguled and winged Or

Motto: *Aides Dieu*
[Help, O God]

Chute

Arms: Gules three Swords fesswise in pale points to the dexter Argent hilts pommels and quillons Or

Crest: On a Wreath of the Colours (Argent and Gules) A Hand in a Gauntlet proper grasping a broken Sword Argent hilt, pommel and quillons Or

Motto: *Fortune de Guerre*
[The fortune of war]

As an early Tudor house with an eighteenth-century owner who was a crony of Horace Walpole, and nineteenth-century squires enthused by their family history, The Vyne can be expected to be an heraldic goldmine. It does not disappoint. The house has a good array of armorial decorations of different dates, all of the highest quality and interest.

The Vyne was begun in the late 1490s by William Sandys, one of Henry VIII's most trusted courtiers, and Lord Chamberlain, who was made a Knight of the Garter in 1518 and became 1st Lord Sandys in 1523. The house is of diapered brick and now U-shaped, but was originally much larger with a base court and gatehouse. Some of Lord Sandys' original interiors survive as does some of the exterior fabric, though this fragment was much remodelled in the seventeenth, eighteenth and nineteenth centuries.

The Chapel is seemingly the least altered Tudor part. The stone battlements are embellished with the carved armorial devices of Henry VIII, Catherine of Aragon, Lord Sandys himself, Sir Reginald Bray (his father-in-law's half-brother) and the Order of the Garter. Inside the Chapel, the splendid oak stalls have a continuous canopy enriched with carved ribs and heraldic bosses. The windows are filled with renaissance stained glass, made in the 1520s by a team of Flemish painters and glaziers,

The cenotaph designed by John Chute (d.1776) in honour of his great-grandfather, the Speaker Chaloner Chute (d.1659), with the arms of Chute in seventeenth-century-style cartouches in the Tomb Chamber at The Vyne.

including David Joris. It is not certain that it was made for The Vyne, and may have been brought from the Holy Ghost Chapel at Basingstoke which Sandys patronised in the 1520s. The principal panels are devoted to biblical subjects, saints and royal portraits, but at the top of each light, within the cusped arches are coats of arms including those of Queen Margaret of Scotland (daughter of Henry VII), Henry VIII and Catherine of Aragon. It is depicted with great clarity and brilliance of colour, and is the best heraldic glass of its date in England. It was apparently saved from puritan iconoclasm during the Civil War by being submerged in the River Shir until the danger had passed, but this may be a romantic legend.

Other rooms in the house retain crisply carved Tudor linenfold panelling. The most complete set is in the Oak Gallery which occupies the whole length of the west wing on the first floor. At the top and bottom of each of the linenfold panels in here and on the doors are delicately carved badges or heraldic devices relating to Lord Sandys and his family, including the goat's head crest and *cross raguly* of the Sandys and the *hemp bray* of Sir Reginald Bray; and the Tudor monarchy with especial prominence given to the Tudor rose and the pomegranate, as at Ightham Mote (q.v.). Over the east door is an outstanding carving of the English royal arms, supported by little renaissance cherubs. Also in the decoration are the arms of Richard Foxe, Bishop of Winchester, Cardinal Wolsey with his Cardinal's hat, and Sandys with the Garter, which helps to date the panelling to between 1518, when Sandys received the Garter, and 1526 when Catherine of Aragon was estranged from Henry VIII.

The Sandys family was impoverished by the Civil War, and the 6th Lord Sandys, who inherited in 1644, was obliged to sell The Vyne in 1653. It was bought by Chaloner Chute, a successful lawyer who became Speaker of the House of Commons during the Commonwealth. He carried out many alterations, demolishing the forecourt and adding the classical portico, probably designed by John Webb, to the North Front. His arms, carved by the master-mason Edward Marshall, adorn the pediment. This is the earliest surviving example in England of a classical portico and the precursor of the architectural taste for placing arms in classical pediments. The idea originally came from Webb's master, Inigo Jones, and became popular in the late seventeenth and eighteenth centuries. Speaker Chaloner Chute, and John Webb, also introduced a series of classical marble chimneypieces into the house, of which the most extraordinary one, now in the Library carved with palm trees (perhaps moved there from a bedroom, as palm trees were a symbol of marital fertility) has a central cartouche of the Chute arms.

In the mid-eighteenth century, The Vyne was inherited by John Chute, a friend of Horace Walpole and member of the Strawberry Hill Committee of Taste. They were enthusiastic, if irreverent, heraldry buffs. Walpole, for instance, designed joke arms with playing cards for White's Club in St James's which are still used there for ornamenting dinner plates. They had various ideas for playing up the antique character of the Chapel area of The Vyne, which in the event were mainly confined to gothicking the Ante-Chapel and constructing a Tomb Chamber. Horace Walpole's suggestion that the 'windows be painted by [Joshua] Price [the leading glass painter of the day] with the pedigree' of the Chute family (i.e. a chronological series of impaled arms) probably never came to anything. The Ante-Chapel, however, now has good sixteenth-century heraldic glass brought in the twentieth century by the late Sir Charles Chute from the Chapel of the Holy Trinity in Basingstoke which William Sandys had built. Sir Charles was the family historian, and bequeathed The Vyne to the National Trust.

The Tomb Chamber is on the south side of the Chapel and was built in 1757 like a little Gothick chantry in honour of the Speaker Chaloner Chute who founded the family. It was designed by John Chute himself and was described by Walpole as a 'little Gothic Columbarium'. The *clou* is the tomb (actually a cenotaph, as the Speaker is buried at Chiswick) with a white marble effigy carved by Thomas Carter. On the sides of the tomb chest are Webb-style cartouches of the Chute arms, their frames copied from Marshall's in the portico pediment. The whole ensemble is a fascinating piece of antiquarianism, and intended to look as if John Webb had designed a contemporaneous tomb for the Speaker with neo-seventeenth-century heraldry within a Sandys-period chantry.

John Chute was a bachelor and the last of the male line. After a couple of generations

A detail of a scagliola table top at The Vyne showing the arms and supporters of Sir Robert Walpole (KG 1726) as a Knight of the Garter impaled with those of his first wife, Catherine Shorter (d.1737).

of cousins the property passed in the nineteenth century to a relation by marriage, William Lyde Wiggett, who took the name Chute and inherited The Vyne in 1827. He made substantial alterations to the house. A characteristic Victorian antiquarian squire interested in genealogy and heraldry, he enhanced the character of the house by creating further antiquarian interiors in the 1840s. On the first floor he created the Library and Tapestry Room out of old bits from elsewhere in the house. The Library has an illuminated pedigree of the Catholic recusant Curfaude family, found blocking a broken pane in a cottage window. Among others, it shows the arms of Edward III, the Duke of Clarence, Cardinal Pole and the Countess of Salisbury. In the Tapestry Room the large 'Jacobean' oak chimneypiece was also made up out of woodwork from the Chapel Parlour, and embellished with a panel of the multi-quartered arms of the Chute family. William Wiggett-Chute 'signed' his alterations at The Vyne by placing stone carvings of the Wiggett and Chute crests on the South Front doorways. A scagliola table shows the arms and supporters of Sir Robert Walpole as a Knight of the Garter impaling those of his first wife, Catherine Shorter.

Wallington Hall

NORTHUMBERLAND

BLACKETT

ARMS: Argent on a Chevron between three Mullets Sable three Escallops Argent

CREST: On a Wreath of the Colours (Argent and Sable) A Falcon's Head erased proper

MOTTO: *Nous Travaillerons en Esperance* [We will labour in hope]

BLACKETT
formerly CALVERLEY

ARMS: Sable an Inescutcheon in an orle of Owls Argent

CRESTS: (1) On a Wreath of the Colours (Argent and Sable) A Horned Owl Argent (2) Issuing from a Crest Coronet Or a Calf's Head erect Sable

TREVELYAN

ARMS: Gules a demi Horse Argent issuing from Water barry wavy Argent and Azure

CREST: On a Wreath of the Colours (Argent and Gules) Two Arms embowed habited Azure cuffed Argent the hands proper holding a Bezant

MOTTO: *Tyme Tryeth Troth*

Sir William Blackett, a rich Newcastle entrepreneur with interests in coal, lead and shipping, bought Wallington in the 1680s from the Fenwicks. He demolished their old house and built a new classical one of stone. The dignified, restrained façades of Wallington therefore date from Sir William's time. He died in 1705 leaving an only son, also Sir William, who had no issue. On the 2nd Baronet's death in 1728 the estate passed to Walter Calverley, the 2nd Baronet's nephew, who, as was often the case, took

The needlework panel worked between 1910 and 1933 by Mary, Lady Trevelyan, depicting the legend of the origin of the arms with the first Trevelyan riding ashore from St Michael's Mount. It also shows her own arms of Bell, those of Fenwick and Blackett and the owl crest of Calverley.

his uncle's name as part of his inheritance. He also married his uncle's illegitimate daughter, which was part of the deal. Walter Calverley Blackett was a man of taste, and in 1738-46 remodelled the interior to the design of Daniel Garrett with plasterwork by the Franchini brothers. Walter died childless in 1886, and the estate was inherited by another nephew, Sir John Trevelyan of Nettlecombe in Somerset. The Victorian Trevelyans were a talented family and strong Liberals, producing M.P.s, historians and civil servants. Sir Charles Trevelyan gave the house to the National Trust in 1941.

The contents of Wallington form a rich assemblage of the possessions of successive members of the Blackett, Calverley, and Trevelyan families who inherited the property, and also of Lord Macaulay whose sister married Sir Charles Edward Trevelyan, owner

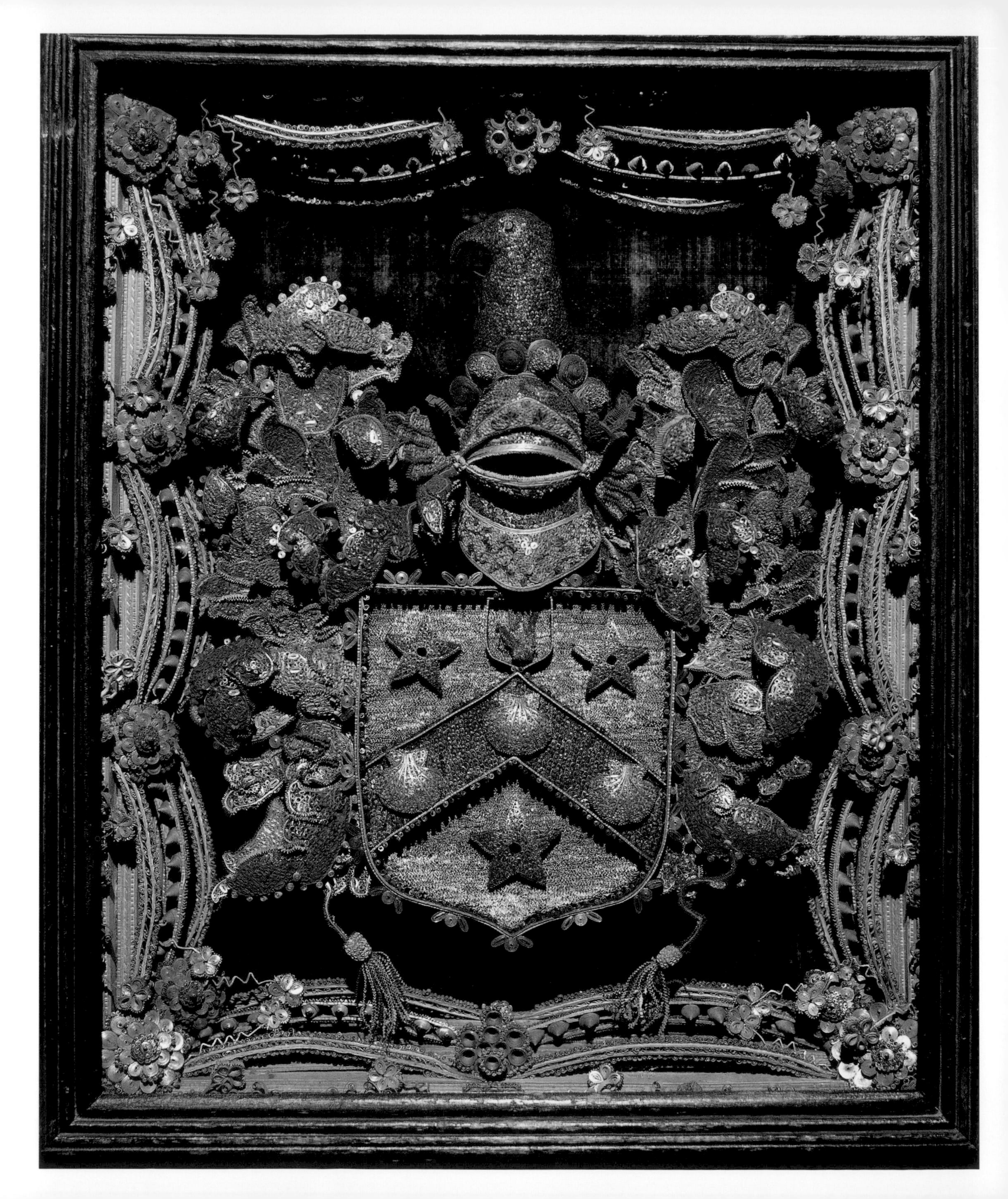

of Wallington from 1879 to 1886. The 1750 silver rococo basket by John Jacobs on the dining room table, for instance, has the owl crest of the Calverleys fully moulded in support of the handles as well as being engraved. It also depicts the quartered arms of Calverley and Blackett with Blackett in pretence. The Calverley owl appears prominently all over Wallington, and is carved in wood in the Victorian Central Hall where it appears four times on the first floor balustrade, as if it had flown in from a Red Indian totem pole. The Central Hall was created from an inner courtyard in 1854 and painted in Pre-Raphaelite taste by William Bell Scott; it has fourteen coats of arms in cartouches all the way round depicting family marriages and connections. The historical scenes above also include heraldry, and in the Chevy Chase scene the Percy arms can be seen. The owl can also be found, carved in stone and perched on the gate piers at the back door, and on the pediment of the two-storeyed pavilion in the walled garden. Two more, superior, owls sculpted out of purest Carrara marble, keep watch at the foot of the main staircase.

In Lady Trevelyan's Parlour, over the fireplace, is a needlework panel, worked by Mary, Lady Trevelyan with four shields showing the arms of the families connected with Wallington: the Fenwicks' red and white martlets; the Blacketts' mullets and scallops; the Trevelyans' horse rising from the waves; and the hawk's bells and lures of the Bells (Lady Trevelyan's family). In the centre is a depiction of the legend which gave rise to the Trevelyan arms: it shows the first Trevelyan swimming on his horse from St Michael's Mount to the mainland of Cornwall. The Calverley owl is prominent with its wings outstretched.

There are other items of particular heraldic interest, including silver presented to Lord Macaulay's father in recognition of his efforts to get the slave trade abolished, which is engraved with a boot, the Macaulay crest. In the Study is an inscribed silver freedom box given by Dundee to Sir George Otto Trevelyan which has the arms of Dundee and Trevelyan. A large Wedgwood dinner service also has the Trevelyan crest. It was a wedding present from Josiah Wedgwood to the Rev. George Trevelyan in 1795.

The best representation of the Blackett arms is a delightful piece of scrolled gilt paperwork or 'quillwork' in the Front Hall, which recalls a lost eighteenth-century art. And peeking out from the broken pediment of the remodelled south doorway can be seen the Trevelyan arms impaling Calverley with its motto, *Tyme Tryeth Troth*, and dolphin supporters.

The most picturesque expression of heraldry at Wallington, and indeed in almost any National Trust house, are the four so-called 'griffins' heads' on the lawn in front of the house looking like submerged monsters awaiting the Resurrection. These are, in fact, dragons' heads and their history could hardly be more improbable. They are the heads of the dragon supporters of the City of London arms. They are splendid examples of vigorous seventeenth-century heraldic carving, and were originally part of displays of the City Arms on Bishopsgate. When the City of London gates were demolished in 1760 – an early example of road-widening vandalism – the stonework was used as ballast for ships. The dragon heads were bought in Newcastle by Sir Walter Blackett to decorate Rothley Castle, an eye-catcher on the Wallington estate. They were removed to their present position in 1928.

An early eighteenth-century rolled paperwork full achievement of the arms of Blackett of Wallington with the badge of the baronetage.

Wimpole Hall

CAMBRIDGESHIRE

Harley

Arms: Or a Bend cotised Sable

Crest: On a Wreath of the Colours (Or and Sable) A Castle triple towered Argent issuing from behind the central tower a demi Lion rampant Gules

Supporters: On either side an Angel proper the habit and wings displayed Or

Motto: *Virtute et Fide* [By Valour and Faith]

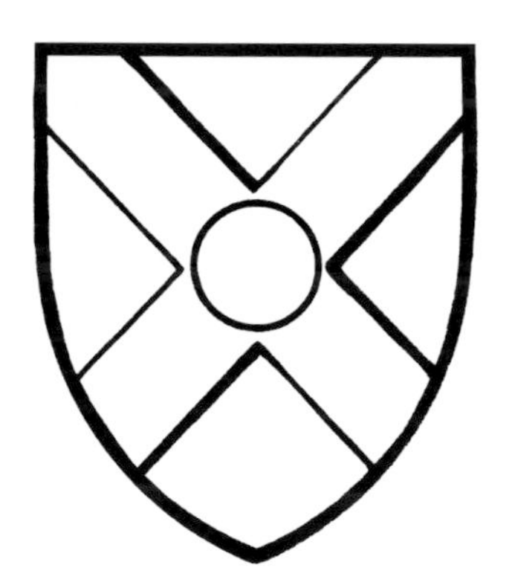

Yorke

Arms: Argent on a Saltire Azure a Bezant

Crest: On a Wreath of the Colours (Argent and Azure) A Lion's Head erased proper collared Gules the collar charged with a Bezant

Supporters: (Dexter) A Lion guardant Or collared Gules the collar charged with a Bezant; (Sinister) A Stag proper attired and unguled Or collared Gules the collar charged with a Bezant

Motto: *Nec Cupias Nec Metuas* [Neither desire nor fear]

Wimpole was bought by John Holles, 1st and last Duke of Newcastle of his creation, in 1710 and passed on his death the following year to his son-in-law, Edward Harley, 2nd Earl of Oxford. Harley was the son of Queen Anne's Minister and a famous bibliophile who added the Library Wing, designed by James Gibbs, for his book collection amounting to over 50,000 volumes, now partly in the British Library. His friend, Matthew Prior, wrote: 'Fame counting his books my dear Harley, shall tell/ No man had so many who knew them so well'. He had no son, and his daughter married the 2nd Duke of Portland, so in 1740 Wimpole was sold to Philip Yorke, 1st Earl of Hardwicke, Lord Chancellor from 1737 to 1756, who further remodelled and extended the house to the design of Henry Flitcroft. Wimpole belonged to the Hardwickes down to 1894. After a period in the ownership of Lord Robartes (later 6th Viscount Clifden) of Lanhydrock, Cornwall (q.v.), it was bought by Mrs Bambridge, the daughter of Rudyard Kipling, who restored the house and bequeathed it to the National Trust. The Kiplings never applied for arms.

The Earls of Hardwicke are the dominant family presence at Wimpole. It is the arms of the Lord Chancellor which fill the pediment in the centre of the South Front. These were installed as part of Henry Flitcroft's remodelling of the exterior of the main block in the 1740s. The arms are impaled with those of his wife, Margaret Cocks, and have only a baron's coronet, as Hardwicke was not promoted to an earldom till 1754. The same representation of the arms can also be seen on his bookplate.

In the Entrance Hall, the polychrome encaustic tile floor inserted by the Victorian architect H. E. Kendall as part of a redecoration for the 4th Earl of Hardwicke in the 1840s incorporates the Hardwicke monogram, coronet and motto. The Axminster carpet of 1845 in the Yellow Drawing Room, one of the architect Sir John Soane's most impressive interiors, also has the Hardwicke monogram and coronet in its border.

The Arrington gates at the entrance to the park and the stables, which were both designed by Kendall in 1851, are embellished with the Hardwicke supporters – a lion and a stag – holding shields of arms made of Blanchard's artificial stone. The arms show Yorke and Liddell for the 4th Earl and his wife, the Hon. Margaret Liddell. Lord Oxford's arms only appear in the architecture at Wimpole painted in grisaille by Sir James Thornhill over the doorway into the Chapel from the Entrance Hall. Many of his books were splendidly bound with gilt representations of his heraldic achievement on the covers. Though few of his volumes now survive in the house, the service books in the Chapel do. The sumptuous prayer books, laid out in the family pew, have the original bindings emblazoned with the arms of Edward, Lord Harley, later 2nd Earl of Oxford, and his wife, Henrietta Cavendish Holles, only daughter and heiress of the Duke of Newcastle.

The most extensive display of heraldry at Wimpole is to be found in the adjoining parish church of St Andrew. This was rebuilt in 1749 by Lord Chancellor Hardwicke to Flitcroft's design, apart from the fourteenth-century Chicheley Chapel, and has the character of a private chapel, but it succeeds the medieval parish church which serves a now vanished village.

The bookplate of Edward, Lord Harley, later 2nd Earl of Oxford (d.1741), who sold Wimpole Hall in 1740, with the arms of his wife, Lady Henrietta Cavendish Holles, in pretence.

A view of the Chapel at Wimpole with the oval armorial bookstamp of Edward, Lord Harley, later 2nd Earl of Oxford, on the boards of the service books.

The Gallery windows have rare eighteenth-century heraldic stained glass with the Yorke family arms. In the central window of the north wall of the Chicheley Chapel is re-set good fourteenth-century glass with thirteen large shields of arms, mainly of local families, but also the royal arms of France and England. The principal impression, however, is 'of an assembly of monuments' to the successive families who have owned the Wimpole estate. The Lord Chancellor himself has the grandest of all, carved by Scheemakers to the design of 'Athenian' Stuart, and there is a large tomb chest for the 3rd Earl of Hardwicke with an effigy in Garter robes carved by Richard Westmacott (the younger) in 1844. All these have the appropriate arms. The Lord Chancellor's are impaled with those of his wife, Margaret Cocks, on a decorative white marble oval silhouetted against a dark obelisk, the 3rd Earl's has a huge coronet on a cushion beside him, and his crest, encircled by the Garter, on the rounded end of the tomb chest. Under the heraldic north window is the tomb of Sir Thomas Chicheley (d.1616) with a shield of impaled arms.

The arms of Chicheley are *Or a Chevron between three Cinquefoils Gules* and their crest is *An heraldic Tyger with a Man's Leg in its mouth*. The Chicheleys of Wimpole were descended from a brother of Henry Chicheley, Archbishop of Canterbury and founder of All Souls College, Oxford.

The Families

Baddesley Clinton

Ferrers

Arms: Gules seven Mascles conjoined 3,3&1 Or a Canton Ermine. Crest: On a Wreath of the Colours (Or and Gules) A Unicorn passant Ermine. Badges: (1) A Unicorn courant Ermine charged on the shoulder with a crescent Sable; (2) A Mascle Or. Motto: *Splendeo Tritus* [I shine though worn].

The Ferrers of Baddesley Clinton were a branch of the great medieval family which at some time held the Earldom of Derby and the Baronies of Ferrers of Chartley and Ferrers of Groby. They were descended from Henry de Ferrieres, a companion of William the Conqueror, Domesday Commissioner and founder of Tutbury Priory in Staffordshire. His son Robert was created Earl of Derby in 1138. Although there is no contemporary evidence, popular accounts state that the first arms borne by the family were *Argent six Horseshoes 3,2&1 Sable*, which also occurs with the tinctures reversed, but the earliest seals and rolls of arms (*c.*1245) show the arms as *Vairy Or and Gules*. William Ferrers, Earl of Derby (d.1254) appears to have compounded these two coats, as his seal shows *Vairy a Bordure charged with Horseshoes*.

William, Earl of Derby married Margaret de Quincy, heiress of Groby in Leicestershire, and while their eldest son Robert, who forfeited the earldom and was the ancestor of the Barons Ferrers of Chartley, retained the Vairy coat, their younger son William, ancestor of the Barons Ferrers of Groby, bore the arms of de Quincy *Gules seven Mascles conjoined 3,3&1 Or*.

William, 5th Lord Ferrers of Groby (d.1445) had a younger son, Sir Thomas Ferrers, who acquired Tamworth Castle by marriage with a Freville heiress. Sir Thomas Ferrers of Tamworth and his wife, Elizabeth Freville, had a younger son Sir Henry Ferrers, whose son Sir Edward Ferrers (d.1535) acquired Baddesley Clinton by marriage with Constance Brome, whose arms were *Sable on a Chevron Argent three Broom Sprigs Vert*.

The arms and crest of Ferrers of Baddesley Clinton are as recorded at the 1682 Visitation of Warwickshire. The arms are those of de Quincy differenced by a Canton Ermine. The Tamworth branch bore the unicorn crest Argent rather than Ermine. The two badges are on the standard of Sir Edward Ferrers (d.1535). The motto *Splendeo Tritus* is a reference to horseshoes.

The Baronies of Ferrers of Chartley and Ferrers of Groby are both Baronies by Writ so can pass through the female line. Ferrers of Groby became a subsidiary title of the Marquessate of Dorset and Dukedom of Suffolk and was forfeited with the other honours of Henry Grey, Duke of Suffolk when he was attainted and beheaded in February 1553/4. Ferrers of Chartley eventually became a subsidiary title of the Marquesses Townshend. On the death of the 3rd Marquess without issue in 1855 the coheirs to the Barony were his two sisters, the elder of whom was married to Edward Ferrers of Baddesley Clinton. Her son, Marmion Edward Ferrers (d.1884), consequently became senior coheir of the Barony of Ferrers of Chartley. In *The Rise of Great Families* (1873) Sir Bernard Burke wrote of Marmion Edward:

> The descendant in the male line of Earls of Derby, older in creation by more than 300 years than the Stanleys, and senior co-heir through his mother of the Barony of Ferrers of Chartley bears no other designation than that of 'Mr Ferrers of Baddesley Clinton' although he has a pedigree and shield of quarterings that would not have disparaged an Elector of Mayence or a Prince-Bishop of Wurzburg.

In 1885, after the death of Marmion Edward, his nephew Henry Ferrers Croxon obtained a Royal Licence entitling him to bear the arms of Ferrers quarterly in the first quarter with those of Croxon. As a result he became Henry Ferrers Ferrers and the arms in the patent following the Royal Licence were quarterly (1&4) Ferrers *Gules seven Mascles conjoined 3,3&1 Or a Canton Ermine;* (2&3) Croxon *Or a Fess nebuly Azure between two Crosses botonny fitchy in chief Azure and a Tun fesswise in base proper*.

In 1941 Gilbert Thomas Ferrers-Walker, who had assumed the additional name of Ferrers by Deed Poll, was granted a quartering for Ferrers of *Gules four Mascles conjoined 3&1 Or within an Orle of the last*. This quartering was borne in the second and third quarters with arms for Walker (granted in 1940) *Gules on a Fess between three Cross crosslets fitchy Or two Round Buckles the tongues erect Azure*, in the first and fourth quarters. The crest granted for Walker was *On a Wreath of the Colours (Or and Gules) A demi Greyhound Argent supporting between the legs a Mascle Or* and a second crest for Ferrers was granted of *On a Wreath of the Colours (Or and Gules) A demi Unicorn Erminois resting the sinister leg upon a Horseshoe inverted Or*.

Belton House

Brownlow, Baronets and Viscount Tyrconnel

Arms: Or an Inescutcheon in an orle of Martlets Sable. Crest: On a

Chapeau Gules turned up Ermine a Greyhound passant Or plain collared Gules. SUPPORTERS (as Viscount Tyrconnel): On either side a Lion reguardant Argent plain gorged Gules. MOTTO: *Esse Quam Videri* [To be rather than to seem to be].

CUST, Baronets, Barons, Earls and Barons Brownlow

ARMS: Ermine on a Chevron Sable three Fountains. CREST: On a Wreath of the Colours (Argent and Sable) A Lion's Head erased Sable plain collared gobony Argent and Azure. SUPPORTERS (as Lord Brownlow): On either side a Lion reguardant Argent collared paly wavy Argent and Azure. MOTTO: *Opera Illius Mea Sunt* [His works are mine]; *Esse Quam Videri* [To be rather than to seem to be].

Richard Brownlow (1553-1638), Chief Prothonotary of the Common Pleas who purchased Belton, obtained a patent from Clarenceux in 1593 confirming his 'ancient arms' and granting him a crest. Such patents were not uncommon in the sixteenth century, although in this case no earlier evidence for the arms has been found. In 1602 a further patent from Norroy added a quartering for Panelly of *Azure a Cross paty floretty Or.* Richard Brownlow's son William was created a baronet in 1641 and consequently the red hand of Ulster, the badge of the baronetage, appears on many versions of the arms. The 5th Baronet was created Viscount Tyrconnel in the Peerage of Ireland in 1718 and his supporters must have been granted by Ulster King of Arms in Dublin, as they are illustrated in the records of that office and there is no grant in England.

Lord Tyrconnel's sister married Sir Richard Cust, 2nd Bt., whose family claimed an ancient lineage although their arms postdate those of Brownlow. They first recorded a pedigree without arms at the 1634 Visitation of Lincolnshire and the arms and crest were granted to Richard Cust in 1663. An earlier grant in 1649 to his father, Samuel Cust, of *Argent on a Chevron wavy Sable a Death's Head Argent* was declared void, like other Commonwealth grants, by a Royal Warrant in 1660.

When Sir Brownlow Cust, 4th Bt. was created Baron Brownlow in 1776, he was granted supporters very similar to those of his great-uncle, Lord Tyrconnel, although the collars on the lions differ. The 2nd Lord Brownlow was raised to an earldom in 1815 and the 1st Earl Brownlow's son, Viscount Alford, changed his surname from Cust to Home-Cust by Royal Licence in 1839. He did not alter his arms. However, in 1849 in compliance with the will of John William (Egerton), 7th Earl of Bridgwater, he changed his surname again by Royal Licence to Egerton and assumed the arms of Egerton *Argent a Lion rampant Gules* and crest of *On a Wreath of the Colours (Argent and Gules) A Lion rampant Gules supporting an Arrow in pale point downwards Or barbed and flighted proper* with the motto *Sic Donec.*

Lord Alford predeceased the 1st Earl so his son succeeded to the title in 1853. He also assumed the name and arms of Egerton by Royal Licence. In the 1853 patent the crest of Egerton is altered by the inclusion of a chapeau and is blazoned *On a Chapeau Gules turned up Ermine A Lion rampant also Gules supporting an Arrow palewise Or pheoned and flighted Argent.* In 1863 the 2nd Earl had a further Royal Licence to change his surname to Egerton-Cust, and thereafter bore quartered arms of (1&4) Cust and (2&3) Egerton with two crests retaining the Egerton crest on a chapeau. On the death in 1921 of the 2nd Earl's brother, who had succeeded him as 3rd Earl and 4th Baron, the earldom became extinct and the barony passed to a second cousin.

BENINGBROUGH HALL

BOURCHIER

ARMS: Argent a Cross engrailed Gules between four Water Bougets Sable. CREST: On a Wreath Or and Vert an Old Man's Head couped at the shoulders habited Vert collared Or the beard and hair proper on his head a crest Coronet Or issuing therefrom a long pointed Cap Gules ending in a tassel hanging forward Or. BADGE: A Bourchier Knot Or.

The illegitimate son of the soldier-courtier John (Bourchier), 2nd Lord Berners (d.1532/3), James Bourchier, married Mary Banester, heiress of Beningbrough. Under the English Law of Arms a right to arms does not pass to an illegitimate child, who must have a new grant of suitably differenced arms and is not entitled to any quarterings which predate the illegitimacy. No member of the Bourchier family of Beningbrough ever had such a grant, so technically they were not entitled to arms. Arms are shown neither on the 1564 Visitation entry nor on a pedigree registered at the College of Arms in 1748.

However, a complicated quartered coat was shown at the 1665 Visitation of Yorkshire with in (1&4) a grand quarter of (i) Bourchier (ii) Lovain *Gules a Fess between 14 Billets palewise Or* (iii) Berners *Quarterly Or and Vert* (iv) Tilney *Argent a Chevron between three Griffins' Heads erased Gules*; (2) Banester *Argent a Cross patonce Sable a crescent untinctured in dexter chief*; and (3) Fyncham *Argent three Bars Sable over all a Bend Ermine.* This was claimed by Barrington Bourchier of Beningbrough, then aged thirty-eight, and there is a note that there was no entitlement because of illegitimacy.

In 1665 the crest appears as it is blazoned above although not all the tinctures are shown. Lord Berners bore the crest without the shoulders clothed in green and gold – the Berners livery colours – and he used the crowned and capped head on a gold and green wreath. The Bourchier family Barons Fitzwarine and subsequently Earls of Bath bore the crest with bare shoulders.

The badge of the Bourchier or Bowser knot is supposed to represent two Bs in cypher, and also appears on the tomb of Fulke (Bourchier), Lord Fitzwarine (d.1479) at Bampton in Devon, and on the brass at Little Easton, Essex, to his uncle, Henry (Bourchier), Earl of Essex (d.1483). The 2nd Lord Berners used a variation in the form of ragged staves twisted into a Bourchier knot.

The arms of the Dawnay family, Viscounts Downe, who inherited Beningbrough in 1827 are *Argent on a Bend cotised Sable three Annulets Argent.*

Blickling Hall

Hobart, Earls of Buckinghamshire

Arms: Sable an Estoile of six rays Or between two Flaunches Ermine. Crest: On a Wreath of the Colours (Or and Sable) A Bull statant per pale Sable and Gules both bezanty armed and in the nose a ring Or. Supporters: (Dexter) A Buck reguardant proper attired and gorged with a radiant collar and a cordon passing between the forelegs and reflexed over the back Or; (Sinister) A Talbot reguardant proper langued Gules with the like collar and cordon. Motto: *Auctor Pretiosa Facit* [The giver makes them valuable].

The arms and crest first appear at the 1563 Visitation of Norfolk and were probably granted to Thomas Hobart of Plumstead, Norfolk, father of Sir Henry Hobart, 1st Baronet, by Clarenceux. This possibly simplified an earlier grant of the same crest to Sir James Hobart (d.1517) with an estoile of more limbs. The supporters were granted to the 5th Baronet in 1725 following his investiture as one of the Knights of the revived Order of the Bath. They pre-date his elevation to the peerage and there is no suggestion that they should be hereditary, which may explain their omission from subsequent entries of the family in the official records of the College of Arms.

The 2nd Earl of Buckinghamshire died in 1793 leaving four daughters and no son, so the earldom was inherited by his half-brother and Blickling eventually became the property of the descendants of his eldest daughter, Henrietta, who married the 6th Marquess of Lothian. The Marquesses of Lothian bore quarterly (1&4) *Azure a Sun in Splendour proper*; (2&3) *Gules on a Chevron Argent three Mullets Gules.*

Buckland Abbey

Drake

Arms: Sable a Fess wavy between two Estoiles Argent. Crest: On a Wreath of the Colours (Argent and Sable) On a Terrestrial Globe a Ship proper trained about the said Globe with hawsers Or by a Hand issuing out of Clouds on the dexter all proper and on an Escroll this Motto *Auxilio Divino* [By divine aid]. Motto: *Sic Parvis Magna* [Thus great things arise from small].

Fuller-Eliott-Drake, Baronets

Arms, Quarterly: (1&4 Drake) Sable a Fess wavy between two Estoiles Argent; (2 Eliott) Gules on a Bend Or a Baton Azure on a Chief the arms of Gibraltar (Azure between two Pillars a Castle Argent from the Gate a Golden Key pendent subinscribed *Plus Ultra* [More beyond]); (3 Fuller) Argent three Bars and a Canton Gules. Crests: (1 Drake) On a Wreath of the Colours (Argent and Sable) On a Terrestrial Globe a Ship proper trained about the said Globe with hawsers by a Hand issuing out of Clouds on the dexter all proper and on an Escroll this Motto *Auxilio Divino*; (2 Eliott) On a Wreath of the Colours (Argent and Gules) A dexter Hand in armour couped above the wrist proper grasping a Scymitar Argent pommel and hilt Or the wrist charged with a Key Sable; (3 Fuller) Out of a Crest Coronet Gules A Lion's Head Argent charged with a Crescent Azure.

The arms of Buckland Abbey were quarterly *Argent and Gules a Crozier in Bend Or* and those of Sir Richard Grenville its purchaser after the Dissolution *Gules three Clarions Or*. The heraldic interest at Buckland is, however, in the arms of Sir Francis Drake who acquired Buckland in the 1580s from the purchaser's grandson, also Sir Richard Grenville, who was mortally wounded in 1591 when commanding *The Revenge*. Drake's arms and crest are in a patent of June 1581, which refers to the arms having been given to Drake by Elizabeth I. Drake may have wanted this coat to be granted as an augmentation to be borne as a quartering with the arms of Drake of Ash *Argent a Wyvern Gules*. He had no known descent from this family. The arms are not quartered on the 1581 patent but despite this Sir Francis Drake used quartered arms on his seal and they appear on at least one portrait.

Whilst there is no doubt as to the arms granted in 1581, there is considerable doubt as to the crest. The question is whether a wyvern, presumably a reference to the arms of Drake of Ash, should be shown in the ship. The wyvern is visible in the ship on Drake's drum and on a coconut cup dated 1580 on which the engraving must be slightly later. It is not mentioned on the 1581 grant but it does appear on several drafts of the text of the grant, which might suggest that Drake was dissatisfied with its omission and sought a further patent. No wyvern appears in the ship at the 1620 Visitation of Devon entry by Sir Francis Drake's nephew, also Francis Drake, who was created a baronet in 1622.

The baronetcy became extinct on the death of the 5th Baronet in 1794. His sister married the 1st Lord Heathfield, whose four-year defence of Gibraltar against combined Spanish and French forces was rewarded by a Royal Licence in 1787 augmenting his ancestral arms of Eliott with those of Gibraltar. The 2nd Lord Heathfield left Buckland Abbey to his nephew, Thomas Trayton Fuller, who obtained a Royal Licence in 1813 to bear quartered arms and the surname Fuller-Eliott-Drake. He was created a baronet in 1821 with an extended limitation allowing the baronetcy to pass to his nephew, who obtained a further Royal Licence in 1870 to assume the surname Fuller-Eliott-Drake and bear the quartered arms of (1&4) Drake (2) Eliott and (3) Fuller with three crests. This baronetcy became extinct in 1915 on the 2nd Baronet's death.

Castle Drogo

Drewe

Arms: Ermine a Lion passant per pale Gules and Or in chief three Ears of Wheat stalked and bladed of the last (i.e. Or). Crest: On a Wreath of the Colours (Argent and Gules) In front of a Bull's Head Sable gorged with a collar gemel and holding in the mouth three Ears of Wheat a Garb fessewise all Or. Motto: *Drogo Nomen et Virtus Arma Dedit* [Drogo is my name and valour gave me arms].

The arms and crest were granted in 1899 to Julius Charles Drew (1856-1931) and the other descendants of his father, the Rev. George Smith Drew sometime Rector of Avington, Hampshire. Julius Drew was described as of Wadhurst Hall in the parish of Wadhurst, Sussex. In 1910 he restored the spelling of his surname to Drewe by deed poll. In the 1914 and subsequent editions of Burke's *Landed Gentry* the claim to descent from Sir Thomas Drewe of Killerton was dropped. Instead the pedigree commences with his greatgrandfather, Thomas Drewe of Sloane Street, Knightsbridge, an architect.

The bull's head crest granted in 1899 is based not on that of Drewe of Killerton, granted to Sir Thomas Drewe's father and blazoned *On a Wreath Argent and Gules On a Mount Vert a Roe Buck rising Or* but on that of Drewe of Drewe's Cliffe in Devon, granted in 1539 and blazoned *On a Wreath Or and Vert A Vervex* [a wether] *Head erased Sable horned and holding in his mouth three Stalks and Ears of Rye Or*. Some printed sources describe the 1539 crest as a bull's head.

Charlecote

Lucy

Arms: Gules semé of Cross Crosslets three Lucies haurient Argent. Crest: Out of a Crest Coronet Gules A Boar's Head Argent gutty Sable between two Wings displayed also Sable billetty Or. Badge: A Lucy haurient Argent. Motto: *By trwt be Delegence*; *Semper Melita Virtus* [Virtue is always sweet]; *By Trwthe And Diligence*.

The arms and crest are of medieval origin and were confirmed at the Visitations of Warwickshire of 1563, 1619 and 1682-3. In 1563 a coat of eight quarters was recorded and in 1619 one of ten quarters. In 1787 the Rev. John Hammond obtained a Royal Licence to take the name and arms of Lucy which were exemplified by subsequent Letters Patent. In 1892 Henry William Ramsay-Fairfax assumed the additional name and arms of Lucy. The Letters Patent exemplified the arms with Lucy in the first and fourth quarters and Fairfax and Ramsay quarterly in the second and third quarters. The grant was made in consequence of his marriage with Ada Christina, eldest daughter and coheir of Henry Spencer Lucy, and the arms of Lucy were granted with a canton Argent as a distinction. The arms were to be borne without the canton by the issue of the marriage. The motto appears in various forms.

Chastleton House

Jones

Arms: Gules a Lion rampant within a Bordure indented Or with a Crescent Sable on a Mullet Or in dexter chief for difference. Crest: On a Wreath of the Colours (Or and Gules) A demi Lion rampant Or armed and langued Azure holding a Mullet Gules.

Whitmore-Jones

Arms, Quarterly: (1&4 Jones) Gules a Lion rampant within a Bordure indented Or and for distinction a Canton Ermine; (2&3 Whitmore) Vert fretty Or. Crests: (1 Jones) On a Wreath of the Colours (Or and Gules) A demi Lion rampant Or holding between the paws a Mullet Gules and for distinction charged on the body with a Fret Gules; (2 Whitmore) On a Wreath of the Colours (Or and Vert) A Falcon standing on the stump of a tree with a branch springing from the dexter side all proper.

The arms were confirmed with a difference and the crest granted by Garter to Walter Jones, described as of the City of Worcester, in March 1602/3. Before the arms were confirmed, the consent of Gilbert Talbot, 7th Earl of Shrewsbury was obtained because the arms without the difference are those of Rhys ap Tewdwr Mawr, Prince of Deheubarth (south-west Wales) (d.1093) whose descendant, Richard Talbot, ancestor of the Earls of Shrewsbury, had adopted these arms from his mother's family. The Jones border is stated to be indented whereas that of Talbot was engrailed, but no distinction would be made between indented and engrailed in medieval heraldry. In the 1602/3 patent the arms were confirmed as the first of six quarters and the text of the patent refers to the other Welsh coats as (2) Pewez (Powys), (3) Vaugham of Toleglas (Vaughan of Tyle Glas), (4) Glamboy (Clanvow) and (5) Barrey &c., omitting the name of the last quarter. (Barrey and the sixth quarter *Argent a Stag statant Gules attired Or* are probably for Gruffudd Gwyr). The Jones family of Chastleton recorded a pedigree at both the 1634 and 1668 Visitations of Oxfordshire, but at the 1574 Visitation Walter Jones's father had been disclaimed as no gentleman, and therefore not entitled to arms.

In 1828 John Henry Whitmore, a younger son of William Whitmore of Dudmaston, succeeded to Chastleton, and obtained a Royal Licence to bear the arms of Jones quarterly in the first and fourth quarters with those of Whitmore. The difference on the arms and crest was appropriate as he had no Jones blood: the last Jones had a Whitmore grandmother.

Chirk Castle

Myddelton, sometime Baronets

Arms, Quarterly: (1&4 Rhirid y Pothan Flaidd) Argent on a Bend Vert three Wolves' Heads erased Argent; (2&3 Rhirid Flaidd) Vert a Chevron between three Wolves' Heads erased Argent. Crest: On a Wreath of the Colours (Argent and Vert) A dexter human Hand couped proper. Motto: *In Veritate Triumpho* [I triumph in the truth].

The Myddelton family descend from the marriage of Rhirid ap Dafydd, who was living in 1393, and Cecily Middleton. They bore the quartered coat of (1&4) the arms attributed to Rhirid ap Dafydd's grandfather, Rhirid y Pothan Flaidd, and (2&3) the arms attributed to the latter's great-grandfather, Rhirid Flaidd.

In 1801, following his marriage to Charlotte Myddelton, Robert Biddulph obtained a Royal Licence to bear the arms of Myddelton quarterly with those of Biddulph and take the name Myddelton Biddulph. In the patent that followed in 1804 the arms are blazoned (1&4) Biddulph *Vert an Eagle displayed Argent a Canton of the last* (i.e. Argent) (2&3) Myddelton *Argent on a Bend Vert three Wolves' Heads erased of the field* (i.e. Argent) and there are two crests: (1) Biddulph *On a Wreath of the Colours (Argent and Vert) A Wolf salient Argent charged on the shoulder with a Trefoil Gules*, (2) Myddelton *On a Wreath of the Colours (Argent and Vert) A dexter Hand couped proper*.

In 1899 Robert Myddelton Biddulph's grandson Richard assumed the surname of Myddelton only, and in 1959 his grandson Ririd Myddelton obtained another Royal Licence – confirmed in a patent of 1960 – reversing the quarterings of 1804, so Myddelton was in (1&4) and Biddulph in (2&3). The order of the crests was also altered, and the Myddelton crest took the principal position to the dexter.

Clandon Park

Onslow, Baronets, Barons and Earls of Onslow

Arms: Argent a Fess Gules between six Cornish Choughs proper. Crest: On a Wreath of the Colours (Argent and Gules) A Falcon Sable beaked legged and belled Or preying on a Partridge lying on its back Or. Supporters: On either side a Falcon proper with bells on the legs Gold the bewits Gules. Motto: *Festina Lente* [On slow!].

Sixteenth-century records in the College of Arms, such as the 1584 Shropshire Visitation, show the birds in the arms as some species of hawk with bells on the legs and they appear in this form in the 1623 Visitation of Surrey; a possible blazon would be *Argent a Fess Gules between six Falcons Sable beaked legged and belled Or*. In John Guillim's *A Display of Heraldry* (4th edition, 1660) the arms of the Onslow family resident in Surrey are said to be *Argent a Fess Gules between six Cornish Choughs proper*, while the arms of the senior line of the family, the Onslows of Onslow in Shropshire, are given in the same source as *Argent a Fess Gules between six Merlions or Sparhawks Sable beaks and legs Or*. The confusion arises because no grant or patent survives and as is customary the Visitation records show only a monochrome sketch with the colours tricked (see p.27) which leaves the identity of the birds open to interpretation.

The blazon of the supporters follows the text of the 1716 grant, when the birds in the arms still have gold beaks, legs and bells. This seems to be the last occasion that the birds in the arms appear as falcons. The editor of the 1724 edition of Guillim on giving the arms of Lord Onslow as *Argent a Fess Gules between six Cornish Choughs proper* adds, 'Some books give them as young hawks, and I believe they are so.' The crest is now given in printed sources as *An Eagle Sable preying on a Partridge Or* but as late as Brydges' edition of *Collins's Peerage* (1812) the crest is given as a falcon belled and feeding on a partridge, although both falcon and partridge are wrongly given as proper. This is an example of a family making unauthorised changes to their heraldry. The motto *Festina Lente* first appears on a grant of supporters in July 1776 to George Onslow when he was created Baron Cranley. These became superfluous when he succeeded to the Barony of Onslow later in the same year. The previous motto was *Semper Fidelis, Laudo Manentem* [Always faithful, I praise him that waits] which sometime occurs as *Semper Fidelis* alone.

Cotehele House

Edgcumbe, Earls of Mount Edgcumbe

Arms: Gules on a Bend Ermines cotised Or three Boars' Heads couped Argent. Crest: On a Wreath Or and Gules A Boar passant Argent a Chaplet about the neck of laurel and oak proper. Badge: A Boar's Head couped and erect Argent armed Or issuing from a Laurel Wreath Vert. Supporters: On either side a Greyhound Argent gutty de poix collared dovetail Gules. Motto: *Au Plaisir Fort de Dieu* [At the all-powerful disposal of God].

The arms first appear at the beginning of the sixteenth century and were entered at the 1531 Visitation of Devon and Cornwall without a crest. The standard of Sir Piers Edgcumbe (d.1539) seems to show a crest of *On a Wreath Or and Purpure A demi Stag bendy of four Gules and Argent with three antlers Or* but this may be a second badge on a crest wreath. The standard also shows the motto *Au Plesir Fort de Dieu* and the boar's head badge, which appears five times. The crest was granted by Clarenceux in March 1573/4 and the blazon is based on the original text. The supporters were granted in 1742 on Richard Edgcumbe's creation as Baron Edgcumbe.

Coughton Court

Throckmorton, Baronets

Arms: Gules on a Chevron Argent three Bars gemel Sable. Crests: (1) On a Wreath of the Colours (Argent and Gules) A Falcon rising Argent beaked legged jessed and belled Or; (2) On a Wreath of the Colours (Argent and Gules) An Elephant's Head couped Sable eared and tusked Or. Motto: *Virtus Sola Nobilitas* [Virtue is the only nobility].

The family take their name from Throckmorton in Worcestershire, where they were tenants of the Bishops of Worcester in the twelfth century. The distinctive arms first appear in the late fourteenth century and before then a seal of a lion rampant and a wyvern was used. The family rose to prominence through the ability and marriage of Sir John Throckmorton (d.1445). A lawyer, Member of Parliament and retainer of the Beauchamp family, Earls of Warwick, he married in 1409 the daughter and coheir of Guy Spiney or Spyne, also a Member of Parliament and a tenant of the Earl of Warwick in the South Warwickshire Manor of Coughton.

The family used two crests which both appear on sixteenth-century standards possibly as badges on crest wreaths, along with a gold crescent badge derived from the arms of Spiney *Sable a Chevron Argent between three Crescents Or*. A variation of the elephant's head crest with red ears and white tusks appears for Sir Robert Throckmorton (d.1581).

Robert Throckmorton of Coughton (d.1650) was created a baronet in 1642 and the baronetcy became extinct on the death of the 12th Baronet in 1994. The 6th Baronet who succeeded in 1819 had in 1792 taken the name and arms of Courtenay only by Royal Licence. The arms of Courtenay of West Molland in Devonshire which were granted to him were *Or three Torteaux* (Roundels Gules) *with for difference On a Crescent Azure another Or* and the crest is blazoned *Out of a ducal Coronet Or a Plume of seven Ostrich Feathers 4&3 Argent*. It is shown with a similar difference of a crescent on a crescent. He died without issue in 1826 and his brother succeeded as 7th Baronet.

Cragside

Armstrong, subsequently Watson-Armstrong, Barons Armstrong

Arms: Gules in fess a Tilting Spear Or headed Argent between two dexter Arms embowed in armour couped at the shoulder fessewise proper the hand extended also proper. Crest: On a Wreath of the Colours (Or and Gules) A dexter Arm embowed in armour fesswise couped at the shoulder and encircled at the elbow by a wreath of oak the hand grasping a Hammer all proper. Supporters: On either side a Figure habited as a Smith holding with the exterior hand a hammer resting on the shoulder all proper. Motto: *Fortis in Armis* [Strong in arms].

The arms and crest were granted in 1859 to Sir William George Armstrong (1810-1900), subsequently Baron Armstrong, the grandson of a Cumbrian yeoman. He is described in the patent as Engineer to the War Department for Rifle Ordnance. The arms are a variation of earlier canting Armstrong coats: *Gules three dexter Arms couped at the shoulder Argent garnished Or* was entered for an Armstrong family at the 1634 Lincolnshire Visitation, and there is a seventeenth-century entry for an Armstrong in the records of the Lyon Office in Edinburgh of *Azure a Fess Or between two Arms couped at the shoulders Argent*.

Lord Armstrong had no children and in 1889 his great-nephew, William Henry Armstrong Fitzpatrick Watson, obtained a Royal Licence to add the name of Armstrong after that of Watson and to bear the arms quarterly with Armstrong in the first quarter. Earlier in 1889 Lord Armstrong's nephew, John William Watson (1827-1909), had been granted arms of *Argent a Fess raguly between two Crosses botonny in chief and a Martlet in base Gules* with a crest of *On a Wreath of the Colours (Argent and Gules) In front of a dexter Arm embowed in armour the hand in a gauntlet proper grasping a Palm Branch slipped Vert*. These arms are shown in the second and third quarters. Both crests were borne, that of Armstrong in the senior position to the dexter. In 1903 the barony was recreated for the great-nephew, and in 1904 he was granted the same supporters. The first Lord Armstrong of the second creation's interest in heraldry can be seen from his petitioning for and receiving a grant of a badge – *A Balista Or* – in 1932. A balista is an ancient military machine for throwing stones, obsolete many centuries before the 1st Lord Armstrong's development of armaments.

Dunham Massey

Booth, Baronets, Barons Delamer and Earls of Warrington

Arms: Argent three Boars' Heads erased and erect Sable. Crest: On a Wreath of the Colours (Argent and Sable) Upon a Garland of Leaves Vert a Lion passant Argent. Supporters: On either side a Boar Sable armed bristled and eyed Or. Motto: *Quod Ero Spero* [What I shall be, I hope].

Grey, Barons Grey of Groby, Earls of Stamford

Arms: Barry of six Argent and Azure. Crest: On a Wreath of the Colours (Argent and Azure) A Unicorn passant Ermine armed maned tufted and unguled Or in front of a Sun in Splendour Or. Supporters: On either side a Unicorn Ermine armed maned tufted and unguled Or. Motto: *A Ma Puissance* [To my power].

Sir Robert Booth or del Bothe (d.1460), who acquired Dunham Massey *c.*1433 was a younger son of John Booth of Barton upon Irwell, Lancashire. The Booths had been at Barton since the marriage *c.*1292 of John del Bothe and Loretta, granddaughter and heiress of Gilbert de Barton. The arms are those of Barton and are a canting reference to the name (Boarton) and were surrendered to the Booths by a male descendant of a cadet branch by a deed dated 30 September 1403 which translates: 'Know all men that I Thomas de Barton have given and by this my present Charter have confirmed to John son of Thomas del Bothe of Barton his heirs and assigns, my arms to be borne by him and them that is to say Argent three Boars' Heads erased Sable...' Such personal deeds disposing of arms before the increasing regulation of heraldry in the fifteenth century leading up to the incorporation of the College of Arms in 1484 are very rare. Before this, in the fourteenth century the Booths bore arms of *A Chevron engrailed and on a Canton a Mullet* which appears on a seal of 1369, and an earlier seal of 1352 shows *A Chevron between three Boars' Heads erect* which appears to combine the two coats.

At the 1567 Visitation of Cheshire and subsequently, the Booth family of Dunham Massey were shown with a crest of *On a Crest Wreath A Lion statant on a Wreath, Chaplet or Garland of Leaves*. When blazoned as a wreath this has sometimes been mistaken for the crest wreath and omitted. The supporters were granted in May 1661 to George Booth a month after his creation as Baron Delamer. In 1690 his son Henry, who had supported William of Orange at the Glorious Revolution, was rewarded by his creation as Earl of Warrington.

In 1736 Lady Mary Booth, granddaughter of the 1st Earl, married Harry Grey, subsequently 4th Earl of Stamford and 5th Lord Grey of Groby. On the death of Henry Grey, 12th Earl and 1st Duke of Kent in 1741, the Earls of Stamford became the senior male representatives of the great medieval family of Grey and consequently were entitled to bear the ancient arms of *Barry of six Argent and Azure* without any marks of difference. Around 1765 the 4th Earl of Stamford, who had previously borne *Barry of six Argent and Azure in Chief three Roundels Gules over all a Label of three points Ermine*, reverted to the simple arms of Grey. The ermine unicorn borne as a crest, badge and supporters by the Stamford branch of the Grey family is derived by descent from the family of Ferrers (q.v. Baddesley Clinton). There is no record at the College of Arms of a formal grant of the supporters.

Dunster Castle

Luttrell

Arms: Or a Bend between six Martlets Sable. Crest: Issuing from a Crest Coronet Or five Ostrich Feathers Argent. Supporters: On either side a Swan Argent ducally gorged and chained Or. Motto: *Quaesita Marte Tuenda Arte* [Gained by strength, held by skill].

A remarkable series of heraldic seals formerly in the Muniment Room at Dunster records the changes in the arms borne by the family. Sir Andrew Luttrell (d.1265) bore three bars. This must have been soon abandoned as his son Geoffrey used a seal in 1261 with six martlets – but no bend – on it. Geoffrey Luttrell's grandson, also Geoffrey, bore *Azure a Bend between six Martlets Argent* and this was borne by his descendants, the Luttrells of Irnham in Lincolnshire, who commissioned the Luttrell Psalter and became extinct in 1419.

The Luttrells of East Quantoxhead, Somerset, descended from Alexander, a younger son of Sir Andrew, bore the arms in their present form. Lady Elizabeth Luttrell, née Courtenay, who bought Dunster in 1376, had married Alexander's great-grandson and bore the arms *in a Bordure engrailed Sable* as did her son, Sir Hugh Luttrell (d.1428). But on his second seal Sir Hugh dropped the engrailed border as he had become the senior male representative of the family following the deaths of Sir John Luttrell of East Quantoxhead in 1403 and Sir Geoffrey Luttrell of Irnham in 1419.

Sir Hugh was the first of the family to use a panache or bush of ostrich feathers issuing from a coronet and supporters of two collared and chained swans. These he copied from Hugh Courtenay, Earl of Devon, his mother's great-nephew, who in 1421 granted him the Courtenay badge of *A Boar Argent armed Or charged for difference on the shoulder with a double Rose Or*. Whilst apparently rejecting the boar, Sir Hugh seems to have adopted his cousin's crest and swan supporters. The boar is only recorded as the crest in the 1623 Somerset Visitation entry which contains a transcript of the 1421 Deed and it is shown as the crest on an early seventeenth-century pedigree roll at Dunster on the Oak Staircase.

Sir John Luttrell (d.1430), son of Sir Hugh, used an otter (loutre) with the letter 'L' below and the letters 'trell' above as his seal. This is a rebus or pun on the syllables in his surname and not truly heraldic. His son, Sir James Luttrell (d.1461), used a fox as a crest as did some later generations, although on occasions it looks more like an otter. This crest never found its way into the records of the College of Arms and like the boar was abandoned in favour of the panache of feathers which dwindled from a bush of feathers to just five.

The arms of Fownes *Azure two Eagles displayed and in base a Mullet Argent* were entered at the 1620 Visitation of Devonshire. Henry Fownes (1723-1780), who married the Luttrell heiress in 1747, took the additional surname of Luttrell. Surprisingly, although his descendants bore Luttrell in the first quarter of their arms, no Royal Licence was ever obtained to sanction this arrangement of the arms.

Erddig

Meller

Arms: Argent three Ouzells or Black Birds proper a Chief indented Sable. Crest: On a Wreath of the Colours (Argent and Sable) A Pied Bull's Head erased proper accolled with an Eastern Diadem crested and holding in his mouth the upper end of a broken Lance Or pointed proper.

Yorke

Arms: Argent on a Saltire Azure a Bezant. Crest: On a Wreath of the Colours (Argent and Azure) A Lion's Head erased proper collared Gules the collar charged with a Bezant. Motto: *Nec Cupias Nec Metuas* [Neither desire nor fear].

The arms of Meller were granted by Letters Patent of Garter and Clarenceux dated 30th June 1707. The patent is unusual as the arms are granted to John Meller, described as of the Middle Temple, Barrister at Law, and the other descendants of his father, also John Meller, and the crest only to the grantee and his descendants. As John Meller had no children, this enabled the children of his sister Anne, wife of Simon Yorke (1652-1723), to quarter the arms on his death in 1733.

John Meller was succeeded by his nephew, Simon Yorke I (1696-1767), who bore without authority the arms of his first cousin, Sir Philip Yorke, Lord Chief Justice of the King's Bench, granted shortly after his elevation to the peerage as Lord Hardwicke in 1733 (q.v. Wimpole Hall). Families in the eighteenth century were better placed to get away with unauthorised use of arms as the Heralds' Visitation system had ended in 1689.

Felbrigg Hall

Windham

Arms: Azure a Chevron between three Lions' Heads erased Or. Crest: On a Wreath of the Colours (Or and Azure) On a Fetterlock Or within the chain thereof Or and Azure a Lion's Head erased Or. MOTTO: *Au Bon Droit* [With good right].

The Windham family arms appear in late medieval sources and there is no record of a grant. The male line of the family continued at Felbrigg till the death of the Right Hon. William Windham in 1810. After the death of his widow in 1824, his half-nephew, William Lukin, Rear Admiral of the White Squadron, obtained a Royal Licence to bear the name and arms of Windham. As he had no Windham blood, he was granted both the arms and crest differenced by an anchor which is erect and in the centre chief point of the arms where it is gold, and charged in blue on the neck of the lion in the crest.

The Lukin family were originally from Essex and entered their pedigree and arms of *Argent a Lion rampant Gules and over all a Bend gobony Or and Azure* at the Visitations of Essex of 1614 and 1634. John Ketton, who purchased Felbrigg in 1863, was not entitled to arms. His daughter Rachel, through whom the property eventually passed, married Thomas Wyndham Cremer, whose father had assumed the Cremer name and arms in 1786. R. W. Ketton-Cremer (d.1969), who gave Felbrigg to the National Trust, was entitled to these arms, blazoned *Argent three Wolves' Heads erased Sable on a Chief Gules three Cinquefoils Argent*.

GAWTHORPE HALL

KAY-SHUTTLEWORTH, Baronets and Barons Shuttleworth

ARMS, Quarterly: (1&4 Shuttleworth) Argent three Weavers' Shuttles Sable tipped and furnished Or; (2&3 Kay) Argent three Ermine Spots in bend between two Bendlets Sable the whole between two Crescents Azure. CRESTS: (1 Shuttleworth) On a Wreath of the Colours (Argent and Sable) A cubit Arm in armour the hand in a gauntlet proper grasping a Shuttle Sable tipped and furnished Or; (2 Kay) On a Wreath of the Colours (Argent and Sable) On a Crescent Or a Goldfinch proper. SUPPORTERS (1902): (Dexter) A Man habited as a Weaver proper holding in the exterior hand a Shuttle Sable tipped furnished and thread pendent Or; (Sinister) A Sailor habited and holding in the exterior hand a Ship's Lantern proper. MOTTO: *Kynd Kynn Knawne Kepe* [Keep your own kin-kind].

The arms of Shuttleworth are first recorded without the crest at the 1567 Visitation of Lancashire. The sketch shows quills of white yarn emerging from the shuttles, and the arms are differenced by a mullet Sable in the centre of the shield. At the 1664 Visitation the mullet has disappeared and the yarn is more clearly depicted against the white background in gold.

The arms of Kay were granted to James Phillips Kay (1804-1877) 'of Battersea, Co: Surrey, Secretary to the Committee of Privy Council on Education' on 31 January 1842 and the limitations were extended to the other descendants of his late father, Robert, of Bury in Lancashire. On 14 February 1842, a Royal Licence permitted James Phillips Kay and Janet, only daughter and heiress of Robert Shuttleworth of Gawthorpe, to use the additional surname of Shuttleworth after that of Kay on their marriage. They married on 24th February 1842 and the quartered arms with two crests granted to James Phillips Kay-Shuttleworth were differenced by a canton Sable on the Shuttleworth arms and a bezant on the arm in armour in the Shuttleworth crest. As is customary when arms and crests are granted to someone who is not of the blood of the family but whose children are, the quartered arms and crest were to be borne by the children without the marks of distinction.

HANBURY HALL

VERNON, sometime Baronets

ARMS: Or on a Fess Azure three Garbs Or and in centre chief a Cross Crosslet fitchy Gules. CREST: On a Wreath of the Colours (Or and Azure) A demi Woman proper habited Or and Purpure crined Or wreathed about the temples with wheat and holding in her arms a Garb Or. MOTTO: *Vernon Semper Viret* [Vernon always flourishes]; *Ver Non Semper Viret* [The spring (season) does not always flourish].

The arms without a crest were recorded at the Visitations of Worcestershire of 1634 and 1683. The baronetcy was created in 1885 and became extinct on the death of the 2nd Baronet in 1940. The arms are a variant of those of Vernon of Haslington, Cheshire, which do not have the cross crosslet fitchy. The crest, for which there is no authority, is also a variation of the Haslington Vernons' in which the demi female figure vested Vert holds a garb under the left arm and a sickle in the right hand. The two families had a thirteenth-century common ancestor, Warin de Vernon of Shipbrook, who is thought to be the brother of William de Vernon, Chief Justice of Chester in 1230, from whom the Vernons of Sudbury descend. Both mottoes are used by the Vernons of Sudbury and Hanbury.

HARDWICK HALL

HARDWICK

ARMS: Argent a Saltire engrailed Azure on a Chief also Azure three Roses

Argent barbed and seeded proper. CREST: On a Wreath of the Colours (Argent and Azure) On a Mount Vert a Stag passant proper gorged with a plain collar Azure charged with Roses Argent.

CAVENDISH, Dukes of Devonshire

ARMS: Sable three Stags' Heads Argent attired Or. CREST: On a Wreath of the Colours (Argent and Sable) A Serpent nowed Vert. SUPPORTERS: On either side a Stag proper wreathed round the neck with a Chaplet of Roses alternately Argent and Azure. MOTTO: *Cavendo Tutus* [Safe by being cautious].

The Visitation records of Bess's arms show the three charges on the chief as roses, but in the architectural detail at Hardwick they are shown as cinquefoils. There is no authority in the records of the College of Arms for the use by Bess of Hardwick of the supporters subsequently borne by the Dukes of Devonshire which are derived from the crest of Hardwick. The arms of Hardwick do not appear on medieval rolls of arms and first occur in the College of Arms in early sixteenth-century records. The arms of Cavendish are also absent from medieval rolls of arms, although they appear on the late fifteenth-century tabarded figure of Robert Cavendish, serjeant at law, (d.1439) in stained glass at Long Melford Church, Suffolk. The Dukes of Devonshire descend from the serjeant's brother. William Cavendish, 1st Earl of Devonshire (1551-1626) inherited Hardwick from his mother, while his elder brother Henry inherited Chatsworth. Till Henry's death in 1616 without legitimate issue, it was appropriate for William Cavendish as a second son to difference his arms with a crescent, which explains why the arms sometimes occur in this form at Hardwick. In addition, as their father, Sir William Cavendish, was also a second son, a crescent was appropriate for all his descendants as long as the senior branch of the family survived.

HUGHENDEN MANOR

DISRAELI, Earl of Beaconsfield

ARMS: Per saltire Gules and Argent a Tower triple towered in chief proper two Lions rampant in fess Sable and an Eagle displayed in base Or. CREST: On a Wreath of the Colours (Argent and Gules) A Tower triple towered issuant from a Wreath of Oak all proper. SUPPORTERS: (Dexter) An Eagle Or (sinister) A Lion also Or each gorged with a Collar Gules and pendant therefrom an Escutcheon Gules charged with a Tower triple towered Argent. MOTTO: *Forti Nihil Difficile* [Nothing is difficult to the brave].

The arms and crest were granted to Benjamin Disraeli, Earl of Beaconsfield, and the other descendants of his father on 16 October 1876 and the supporters on the following day. To be eligible for supporters one must already be entitled to arms, and it was customary for these to be granted separately. The arms are based on those used without authority by the family. In 1868 Disraeli's wife had been created Viscountess Beaconsfield in her own right and she was granted arms in 1869 of *Argent a Slip of Vine fructed and leaved proper between two Flaunches Sable each charged with a Boar's Head erased Argent*. In 1869 she was granted the supporters that were subsequently granted to her husband, although in the blazon the towers on the red shields hanging from the animals' necks are not described as triple towered. She died in 1872, four years before her husband was elevated to the peerage.

ICKWORTH

HERVEY, Marquesses of Bristol

ARMS: Gules on a Bend Argent three Trefoils slipped Vert. CREST: On a Wreath of the Colours (Argent and Gules) An Ounce passant Sable spotted ducally collared and chain reflexed over the back Or holding in the dexter paw a Trefoil slipped Vert. SUPPORTERS: On either side an Ounce Sable bezanty each ducally collared and chain reflexed over the back Or. MOTTO: *Je N'Oublieray Jamais* [I shall never forget].

The arms first appear in the early fifteenth century. In the Visitation records the arms are often quartered with those of Nyernute *Sable a Lion rampant Argent in a Border gobony Argent and Sable*, derived from the fifteenth-century marriage of John Hervey of Thurleigh, Bedfordshire (d. *c.*1445) to Joan, daughter and coheir of Sir John Nyernute. Sir George Hervey of Thurleigh (d.1522) bore the crest as a badge and also badges of *A Garb of Trefoils Vert bound with a Torse Argent and Sable* and *An Ounce's Head affronty erased at the neck Azure ducally gorged with a line reflexed behind the neck and ending in a ring Or*. Sir George Hervey was succeeded by his illegitimate son, Gerard Smart or Hervey, and the latter's son, John Hervey of Thurleigh, had his arms confirmed in 1566 with a crest based on the third badge of *On a Wreath An Ounce's head affronty couped at the neck Azure plain collar studded with a chain reflexed around the neck and ending in a ring Or*. The legitimate line of the family descend from Sir George Hervey's uncle, Thomas Hervey (died *c.*1470) who married Jane, daughter and eventual heir of Henry Drury of Ickworth. The supporters were granted on 2 February 1703/4 to the 1st Earl of Bristol when he was created Lord Hervey of Ickworth.

Ightham Mote

Selby

Arms: Barry of eight Or and Sable. Crest: On a Wreath of the Colours (Or and Sable) A Saracen's Head couped at the shoulders proper vested Gules wreathed around the temples with a Torse Or and Sable the ends tied on the sinister side in a bow. Motto: *Fort et Loyal* [Bold and loyal].

The arms and crest appear on a funeral certificate at the College of Arms for Sir William Selby of The Moate (d.1637/8). He married Dorothy Bonham and is described as nephew and heir of Sir William Selby also of The Moate, and his father, Sir John Selby, was of Berwick in Northumberland. The arms first appear on fourteenth-century rolls of arms and the number of horizontal divisions of the shield varies, often being more than eight. In 1783 John Browne, who had inherited the property, took the name of Selby by Act of Parliament but did not establish a right to the arms. His son, Thomas Selby (1752-1820), disinherited his own son and left the property to a distant relation, Prideaux John Selby (1789-1867) of Twizell House, Northumberland, whose connection was through a sixteenth-century common ancestor. The executors of his grandson, Charles Selby Bigge (d.1889), sold Ightham Mote in 1889.

Kedleston Hall

Curzon, Barons Scarsdale, sometime Marquess Curzon and subsequently Viscounts Scarsdale

Arms: Argent on a Bend Sable three Popinjays Or plain collared beaked and legged Gules. Crest: On a Wreath of the Colours (Argent and Sable) A Popinjay rising wings expanded and inverted Or plain collared beaked and legged Gules. Badge: A Cockatrice wings elevated the tail nowed and terminating in a dragon's head Gules feet and wattles Azure. Supporters: (Dexter) The Figure of Prudence represented by a Woman habited Argent mantled Azure holding in her sinister hand a Javelin entwined with a Remora proper; (Sinister) The Figure of Liberality represented by a like Woman habited Argent mantled Purpure holding a Cornucopia proper. Motto: *Let Curzon holde what Curzon helde*; *Recte et Suaviter* [Rightly and agreeably].

The arms are medieval. The badge was originally associated with the senior branch of the family seated at Croxall in Staffordshire, which failed in the male line in the seventeenth century, and the heiress married Edward (Sackville), 4th Earl of Dorset. A cockatrice with a dragon's head at the end of its tail is now usually referred to in heraldry as a basilisk or Amphisian cockatrice. Lord Scarsdale's supporters were granted when the Barony of Scarsdale was created in 1761. The Latin motto was shown on the patent of supporters in 1761. The English motto is on the 1794 grant of supporters when Lord Scarsdale's brother was created a viscount, and appears on a circlet surrounding Lord Curzon's (d.1925) quartered arms on the metal screen of his Memorial Chapel in the church. In 1513 John Curzon of Croxall bore the motto *Bone Eure Me Comforte* and arms of *Azure on a Bend between two Lions rampant Argent three Popinjays Vert collared beaked and legged Gules*. This and other variations of the arms borne by branches of the family can be seen on the extensive nineteenth-century pedigree hanging in the Family Corridor at Kedleston.

Knightshayes Court

Heathcoat-Amory, Baronets

Arms, Quarterly: (1&4 Amory) Argent two Bars Gules on a Bend engrailed with plain Cottises Sable two Annulets Argent; (2&3 Heathcoat) Vert three Piles one reversed in base between the others issuant from the chief Or each charged with a Pomme thereon a Cross Or. Crests: (1 Amory) On a Wreath of the Colours (Argent and Gules) The Battlements of a Tower Or therefrom issuant a Talbot's Head Azure charged with two Annulets fessewise and interlaced Or; (2 Heathcoat) On a Wreath of the Colours (Or and Vert) Upon a Mount Vert between two Roses springing from the same Gules stalked and leaved proper a Pomme charged with a Cross Or. Motto: *Amore Non Vi* [By love not force].

The arms for Amory were granted in 1874 following a Royal Licence by which John Heathcoat Heathcoat-Amory (1829-1914) was authorised to take the additional surname of Heathcoat and bear the arms of that family quarterly with those of Amory. He was created a baronet later in the same year. His grandfather, John Heathcoat (1783-1861), had been granted the Heathcoat arms and crest in 1824. The distinct charge of a pomme, or green roundel, charged with a gold cross, is derived from the arms granted in 1708 to the unrelated Sir Gilbert Heathcote and his brothers.

The 'ancient' arms of Amory *Barry nebuly Argent and Gules over all a Bend engrailed Sable* are an unofficial variation achieved by engrailing the bend of *Barry nebuly Argent and Gules over all a Bend Sable* recorded in 1620 at the Visitation of Devonshire for John Amory of the parish of Bishop's Nympton. The origin of the coat can be seen in two adjacent shields on the Great Parliamentary Roll of *c.*1312. Sir Richard d'Amory bore *Barry wavy Argent and Gules* and his younger brother, Sir Roger d'Amory, bore *Barry wavy Argent and Gules and over all a Bend Sable.* Both brothers were summoned to Parliament as barons in the reign of Edward II.

KNOLE

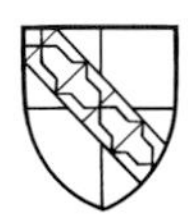

SACKVILLE, sometime Dukes of Dorset

ARMS: Quarterly Or and Gules a Bend Vair. CREST: Out of a Coronet composed of Fleurs de lys Or an Estoile Argent. BADGE: A Leopard Argent spotted Sable. SUPPORTERS: On either side a Leopard Argent spotted Sable. MOTTO: *Aut Nunquam Tentes aut Perfice* [Either never attempt, or accomplish].

The arms first occur in the thirteenth century and appear in medieval rolls of arms both as *Quarterly Gules and Or a Bend Vair* and as *Quarterly Or and Gules a Bend Vair.* Since the sixteenth century the latter has been the usual coat. In many early sources the crest is shown as *On a Wreath Or and Gules A Ram's Head erased Sable armed Or.* Thomas Sackville was created Lord Buckhurst in 1567 and 1st Earl of Dorset in 1604. The supporters presumably date from 1567 although there is no surviving record of a grant in the College of Arms. The supporters also occur as a badge. Other mottoes used were *Tout Jours Loyal* [Always loyal] and *Per Angusta ad Augusta* [Through difficulties to honours].

The 7th Earl of Dorset was created Duke of Dorset in 1720, and both titles became extinct on the death of the 5th Duke in 1843. The representation of the family continued through the 4th Duke's sister, Countess De La Warr, and in 1843 she and her husband, George John (West), 5th Earl De La Warr, obtained a Royal Licence to bear the additional name and arms of Sackville quarterly with those of West. In 1864 she was created Baroness Buckhurst with a remainder to her second surviving and younger sons with a proviso that if that younger son inherited the Earldom of De La Warr, the Barony of Buckhurst should then pass to the next son. In 1870 Countess de La Warr died and her second surviving son, Reginald Windsor Sackville-West, succeeded her as Lord Buckhurst. In 1871 he took the name and arms of Sackville alone. In 1873 his elder brother who had succeeded as 6th Earl De La Warr in 1869 died and Lord Buckhurst became 7th Earl De La Warr. The House of Lords, however, ruled in 1876 that the Barony of Buckhurst should not pass to the next brother, as 'a dignity cannot be removed upon the occurrence of a collateral event'. The 1864 grant of the peerage was therefore held to be invalid as far as the shifting remainder was concerned. Knole, however, passed to his next brother, Mortimer Sackville-West, who was created Baron Sackville of Knole in 1876, when he was granted supporters of *On either side a Griffin Azure beaked and eared Or ducally gorged also Or pendent therefrom an Escutcheon that on the dexter charged with the arms of West and that on the sinister with the arms of Sackville.* The arms of West are *Argent a Fess dancetty Sable* and the crest *Out of a ducal Coronet Or A Griffin's Head Azure beaked and eared Or.*

LACOCK ABBEY

SHARINGTON

ARMS: Gules two Crosses paty in pale Or voided Sable between two Flaunches checky Argent and Azure. CREST: On a Wreath Argent and Azure A Scorpion Or its tail erect gobony Or and Argent between two Elephants' Tusks per fess the upper part checky Argent and Azure the lower part Gules charged with a Cross paty Or voided Sable. BADGE: A Scorpion its tail erect Argent.

TALBOT

ARMS: Gules a Lion rampant within a Bordure engrailed Or. CREST: On a Chapeau Gules turned up Ermine A Lion passant Or.

Sir William Sharington, M.P. (*c.*1495-1553), who purchased Lacock in 1540, came from Sharrington in Norfolk. The arms and crest were recorded by his younger brother, Sir Henry Sharington (*c.*1518-1581), also an M.P., at the Visitation of Wiltshire and were probably the subject of a lost Tudor grant. Sir Henry's daughter Olive married in 1574 Sir John Talbot of Salwarp, Worcestershire, the grandson of the second son of the 2nd Earl of Shrewsbury, and in 1856 their senior male descendant succeeded as 18th Earl of Shrewsbury. Lacock passed out of the male line of the Talbot family when John Ivory succeeded his maternal grandfather, Sir John Talbot, M.P., in 1714. Although he assumed the additional name of Talbot, he did not take any formal steps to assume their arms. A Royal Licence to assume the name and arms of Talbot was, however, obtained in 1778 when John Ivory Talbot's sixteen-year-old grandson, William Davenport, succeeded to the property on the death of his uncle, John Talbot. The arms and crest are stated to be differenced by a crescent, but no crescent is shown in the 1778 College of Arms painting.

LANHYDROCK

ROBARTES, sometime Earls of Radnor

ARMS: Azure three Estoiles Or a Chief wavy also Or. CREST: On a Wreath of the Colours (Or and Azure) A Lion rampant Or holding a flaming Sword erect proper pommel and hilt Or. SUPPORTERS: On either side a Goat Argent ducally gorged Azure armed and unguled Or. MOTTO: *Quae Supra* [Things which are above].

Richard Robartes, the builder of Lanhydrock, was knighted in 1616, created a baronet in 1621 and Baron Robartes of Truro in 1625. In 1614 when he was Sheriff of Cornwall he was granted arms by Clarenceux of *Azure on a Chevron Argent three pierced Mullets Sable* with a crest of *On a Wreath* (untinctured in the records but which was presumably of the colours Argent and Azure) *A demi Lion Azure holding in the dexter paw a Mullet Argent pierced Sable*. These arms and crest were apparently altered by Sir William Segar, Garter, when he granted supporters to Lord Robartes. A certificate by Richmond and Lancaster Heralds stating that there was no record of the grant of supporters was produced in 1634 at the request of Lord Lambart (later 1st Earl of Cavan), who had married Lord Robartes' daughter, and the arms with the estoiles appear on a funeral certificate for Lady Robartes who died on 12 April 1626. There is a record of another patent dated 16 December 1630 from Segar in which he certified that *Ermine a Lion rampant Sable* was the coat of the family of Roberts of County Flint from which family Lord Robartes 'claymeth to be descended'. He allowed Lord Robartes these arms differenced *within a Bordure Sable bezanty* 'as having relation to his habitacon & seate of honor in the County of Cornwall' to be borne quarterly with his usual coat of arms.

The 2nd Lord Robartes was created Earl of Radnor in 1679. The title became extinct in 1757 on the death of the 4th Earl. On inheriting Lanhydrock in 1822 Thomas James Agar, a grandson of the 1st Viscount Clifden and a descendant of the 3rd Earl of Radnor's sister, obtained a Royal Licence to bear the additional surname of Robartes and the arms and crest of the family. In 1869 as Thomas James Agar-Robartes he was created Baron Robartes and granted supporters of *On either side a Goat Argent ducally gorged and charged on the shoulder with an Estoile Azure*. In 1899 the 2nd Lord Robartes of the 1869 creation succeeded as 6th Viscount Clifden and thereafter used the supporters associated with that title. Both titles became extinct on the death of the 8th Viscount Clifden in 1974.

LYME PARK

LEGH, Barons Newton

ARMS: Gules a Cross engrailed Argent with an augmentation of On an Inescutcheon Sable semy of Mullets Argent an Arm embowed in armour Argent the hand grasping a Standard Silver. CREST: Issuant out of a Crest Coronet Or a Ram's Head Argent armed Or in the mouth a sprig of Laurel Vert. SUPPORTERS (1892): On either side a Mastiff proper collared Sable. MOTTO: *En Dieu est Ma Foi* [In God is my faith].

Piers Legh, who with his wife was granted Lyme in 1398, was a supporter of Richard II and beheaded by Henry IV in 1399. He was a son of Robert Legh of Adlington by his second wife Matilda de Norley, and the arms of *Gules a Cross engrailed Argent* were those of the Norley family. The Legh surname was adopted by Robert Legh's father, John de Venables, from his mother Agnes, daughter and heiress of Richard de Legh. The Legh family of Adlington (which came to the family through the marriage of John (de Venables) Legh to Ellen Coroun) kept the arms of Venables *Azure two Bars Argent* differenced with a *Bend over all gobony Or and Gules*, while at the 1566 Visitation of Cheshire, the Leghs of Lyme bore the coat of Coroun or Corona *Azure a Roundel Argent between three Coronets Or all within a Bordure Argent* in the first quarter before *Gules a Cross engrailed* in the second on that occasion in a bordure also engrailed. Although there are instances of the engrailed cross of Legh of Lyme in a border, it is more usually not.

The family's maternal descent and the number of other distinguished families of Legh and Leigh in Cheshire may explain why the Leghs of Lyme adopted the arms of Norley. The ram's head crest was also derived from a maternal ancestor, being based on that of the Baggiley family. Piers Legh's wife Margaret was the only child of Isabel de Baggiley and Sir Thomas Danyers, the hero of Crécy. Although often wrongly stated to have been granted by Richard II, the augmentation to the arms in honour of Sir Thomas Danyers' heroism at Crécy was not granted until 1575. Unfortunately, the patent incorrectly attributes his act to his son-in-law, Piers de Legh, who was then unborn.

The Crécy augmentation was retained in the seven grants in 1806 to the illegitimate children of Thomas Peter Legh (1753-1797) although slightly varied by the substitution of estoiles for mullets. The arms and crest granted to the second illegitimate son, William Legh (d.1834), father of the 1st Lord Newton, were *Gules a Cross engrailed Argent in the chief point on an Inescutcheon Sable semy of Estoiles an Arm in armour embowed Argent the hand proper holding a Pennon Silver all within a Bordure wavy Or* with a crest *Out of a Crest Coronet Or a Ram's Head Argent armed Gules in the mouth a Slip of Laurel proper over all a Pallet wavy Azure*. The supporters referred to Lyme mastiffs, a celebrated breed, and tradition has it that Margaret Danyers' son, Piers Legh II, had one of these dogs with him at Agincourt in 1415. This Sir Piers Legh, who was either knighted at Agincourt or soon after, acquired the family's Lancashire estates by his marriage to Joan Haydock. The arms of Haydock *Argent a Cross and in dexter chief a Fleur de lys Sable* recording this inheritance occur in quartered versions of the arms and at one stage in the late fifteenth century appear in the first quarter.

Lyveden New Bield

Tresham

Arms: Per saltire Sable and Argent six Trefoils (2&1 and 1&2) Or. Crest: On a Wreath Or and Sable A Boar's Head erased at the neck Sable ducally gorged Or holding by the stalk in the mouth a Trefoil fessways slipped Vert. Motto: *Fecit mihi magna qui potens est* [He that is mighty hath done to me great things].

The Tresham family rose to prominence in the early fifteenth century and their arms do not appear on medieval rolls of arms. Both Sir William Tresham of Rushton (1400-1450) and his son, Sir Thomas Tresham (1422-1471), were Speakers of the House of Commons; the former, a Yorkist, was killed by Lancastrians, and the latter – a Lancastrian – was beheaded by Edward IV. The family's many quarterings were acquired by the marriage of Sir Thomas Tresham's son John to Isabel, one of ten daughters and coheirs of Sir James Harrington of Brixworth, Northants (d.1497), and of their son, Sir Thomas Tresham (d.1559), to Anne Parr of Horton, a cousin of Henry VIII's last Queen. This Sir Thomas Tresham sat in Mary I's House of Lords as Grand Prior of the Order of St John of Jerusalem. His grandson, also Sir Thomas Tresham (d.1605), the recusant and mystic who built Lyveden New Bield, was the father of Francis Tresham (d.1605) who betrayed the Gunpowder Plot and died in the Tower of London. The Tresham family of Rushton did not record a pedigree at any of the three Visitations of Northamptonshire, although the Tresham family of Newton descended from a younger son of Sir William Tresham (d.1450) recorded arms and a crest in 1564 and 1618. The motto is possibly taken from Luke Chapter I. 49.

Montacute House

Phelips

Arms: Argent a Chevron between three Roses Gules barbed and seeded proper. Crest: On a Wreath of the Colours (Argent and Gules) A Square Fire Basket Or containing Flames proper. Motto: *Pro Aris et Focis* [For our altars and our homes].

The arms are often quartered with O*r on a Chevron Vert three unidentified Birds' Heads erased Argent*, a coat attributed in early sixteenth-century sources in the College of Arms to a family named Crafford, but there is no known marriage to an heiress of that name. The arms without the quartering and the crest were entered for the family at the Visitation of Somerset in 1623 when the surname is spelt Phillips. It occurs as Phillipps on a 1638 funeral certificate for Elizabeth, widow of Sir Edward Phelips (*c*.1560-1614), the builder of Montacute.

The origins of the arms of Phelips are obscure. The coat first appears in a roll of arms of *c*.1510 called Creswick's Book, now in the British Library, which appears to be a copy of an earlier collection of arms made between 1445 and 1450. There is no record of a grant of the arms to an ancestor of Sir Edward Phelips. Both his father, Thomas Phelips, and grandfather, Richard Phelips, were Members of Parliament, the latter first sitting for Poole in Dorset in 1512. The pedigree cannot be traced back beyond his great-grandfather, Thomas Phelips, who died in 1501. The crest sometimes, but not in the records of the College of Arms, occurs as a fire basket on wheels.

Nostell Priory

Winn, Barons St Oswald

Arms: Ermine on a Fess Vert three Eagles displayed Or. Crest: On a Wreath of the Colours (Argent and Vert) A demi Eagle wings displayed Or plain collared Ermine. Supporters: On either side a Dragon reguardant Vert gorged with a Riband Or pendant therefrom an Escocheon Gules charged with a Rose Argent. Motto: *Tout Pour Dieu et ma Patrie* [All for God and my Country].

The arms and crest first appear in a patent by Garter dated 10 May 1604 to George Winn, described as servant and draper to Elizabeth I. They are a variation of the arms of Wynn of

Gwydir *Vert three Eagles displayed in fess Or* which were attributed to their ancestor, Owain Gwynedd, Prince of Gwynedd (d.1170). Following the death intestate of Sir Rowland Winn, 6th Bt. in 1805, his nephew John Williamson assumed the name and arms of Winn by a Royal Licence in 1815. He died two years later, and in 1818 his younger brother, Charles Williamson, obtained a further Royal Licence allowing him and his sister Louisa to bear the name and arms of Winn. Charles (Williamson) Winn's son Rowland was created 1st Lord St Oswald in 1885, when the supporters were granted.

Nunnington Hall

Graham, Viscount Preston

Arms, Quarterly: (1&4 Graham) On a Chief Sable three Escallops Or; (2&3 Stuart) Or a Fess checky Argent and Azure in chief a Chevron Gules over all in the centre point a Crescent Gules. Crest: On a Wreath Or and Sable A Demi-Vol Or. Supporters: (Dexter) An Eagle (sinister) A Lion both Ermine armed Gules crowned Or. Motto: *Reason contents me.*

The quartered arms of the Grahams, who claimed descent from a younger son of Malise, 1st Earl of Menteith, were originally differenced with a *border engrailed Azure*. They first occur in the records of the College of Arms in an undated entry for Sir Richard Graham, later 1st Bt., in a certificate from the 7th Earl of Menteith and Islay Herald in Scotland, Thomas Drysdale, (which dates the entry between 1617 and 1627) confirming their common ancestry. The arms are next recorded at the 1665 Visitation of Cumberland for Sir Richard Graham, 3rd Bt.

The border was removed in 1681 with the consent of the 8th Earl of Menteith and by the authority of Lyon King of Arms when the 3rd Baronet was created Viscount Preston and Lord Graham of Esk in the peerage of Scotland. These quarterly arms differenced by a crescent in the centre were confirmed by a patent from Lyon King of Arms which also granted the supporters. A warrant issued by the Deputy Earl Marshal, Lord Ailesbury, in the same year ordered that copies of Lord Menteith's declaration and the Lyon grant should be entered in the records of the College of Arms. The crest is usually blazoned *Two Wings addorsed Or*; the term a Demi-Vol Or is used in Lyon's grant although the depiction is no different.

William Rutson, who purchased Nunnington in 1839, was granted arms in 1850 when High Sheriff of the county. These are blazoned Arms *Per fess indented Or and Sable three Bulls' Heads couped counterchanged the two in chief charged with a Bezant and that in base with a Pellet* and crest *On a Wreath of the Colours (Or and Sable) A Griffin's Head couped per Bend Sable and Or and entwined by a Serpent proper*. The motto shown on the patent is *Spectemur Agendo* [Let us be viewed by our actions].

Osterley Park

Child-Villiers, Earls of Jersey

Arms, Quarterly: (1&4 Villiers) Argent on a Cross Gules five Escallops Or; (2&3 Child) Gules a Chevron engrailed Ermine between three Eagles close Argent each gorged with a ducal Coronet Or. Crests: (1 Villiers) On a Wreath of the Colours (Argent and Gules) A Lion rampant Argent ducally crowned Or; (2 Child) On a Wreath of the Colours (Argent and Gules) On a Rock proper an Eagle rising Argent gorged with a ducal Coronet Or and holding in the beak an Adder proper. Supporters: On either side a Lion rampant Argent ducally crowned Or plain gorged Gules the collar charged with three Escallops Or. Motto: *Fidei Coticula Crux* [The cross is the touchstone of faith].

The arms of Villiers appear in medieval rolls of arms. The supporters were granted in 1691 to the 1st Earl of Jersey on his creation as Viscount Villiers. The arms and crest of Child were granted without a motto to Sir Francis Child (1642–1713) on 28 January 1700/1. In 1819 the 5th Earl of Jersey, who had married in 1804 Lady Sarah Sophia Fane, the heiress of Osterley, obtained a Royal Licence to assume the additional name of Child and bear the arms of Child quarterly with those of Villiers with both crests. As he had no Child blood, the grant to him of the quartering for Child differenced the arms by the addition of an escallop in centre chief and the Child crest was differenced with an Ermine spot on the breast of the eagle. The issue of his marriage were to bear the quartering and crest without the difference but surprisingly it still appears in Debrett's *Peerage*.

Oxburgh Hall

Paston-Bedingfeld, Baronets

Arms, Quarterly: (1&4 Bedingfeld) Ermine an Eagle displayed Gules; (2&3 Paston) Argent six Fleurs de Lys 3,2&1 Azure a Chief indented Or. Crests: (1 Bedingfeld) On a Wreath of the Colours (Argent and Gules) An Eagle displayed Or; (2 Paston) On a Wreath of the Colours (Or and Azure) A Griffin sejant wings elevated Or gorged with a Collar Gules therefrom a line held in the beak and terminating in a ring also Gules.

Badge: A Fetter the thong Gules edged and studded and with buckles at both ends chained together Or. Motto: (Bedingfeld) *Despico Terrena Solem Contemplor* [I despise earthly things and contemplate the sun]; (Paston) *De Mieulx je pense en mieulx* (From better I think to better).

The arms first appear in rolls of arms of the fifteenth century and in these and early sixteenth-century sources the eagle is shown with distinctive gold legs and beak as it also appears on an armorial pedigree of 1710. Betham's *Baronetage* of 1802 suggests that Sir Adam de Bedingfeld, Steward of the Honour of Eye in 1269 sealed with these arms. If so, the arms may derive from those of their early medieval feudal overlords, the Norman family of de Limesi, who held the Manor of Bedingfield in Suffolk and different members of which bore *Gules an Eagle displayed Or*, *Gules three Eagles displayed Or* and *Gules six Eagles displayed Or*. Oxburgh was inherited by Margaret Bedingfeld on the death of her brother, Sir Thomas Tudenham, in 1462 and the Tudenham arms *Paly bendy lozengy Argent and Gules* regularly occur as a quartering.

In 1830 Sir Henry Richard Bedingfeld, 6th Bt. (1800-1862) and his wife, who was a Paston heiress, obtained a Royal Licence to bear the additional name and arms of Paston. Quartered arms were exemplified with two crests in Letters Patent of the same year. The Bedingfeld red eagle is shown without a gold beak and legs so that, despite the historical evidence supporting their inclusion, the 1830 grant is authority for their omission. No motto appears on the 1830 patent although since 1830 the Paston motto has been used.

The badge was only formally granted to the 9th Baronet in 1987, but first appears on the tomb of Sir Henry Bedingfeld (d.1583) at Oxburgh. He was Governor of the Tower of London, and it is thought to relate to his having been the gaoler of Princess Elizabeth, later Elizabeth I. Mary I is said to have found in Bedingfeld a man with the qualities necessary to be her sister's gaoler – honesty, loyalty, obedience and perhaps a certain lack of initiative. Interestingly, Sir Henry's father had been Catherine of Aragon's custodian at Kimbolton Castle.

Petworth

Percy, Earls of Northumberland

Arms, Quarterly: (1&4) (i&iv Percy often wrongly called Louvain) Or a Lion rampant Azure; (ii&iii Lucy) Gules three Lucies haurient 2&1 Argent; (2&3 old Percy) Azure five Fusils conjoined in fess Or. Crest: On a Chapeau Gules turned up Ermine A Lion statant the tail extended Azure. Badge: A Crescent Argent. Supporters: (Dexter) A Lion rampant Azure; (Sinister) A Lion rampant guardant Or ducally crowned Argent gorged with a Collar gobony Argent and Azure. Motto: *Esperaunce en Dieu* [Hope in God].

Seymour, Dukes of Somerset

Arms, Quarterly: (1&4 Augmentation) Or on a Pile Gules between six Fleurs de lys Azure three Lions passant guardant Or; (2&3 Seymour) Gules a pair of Wings inverted conjoined in lure Or. Crest: Issuing from a Crest Coronet Or a Phoenix in flames proper. Supporters: (Dexter) A Unicorn Argent armed maned tufted and unguled Or gorged with a ducal Coronet per pale Or and Azure a Line attached thereto gobony Or and Azure; (Sinister) A Bull Azure armed unguled and ducally gorged Or a Line Or attached to the collar. Motto: *Foy pour Devoir* [Faith for duty].

Wyndham, Earls of Egremont, Barons Leconfield and Egremont

Arms (from 1856): Azure a Chevron between three Lions' Heads erased within a Bordure wavy Or. Crest: On a Wreath of the Colours (Or and Azure) A Lion's Head erased Or within a Fetterlock the lock Gold and the bow countercompony Or and Azure the head charged with a Saltire wavy Gules. Supporters: (Dexter) A Lion Azure winged invertedly and plain collared Or; (Sinister) A Griffin Argent gutty de sang plain collared Gules. Motto: *Au Bon Droit* [With good right].

Petworth was given in 1150 by Henry I's widow Adeliza to her half-brother, Josceline de Louvain, who married Agnes, daughter and coheir of William de Percy. Their children bore their mother's name of Percy and arms of *Azure five Fusils conjoined in fess Or*. The fusils are sometimes called mill-picks and may be a pun on piercing. The arms of *Or a Lion rampant Azure* seem to have been adopted by Henry, Lord Percy (*c*.1273-1314) on his marriage to Eleanor, daughter of John FitzAlan, Earl of Arundel whose arms were *Gules a Lion rampant Or*. Henry Percy, 1st Earl of Northumberland (1342-1408) married Maud (d.1398), daughter and ultimate heir of Thomas, 2nd Lord Lucy in about 1381. Maud was responsible for what was in effect an early name and arms clause, as by a final concord levied in 1384, the castle and honour of Cockermouth were settled on her husband's children by his first wife provided they bore the lion coat of Percy quarterly with the arms of Lucy on all banners, pennons, coat-armour, and other representations of arms whenever they displayed arms, 'whether in deeds of war or elsewhere'. If they ceased doing so the property should 'remain' to the right heirs of Maud. Consequently when on 6 May 1531 Henry Algernon, 5th Earl of Northumberland (*c*.1502-1537) displayed his Garter banner in St George's Chapel, Windsor without the quartered arms,

Maud's heir, Sir John Melton, brought proceedings to enforce the final concord of 1384. Lord Northumberland obtained an Act of Parliament in 1536 to defeat the Melton claim whereby the King was granted a remainder. Cockermouth passed to the Crown on his death in 1537 and was only returned to the 6th Earl in 1557.

In compliance with Maud's wishes, the lion coat of Percy (often wrongly called Louvain) and Lucy are usually borne in a Grand Quarter (i.e. quartered together in one quarter) and the earlier arms of Percy *Azure five Fusils conjoined in fess Or* normally appear in the second quarter.

In 1750 Sir Hugh Smithson (1714-1786), who had succeeded his father-in-law as 2nd Earl of Northumberland of the third creation, assumed the name and arms of Percy by Act of Parliament. His sinister supporter is shown crowned with a gold ducal coronet. The old Earls of Northumberland usually bore this supporter with a silver coronet.

The Seymour augmentation with elements from the royal arms was granted by Henry VIII on his marriage to Jane Seymour in 1536. It was borne by her brother Edward (d.1552), who became Duke of Somerset, and his descendants. The arms of Seymour of *two wings conjoined in lure* appear on a seal of William Seymour in 1372. The supporters are sometimes shown with gold chains rather than lines attached to the coronets. The phoenix crest which is shown multi-coloured in College of Arms records may allude to Jane Seymour's death in giving birth to Edward VI. Other crests such as *two wings conjoined as in the arms* and a *bird's head and wings* also occur.

Charles Seymour, 6th Duke of Somerset (1662-1748), who married the Percy heiress in 1682, bore an unusual form of her arms on an escutcheon of pretence consisting of three quarters: (1) the Percy lion coat commonly called Louvain; (2) Lucy; and (3) across the whole bottom half of the shield the Percy fusils coat.

Sir Charles Wyndham, 4th Bt. (d.1763) inherited Petworth on the death of his uncle, the 7th Duke of Somerset, in 1750 and also succeeded him as 2nd Earl of Egremont. He bore the same arms and crest as the Windham family of Felbrigg with whom he shared descent from Sir John Wyndham (d.1645), grandfather of the 1st Baronet. In 1750 he was granted supporters of dexter *A Lion rampant Azure winged invertedly Or*; sinister *A Griffin Argent gutty de sang*.

In 1837 the 3rd Earl of Egremont died leaving three sons born before his marriage to their mother. In 1856 they obtained a Royal Licence to bear the arms and crest of Wyndham suitably differenced for illegitimacy. The eldest son, George Wyndham of Petworth who was created Lord Leconfield in 1859, was granted the arms in a gold wavy bordure; the second son, Henry Wyndham of Cockermouth Castle, in a white wavy bordure; and the third son, Charles Wyndham of Rogate, in an ermine wavy bordure. They were similarly granted variations of the crest. The blazon of the crest granted to the eldest son is *On a Wreath of the Colours (Or and Azure) A Lion's Head erased Or within a Fetterlock the Lock Gold and the bow countercompony Or and Azure the head charged with a Saltire wavy Gules*. Henry Wyndham's crest was varied with a black wavy saltire on the lion's head and Charles Wyndham's with a blue wavy saltire on the lion's head. When supporters were granted to the eldest son on his creation as Lord Leconfield the 1750 supporters were differenced by the addition of collars.

Plas Newydd

Paget, Marquesses of Anglesey

Arms: Sable on a Cross engrailed between four Eagles displayed Argent five Lions passant Sable. Crest: On a Wreath of the Colours (Argent and Sable) A demi heraldic Tyger rampant Sable ducally gorged tufted and maned Argent. Supporters: On either side an heraldic Tyger Sable ducally gorged tufted and maned Argent. Motto: *Per il suo contrario* [By its opposite].

William Paget, subsequently Sir William Paget and 1st Lord Paget (*c*.1506-1563) was granted arms of *Azure a Cross engrailed Or between four close Eagles Argent* with the crest *On a Wreath Argent and Gules A demi heraldic Tyger per pale Or and Sable charged with four Gouttes counterchanged armed and langued Gules supporting in his paws a Branch of Peach Tree leaved Vert fructed proper* in June 1541 by Clarenceux. He was then Clerk to the Privy Council.

In 1552 he was degraded from the Order of the Garter chiefly – according to the King – because he was no gentleman of blood 'neither of father's side, nor mother's side'. He is also said to have been deprived of his arms and crest. In the following year the arms and crest subsequently associated with the family were granted to him by Letters Patent from the King, Edward VI. The Royal Patent confirms arms previously granted without authority by an unnamed King of Arms. This is not the grant of 1541 but one of arms and a crest as on the Royal Patent which occurs in a list of grants made by Sir Christopher Barker, Garter. As Barker died in 1550 it must predate Paget's degradation from the Order of the Garter, to which he was restored by Mary I in 1553.

In 1769 Henry Bayly (1744-1812) succeeded as 10th Lord

Paget and assumed the name and arms of Paget by Royal Licence in 1770. His mother, Caroline Paget, who had married Sir Nicholas Bayly, 2nd Bt. of Plas Newydd in 1737, was a great-niece of the 7th Lord Paget and as the barony was created by Writ of Summons it could pass through the female line. The supporters, which had passed to Henry Bayly with the peerage, are shown on the patent exemplifying the arms but did not need to be granted. The 10th Lord Paget was created Earl of Uxbridge in 1784 and his son Henry William, 2nd Earl of Uxbridge (d.1854) who lost his leg at Waterloo, was created Marquess of Anglesey in 1815. Although printed sources sometimes describe the lions on the shield as *passant guardant*, both the Royal Patent of 1553 and the exemplification of 1770 show them just as *passant*.

The arms of Bayly were entered in the Ulster Office in 1730. A quartered coat was shown for the 1st Baronet, Sir Edward Bayly (d.1741), with in (1&4) Bayly *Gules a Chevron Vair between three Martlets Or* (2) Bagenal (for the 1st Baronet's grandmother) *Barry of four Ermine and Or a Lion rampant Azure* (3) Hall (for his mother) *Argent crusilly Azure three Talbots' Heads erased Sable langued Gules*. On the fourth quarter is an escutcheon of pretence showing the arms of his wife, Dorothy Lambert, *Gules three Cinquefoils Argent*. The crest is shown as *On a Wreath Argent and Gules An Antelope sejant Vert gorged with a ducal Crown and chained and armed Or*. However, the Bayly family of Plas Newydd seem to have either disregarded or forgotten this entry in the Ulster Office as they bore arms of *Azure nine Estoiles (3,3,2&1) Argent* which are the arms of Scottish families of Baillie and their use of them must be associated with the tradition that their ancestor, Lewis Bayly (d.1631), Bishop of Bangor, came from Scotland with James I.

Powis Castle

Herbert, sometime Marquesses and now Earls of Powis

Arms: Per pale Azure and Gules three Lions rampant Argent. Crest: On a Wreath of the Colours (Argent and Azure) A Wyvern with wings elevated and addorsed Vert gorged with a ducal Coronet Or and holding in its mouth a dexter Human Hand couped at the wrist Gules. Supporters (borne by Earls and Marquesses of Powis of the 1st creation): (Dexter) A Panther guardant Argent spotted with various colours with Fire issuing out of its mouth and ears proper and gorged with a ducal Coronet Azure; (Sinister) A Lion guardant Argent gorged with a ducal Coronet Gules. Motto: *Ung Je Serviray* [One will I serve].

The Herbert family are of Welsh descent and the first ancestor to bear these arms was Sir William ap Thomas of Raglan who died in 1446. He, however, bore a crest of *a moorish woman's head and shoulders with a wreath about her forehead*, which is carved on his monument in St Mary's Church, Abergavenny.

Sir William ap Thomas's son was the ardent Yorkist Sir William Herbert KG, created Earl of Pembroke in 1468, but captured and beheaded by the Lancastrians in 1469. His illegitimate son, Richard Herbert of Ewyas (d.1510), whose tomb – also in St Mary's Church – shows the Herbert arms differenced by a bendlet sinister, denoting illegitimacy, and a crescent for further difference, was the father of William Herbert, created Earl of Pembroke in 1551, from whose second son, Sir Edward Herbert (d.1594/5), the Earls of Powis descend. William Herbert, 1st Earl of Pembroke had a grant in 1542/3 of the basic Herbert coat differenced by *a Bordure gobony Or and Gules bezanty*. His descendants, however, dropped this border. The earliest noted use of the motto is on a tapestry of *c*.1565 in the Victoria and Albert Museum, London, where it appears above the 1st Earl of Pembroke's quartered arms with supporters and the Garter but no crest. The first records of the wyvern crest are in the late fifteenth century. There is no record in the College of Arms of a grant of supporters to William, son of Sir Edward Herbert (d.1594/5), who was created Baron Powis in 1629 and whose grandson the 3rd Lord Powis was created Earl of Powis in 1674, or to his immediate successors.

Henry Arthur Herbert, 1st Earl of Powis of the second creation (1703-1772) had a legitimate descent from a younger brother of Sir William Herbert KG, created Earl of Pembroke in 1468, so was actually entitled to the arms without the border. He was granted supporters of dexter: *A Lion rampant Argent about the neck a Collar the buckle and pendant Or to which is affixed a plain Shield Gold charged with a Lion's Paw erased in bend Gules*; sinister: *A Panther guardant Argent spotted of various colours with Fire issuing at the mouth and ears proper and a like Collar about the neck to which is affixed a plain Shield Gold charged with a Lion rampant Gules*. The present Earls of Powis are descended in the male line from Robert Clive whose military exploits secured India for the East India Company. There is no record of a grant of supporters in England when he was created Baron Clive of Plassey in the Peerage of Ireland in 1762. There is, however, a painting of his arms with supporters of (dexter) *An Elephant*, (sinister) *A Griffin wings expanded both Argent the latter gorged with a ducal Coronet Gules and charged with five Mullets in saltire Sable* in the records of the former Ulster Office of Arms. His son, Edward Clive, married the sister and heir of the 2nd Earl of Powis who died in 1801 and was himself created Earl of

Powis of the 3rd creation in 1804. In 1807 his son, subsequently the 2nd Earl of Powis of the 3rd and present creation, assumed the name, arms and crest of Herbert by Royal Licence. Neither he nor his father had a new grant of supporters so the Earls of Powis now bear the arms, crest and motto of Herbert and the supporters of Lord Clive, which is one of their subsidiary titles. The motto of Clive was *Audacter et Sincere* [Boldly and sincerely] and their arms and crest which were recorded at the Visitation of Shropshire 1623 are arms: *Argent on a Fess Sable three Mullets Or*; crest: *On a Wreath of the Colours (Argent and Sable) A Griffin statant Argent ducally gorged Gules.*

Rufford Old Hall

Hesketh, subsequently Fermor-Hesketh, Baronets, subsequently Barons Hesketh

Arms: Argent on a Bend Sable three Garbs Or. Crest: On a Wreath of the Colours (Argent and Sable) A Garb Or banded Azure. Badge: A double-headed Eagle displayed Purpure armed Gules enfiled with a Circlet Or charged with four Pearls proper. Supporters: On either side a Griffin Or gorged with a Collar Gules thereon a Fleur de lys Gold and charged on the shoulder with a Rose Gules barbed and seeded proper. Motto: *Hora è Sempre* [Now and always].

The arms are of medieval origin and are said to derive from the arms of Fitton. Sir William Hesketh married Maud Fitton in 1276 and the Rufford property came from her. The coat appears on medieval rolls attributed to both Hesketh and Fitton. The suggestion that the original arms of Hesketh were *Argent a double-headed Eagle proper* seems to be based on a seventeenth-century manuscript in the College of Arms entitled *Grafton's Lancashire*, but a double-headed eagle does not appear attributed to Hesketh in any medieval roll of arms. Sir Robert Hesketh (d.1541), the builder of Rufford Old Hall, was illegitimate and not therefore entitled to his father's arms and quarterings. This may explain why his son, Sir Thomas Hesketh, had a confirmation of arms and alteration of the crest from Norroy in 1561. The altered crest is blazoned *On a Wreath Or and Azure An Eagle with two heads displayed Gules beaked membered and charged on the breast with a Garb Or.* Surprisingly, despite the use of this crest on the outside of the building at Rufford, the original garb crest was recorded at the 1567 Visitation of Lancashire and subsequently.

The 2nd Baronet assumed the name of Juxon in lieu of Hesketh by Royal Licence in 1792 and bore the arms of that family quarterly in the first and fourth quarters with Hesketh in the second and third. In 1867 the 5th Baronet assumed the additional name and arms of Fermor by Royal Licence and the arms of Fermor were borne quarterly in the second and third quarters with Hesketh in the first and fourth. The 8th Baronet was created a peer in 1935 when he was granted the supporters and badge which refers to the so-called original arms of Hesketh and the 1561 crest.

St Michael's Mount

St Aubyn, Baronets and Barons St Levan

Arms: Ermine on a Cross Gules five Bezants. Crest: On a Wreath of the Colours (Argent and Gules) A Rock therefrom a Cornish Chough rising all proper. Motto: *In Se Teres* [Polished and rounded in himself].

The arms appear on a seal attached to a deed of 1412 in the Public Record Office. The coat appears earlier with a plain field but by the fifteenth century seems to have settled in the form blazoned.

The family entered pedigrees at all three Visitations of Cornwall in 1531, 1573 and 1620. In 1573 and 1620 a coat of six quarters was entered the second for Kemyell *Argent three Dolphins naiant in pale Sable* and the fourth for Tremere *Argent three interlaced Reaping Hooks Sable* are the most recognisable. The sixth quarter, *Gules a Fess checky Or and Azure*, records a descent from the Whittington family of Pauntley, Gloucestershire, to which the celebrated Dick Whittington (d.1423) also belonged. The crest was granted by Garter to Thomas St Aubyn in March 1545/6. Originally blazoned *A Sea Pye in his proper couller beked and membred gouls volant of on a rocke in the proper couller*, this sea pie seems to have been considered a Cornish chough, although the *Dictionary of Heraldry* (1890) identifies it as an oyster catcher and the *Glossary of Terms used in Heraldry* (1894) describes 'a maritime bird of a dark brown colour with a white breast'. In the 1545/6 grant it is shown on a wreath Argent and Sable, although as was customary in England in the sixteenth century the mantling was Gules and Argent.

Sir John St Aubyn was created a baronet in 1671. The baronetcy became extinct on the death of the 5th Baronet, Sir John St Aubyn, in 1839 without legitimate issue. In 1829 he was granted a Royal Licence on behalf of nine of his illegitimate children allowing them to continue to use the surname St Aubyn. In his will he directed that his property should be held in trust for twenty-one years before his eldest son James inherited, with the remainder to his son Edward. In 1861 following a Royal Licence James St Aubyn was granted the arms, differenced by a gold wavy border, with the crest *debruised by a Bendlet wavy sinister Or* to signify his illegitimacy. He died without issue in 1862. In the same year, Edward St Aubyn obtained a further Royal Licence to bear the arms and crest suitably differenced by a red wavy border and an ermine wavy bendlet sinister.

In 1866 Edward St Aubyn was created a baronet and in 1887 his son the 2nd Baronet was created Lord St Levan. The supporters of *On either side a Lion Or each gorged with a Chain Sable therefrom pendent an Escocheon that on the dexter per fess Azure and Argent in chief a Naval Crown encircled by two branches of Oak in saltire slipped Or and in base a Ship in frame proper that on the sinister Sable charged with five Bezants in cross* were granted in 1888. The arms and crest now borne by the family are those granted in 1862. Mottoes seldom appear in the Visitation records and the St Aubyn motto is no exception. It appears on eighteenth-century bookplates.

Saltram

Parker, Earls of Morley

Arms: Sable a Stag's Head caboshed between two Flaunches Argent. Crest: On a Wreath of the Colours (Argent and Sable) A Cubit Arm vested Azure cuffed and slashed Argent the Hand proper holding a Stag's Attire Gules. Supporters: (Dexter) A Stag Argent Collar Or suspending a Shield Vert charged with a Horse's Head couped Argent bridled Or; (Sinister) A Greyhound Sable Collar Or suspending a Shield Gules thereon a ducal Coronet Or. Motto: *Fideli Certa Merces* [Reward is certain to the faithful].

According to a note made at the 1620 Visitation of Devonshire the arms and crest were granted in 1547. The arms as granted had pheons on the flaunches and might be blazoned *Sable a Stag's Head cabossed between two Flaunches Sable each charged with two Pheons in pale points downwards Sable.* The grantee is recorded as John Parker of North Molton and the arms appear in this form with the crest in the 1564 Devonshire Visitation entry. A later copy of the Visitation omits the pheons and the arms were allowed at the 1620 Visitation and subsequently without them. The arms do not appear without the pheons in medieval sources so this is not a reversion to a medieval coat. The supporters were granted in 1784 when John Parker of Saltram was created Baron Boringdon. He was the father of the 1st Earl of Morley. The motto appears on the grant of supporters.

Sizergh Castle

Strickland

Arms: Sable three Escallops Argent. Crest: On a Wreath of the Colours (Argent and Sable) A Holly Tree fructed proper. Motto: *Sans Mal* [Without evil].

The arms are of medieval origin and the escallops may refer to the abundance of cockles at nearby Morecambe Bay. The crest originated as a faggot or bundle of sprigs of holly, which grew in profusion in Westmorland and the Furness fells.

The motto has been used since the sixteenth century. In the mid-sixteenth century, the family bore without any apparent authority supporters of dexter *a Stag collared and chained*, and sinister *a Bull charged on the breast with a mullet*. The stag is said to be derived from the Ward family and the bull from that of Neville. Both therefore came from the marriage of Sir Walter Strickland and Katherine Neville in 1515 as her mother was a Ward heiress. It was her son Walter who was responsible with his wife Alice Tempest for their appearance on the carved heraldic chimneypieces at Sizergh. Remarkably, the family avoided recording a pedigree at Visitations of the northern counties in which they held land, despite their undoubted standing and antiquity.

The supporters of dexter: *A Figure habited as a Knight in complete Armour supporting in the dexter hand a Banner of St George all proper representing the bearer of that banner at the Battle of Agincourt*; sinister: *A Figure habited and in Armour proper cloaked Sable charged on the left shoulder with a Maltese Cross Argent at the feet an Anchor also proper representing the Admiral of the Galleys of the Knights Hospitallers at the time they retreated from the Island of Rhodes* were granted in 1916 to Sir Gerald Strickland (later 1st Lord Strickland) as a Knight Grand Cross of the Most Distinguished Order of St Michael and St George. They allude to the Strickland who bore the Banner of St George at Agincourt and to the Bologna family, one of whom was Admiral of the Galleys of the Knights Hospitallers, from whom he was descended through his mother. Lord Strickland's daughter and her husband, Henry Hornyold, assumed the additional name of Strickland by Royal Licence in 1932 and were granted quartered arms and two crests with the arms of Strickland in the first and fourth quarters.

Snowshill Manor

Wade

ARMS, Quarterly: (1 Wade) Azure a Saltire between four Escallops Or; (2 Wade) Or a Chevron between three Falcons' Heads erased Sable; (3 Comyn) Gules three Garbs of Cummin Or; (4 Fleming) Barry of six Argent and Azure in chief three Maunches Gules. CREST: On a Wreath Or and Sable A Rhinoceros Argent.

Charles Paget Wade (1883-1956), who gave Snowshill to the National Trust, used without any authority the quartered arms which were exemplified in a patent by Clarenceux to Sir William Wade (1546-1623) some time after he became Clerk of the Privy Council in 1582. This was not the first grant to William Wade, and the heraldic history of the family begins with a grant to his father, Armagil Wade (d.1568) who was on Hore's voyage to North America in 1536 and subsequently became a Clerk of the Privy Council in 1547, the year he also became M.P. for Chipping Wycombe and was granted arms and a crest by Gilbert Dethick, Norroy. These are blazoned *Or on a Chevron between three Falcons' Heads erased Sable three Garbs of Cummin Argent* with a crest of *On a Wreath of the Colours (Or and Sable) A demi Griffin vairy Argent and Sable beaked and membered Gules and holding between his claws a Garb of Cummin Argent*. In 1574 a simplified version of these arms was confirmed by Dethick as Garter with a quartering and a crest granted of *A Rhinoceros Argent* to Armagil Wade's son William then described as of the Middle Temple. These arms are blazoned (1&4) *Or a Chevron between three Falcons' Heads erased Sable*; (2&3) *Gules three Garbs Or*. There is a statement in the patent that his father was descended from the ancient house of the Wades of Yorkshire. Dethick extracted the garbs from the chevron and turned them into a quartering supposedly for Armagil Wade's mother's family of Comyn. Finally, the later patent after 1582 introduced a new coat for Wade in the first quarter, the simplified version of the 1547 coat was moved into the second quarter and another quartering described as Fleming, the origin of which is not stated, appears in the fourth quarter. Neither of the coats in the first and second quarters occur in medieval rolls of arms so they were not the arms of an ancient Wade family. The position of the rhinoceros is not stated although it is usually shown as passant or statant and is clearly Argent; printed sources often describe it wrongly as Or. Mottoes do not occur on any of the patents.

Charles Paget Wade was not entitled to bear these arms because he was not descended from this family of Wade in an unbroken male line. His grandfather, Solomon Abraham Wade (d.1881), was buried at Bromley, Kent, but there is a monument to his memory at St Peter's, Basseterre in St Kitts and it is in the West Indies that his ancestry disappears. His heraldic dreams echo those of William Wade and the only difference is that Wade successfully persuaded the late sixteenth-century heralds to confirm his.

The arms in the pediment over the front door *Azure a Fess between three Garbs Or* are those used by William Sambach. He did not establish any entitlement to them and they are a variation of the arms of the Cheshire family of Sandbach of Sandbach which are shown in a number of late medieval rolls of arms as *Azure a Fess Gules between three Garbs Or*. This is a very rare example of breaking the rule that a colour may not be placed on a colour as the red fess appears on a blue background.

Speke Hall

Norris

ARMS: Quarterly Argent and Gules in the second and third quarters a Fret Or over all a Fess Azure. CREST: On a Wreath Argent and Azure An Eagle rising Sable beaked and legged Or.

Watt

ARMS: Per pale Or and Azure a Fess nebuly between four Fleurs de lys two in chief and two in base all counterchanged. CREST: On a Wreath of the Colours (Or and Azure) A Greyhound sejant Argent semy de Lys Azure supporting with the dexter paw two Arrows saltireways points downwards proper. MOTTO: *Vigueur de Dessus* [Strength is from above].

The Norris family recorded a pedigree, arms and a crest at the Visitations of Lancashire in 1567 and 1664. No entries were made at the Visitations of 1531 and 1613. In the 1567 entry the coat is shown as *Quarterly Gules and Argent in the first and fourth quarters a Fret Argent over all a Fess Azure*. A fret in the first and fourth quarters appears on the brass to Henry Norris of Speke in Childwall Church. He fought at Flodden and died in 1524. In the 1664 entry the eagle in the crest is shown as proper and rising from a mount Vert.

The arms and crest of Watt were granted to Francis Watt (1813-1870) of Bishop Burton in the East Riding of Yorkshire in 1856, and the other descendants of his deceased father, Richard Watt (d.1855) of Speke Hall. Prior to this the Watt family used the arms granted by Garter in 1616 to the unrelated Hugh Watts of Shankes in Somerset. The arms in the original grant are blazoned *Asure three broad Arrowes, fethered, and headded sylver; and on a cheife gould as many Moores heads couped, theire left eares ringed.* The crest granted in 1856 is based on the 1616 grant to Watts whose crest was *On a Healme and wreathe of his coullors, a greyhound seigeant Silver, collored Asure, houlding a Broad-Arrowe in the right foote.* The 1616 blazon illustrates how the style of blazon has changed since the seventeenth century, as punctuation was then used, and silver and gold appear instead of Argent and Or.

Stourhead

Hoare, Baronets

Arms: Sable within a Bordure engrailed an Eagle displayed with two heads Argent on the breast an Ermine Spot. Crest: On a Wreath of the Colours (Argent and Sable) An Eagle's Head erased Argent charged with an Ermine Spot. Motto: *In Ardua* [On high].

The arms and crest were granted in 1776 to Henry Hoare (1705-1785) of Stourhead, and the other descendants of his grandfather, Sir Richard Hoare (1648-1718), Lord Mayor of London in 1712. The text of the patent states that the armorial ensigns of the family had not been duly recorded at the College of Arms, which implies that arms had been used before the grant and the evidence supports this. A much earlier entry of the arms without the Ermine spot appears on a mounted figure named Hoore on the military roll of *c.*1446.

As the limitations of the grant were extended to the other descendants of his grandfather, it included his nephew and son-in-law, Sir Richard Hoare (d.1787), 1st Baronet. His son was Sir Richard Colt Hoare, 2nd Baronet (d.1838), the distinguished antiquary and local historian of Wiltshire who succeeded his maternal grandfather at Stourhead.

Stowe

Temple, Baronets and Viscount Cobham

Arms (from 1688), Quarterly: (1&4) Or an Eagle displayed Sable; (2&3) Argent two Bars Sable each charged with three Martlets Or. Crest: On a ducal Coronet A Martlet Or. Supporters (1714/15): (Dexter) A Lion per fess embattled Or and Gules; (Sinister) A Horse Argent powdered with Eagles displayed Sable. Motto: *Templa quam dilecta* [How beloved are the temples].

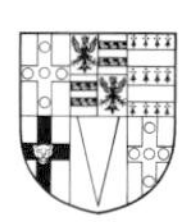

Temple-Nugent-Brydges-Chandos-Grenville, Duke of Buckingham and Chandos

Arms, Quarterly: (1&6 Grenville) Vert on a Cross Argent five Roundels Gules; (2) (i&iv Leofric) Or an Eagle displayed Sable; (ii&iii Temple) Argent two Bars Sable each charged with three Martlets Or; (3 Nugent) Ermine two Bars Gules; (4 Brydges) Argent on a Cross Sable a Leopard's Face Or; (5 Chandos) Or a Pile Gules. Crests: (1 Grenville) On a Wreath of the Colours (Argent and Vert) A Garb Vert; (2 Brydges) On a Wreath of the Colours (Argent and Sable) The Bust of a Man's Head in profile couped below the shoulders proper vested paly Argent and Gules semy of Roundels counterchanged round the temples a Wreath Argent and Azure; (3 Chandos) On a Wreath of the Colours (Or and Gules) A Saracen's Head affronty proper couped at the shoulders wreathed round the temples Argent and Purpure. Supporters: (Dexter) A Lion per fess embattled Or and Gules; (Sinister) A Horse Argent powdered with Eagles displayed Sable.

In February 1569/70 Peter Temple of Burton Dassett, Warwickshire, received a patent from Garter, Clarenceux and Norroy confirming arms of *Argent on a Chevron Sable between three Crescents Gules five Martlets Argent* and granting a crest of *On a Wreath of the Colours (Argent and Sable) A Hound sejant Sable collared Or.* In 1576 a further patent from Clarenceux 'assigned' a simpler coat of *Sable a Chevron Ermine between three Martlets Argent* and granted the same crest as in 1569/70. In 1593 Clarenceux confirmed the 1576 arms and crest to Peter Temple's son, John Temple of Stowe (1542-1603). However, at the Visitation of Buckinghamshire in 1634 John Temple's son, Sir Thomas Temple of Stowe, 1st Bt. (d.1637) was entered with arms without a crest of *Argent two Bars Sable each charged with three Martlets Or.* There is no explanation in the records of the College of Arms for this change.

In 1688, complying with a warrant from the Earl Marshal which refers to the evidence of fifteenth century and undated seals, the arms were exemplified by Clarenceux for Sir Richard Temple, 3rd Bt. (1634-1697) with *Or an Eagle displayed Sable* in the first and fourth quarters. Edmondson's *Baronagium* (1764) attributes this coat to Leofric, Earl of Mercia (d.1057) and shows the 3rd Baronet's purported descent in an unbroken male line from Leofric. Genealogists from the nineteenth century onwards have revealed this as a fiction. The Temples did not rise above the rank of minor gentry before the end of the fifteenth century.

The arms with the martlets on the bars appear on a shield accompanying an inscription at Shepey Magna in Leicestershire which records the death of Nicholas Temple in 1506. In different tinctures, these are the arms of the Leicestershire family of Burdet and if the seals referred to in the Earl Marshal's warrant are disregarded it appears that Nicholas Temple adopted a variation of the arms of a family related to him or his wife. The coat was then forgotten and only revived in the early seventeenth century after three patents of different arms. The senior line of the family were recorded with the 1576 grant at the 1619 Visitation of Leicestershire although they were not descended from Peter Temple of Burton Dassett. This branch of the family lost their property when it was confiscated from the regicide Peter Temple at the Restoration. In contrast, the Stowe line who were entitled to the arms stopped using them.

Following his creation as Baron Cobham, Sir Richard Temple of Stowe, 4th Bt. (1675-1749) was granted supporters in 1714/15. The patent states that they were to be borne by him and the heirs male of his body. In 1718 he became Viscount Cobham with a special remainder to his two sisters: Hester, married to Richard Grenville, and Christian, wife of Sir Thomas Lyttelton, 4th Bt., and their descendants in the male line. Hester (d.1752) succeeded him and was created Countess Temple. Her successor was her son, Richard (Grenville-Temple), 2nd Earl Temple (d.1779) who bore a quartered coat of (1&4) Grenville (2&3) the quartered coat of Temple of 1688. The 2nd Earl Temple was succeeded by his nephew George, 3rd Earl Temple and 1st Marquess of Buckingham (1753-1813). He assumed the additional surnames and arms, but not the crests, of Temple and Nugent by Royal Licence of 1779 exemplified in a patent of 1780 which also shows the supporters of 1714/15.

By a Royal Licence dated 1799 Richard Temple-Nugent-Grenville (d.1839) who, as eldest son of the Marquess of Buckingham, bore the courtesy title of Earl Temple, was permitted to take the additional surnames of Brydges-Chandos and the arms and crests of those families following his marriage in 1796 to Lady Anna Eliza Brydges, heiress of the 3rd and last Duke of Chandos. These were exemplified in a patent dated 1800. In 1822 he was created Duke of Buckingham and Chandos, a title that became extinct on the death of his grandson the 3rd Duke in 1889. The Viscountcy of Cobham passed to the heir male of Christian Lyttelton (née Temple) and the 5th Lord Lyttelton became 9th Viscount Cobham. Although the wording of the 1714/15 patent suggests that the supporters should not have passed with the Viscountcy of Cobham they were entered in the records of the College of Arms in 1780 on both a pedigree and the exemplification of quartered arms for the 3rd Earl Temple. Since 1889 the Viscounts Cobham have borne the supporters granted to Lord Lyttelton in 1794 of *two Mermen holding Tridents*.

Tattershall Castle

Cromwell, Barons Cromwell

Arms: Argent a Chief Gules and over all a Bend Azure. Crest: On a Chapeau Gules turned up Ermine A Panache of Ostrich Feathers Argent. Badge: A Purse Argent tasselled and buttoned Or. Supporters: On either side a Wild Man proper each with a Club over his shoulder. Motto: *Nay Je Droit* [Have I not the right].

The arms first appear in the thirteenth century and are on Segar's Roll of *c.*1285 for Ralph Cromwell (d.1298). The builder of Tattershall, Ralph, 3rd Lord Cromwell, was Lord High Treasurer between 1433 and 1443 and adopted the Lord High Treasurer's purse as a badge. At Tattershall the purse has now been painted *Or tasselled and buttoned Gules*. The Common Gromwell (*Lithospermum officinale*) which appears in various places carved in the decoration at Tattershall is a rebus, and is also seen in the background of the Lord High Treasurer's seal of *c.*1437, as are the supporters. The panache of feathers on the crest resembles a garb on the Lord High Treasurer's seal.

The arms of Vipont put up at Tattershall by the 3rd Lord Cromwell appear in the unusual form of *ten Annulets (4,3,2 &1)*. Ralph Cromwell's brother John, Lord Cromwell, married a Vipont heiress *c.*1300 and bore her arms *Or six Annulets (3,2&1) Gules* with the tinctures reversed. Although Vipont heraldry appears at Tattershall there is no descent from this family.

Tatton

Egerton, Barons Egerton

Arms: Argent a Lion rampant Gules between three Pheons Sable. Crest: On a Wreath of the Colours (Argent and Gules) A Lion rampant supporting an Arrow palewise point downwards Or pheoned and flighted Argent. Supporters: (Dexter) A Griffin Argent gorged with a ducal Coronet Azure and pendent therefrom a Pheon Sable; (Sinister) A Lion Gules gorged with a plain collar Argent and pendent therefrom a Pheon Sable. Motto: *Sic Donec* [Thus until].

Thomas Egerton, 1st Viscount Brackley (1540-1617), illegitimate son of Sir Richard Egerton of Ridley in Cheshire, inherited Tatton in 1598 from Richard Brereton who had married his father's legitimate daughter. The arms of Egerton of Ridley first appear in the early sixteenth century. The crest of that family appears on the standard of Lord Brackley's grandfather, Sir Ralph Egerton, *c.*1530 as *A Lion's Gamb Gules grasping a Sword Argent hilt and pommel Or* and his motto was *Fin Faict Tout* [The end is all]. Thomas Egerton's first grant of arms was from Norroy in 1583 when he was Solicitor-General. He was granted the arms of Egerton quartering those of Bassett of Blore (for his paternal grandmother) *Or three Piles conjoined in base Gules on a Canton Argent a Griffin segreant Sable* and both coats are in an engrailed border Sable as a mark of his illegitimacy. The crest granted to him was based on that of Egerton of Ridley. In May 1596 as Master of the Rolls and Lord Chancellor, he received a further grant from Garter confirming the arms and granting the distinctive crest of a lion rampant and arrow.

Lord Brackley's son, the 1st Earl of Bridgwater, continued the use of the engrailed border, which appears on his funeral certificate of 1649, but it was dropped without any apparent authority by the 2nd Earl some time before 1663 when it does not appear on his wife's funeral certificate. The motto *Sic Donec* appears on a painting of the Lord Chancellor's arms in 1616 and has been used since then.

The first Egerton to live at Tatton was Thomas Egerton (1651-1685), a younger son of the 2nd Earl of Bridgwater. His grandson, Samuel Egerton, died in 1780 without surviving issue when his heir was his sister, Hester Tatton (1708-1780). She took the name of Egerton by Royal Licence but died before the arms of Egerton could be assigned to her and it was not till 1806 that her grandson, Wilbraham Egerton (d.1856), had an exemplification of the arms and crest pursuant to his grandmother's Royal Licence. Wilbraham Egerton's son, William Tatton Egerton (d.1883), was created 1st Baron Egerton in 1859 and in the same year he was granted the supporters. On this grant, the crest is shown for the first time *on a cap of maintenance Gules turned up Ermine* rather than on a crest wreath.

Uppark

Fetherstonhaugh, Baronets

Arms: Gules on a Chevron between three Ostrich Feathers Argent a Roundel Sable. Crest: On a Wreath of the Colours (Argent and Gules) An Antelope statant Argent armed Or.

Sir Matthew Fetherstonhaugh, 1st Bt. (1714-1774), who purchased Uppark in 1747 and his son, Sir Henry Fetherstonhaugh (d.1846), 2nd and last Baronet, never established a legal right to arms. The arms which they used were those of the Fetherston baronets of Blakesware in Hertfordshire recorded without a crest at the Visitation of London of 1635. The crest is that used by the Fetherston baronets of Ardagh in County Longford, although it was not registered in the Ulster Office till 1907.

The head-in-the-sand approach to establishing legal entitlement to their arms is emphasised by the unauthorised use of supporters – appropriately two ostriches. Arms have, however, been registered by the heirs of the 2nd Baronet. In 1848 his widow, née Mary Ann Bullock, was granted arms for Bullock of *Ermine fretty Azure on a Fess engrailed also Azure three Roses Argent barbed and seeded proper*. In 1896 the Hon. Keith Turnour (d.1930), who assumed the additional name of Fetherstonhaugh by Royal Licence, was granted a quartering to be borne in the first and fourth quarters for Fetherstonhaugh of *Per pale Gules and Sable a Chevron between four Ostrich Feathers three in chief and one in base Argent* with a crest for Fetherstonhaugh of *On a Wreath of the Colours (Argent and Gules) An heraldic Antelope's Head couped Gules armed Or gorged with a collar Vair and holding in the mouth an Ostrich Feather in bend Argent*. The same arms as a quartering and crest were granted in 1932 to Admiral the Hon. Sir Herbert Meade-Fetherstonhaugh (d.1964) after he also took the Fetherstonhaugh name by Royal Licence on inheriting the property. The crest is a variation of that of Fetherston of Fetherstonhaugh *On a Wreath of the Colours (Argent and Gules) An heraldic Antelope's Head erased Gules armed Or* recorded at the 1665 Visitation of Cumberland.

The Vyne

Sandys, Baron Sandys

Arms: Argent a Cross raguly Sable. Crest: On a Wreath of the Colours (Argent and Sable) A Goat's Head couped at the neck Argent armed and between two Wings Or. Badge: A Goat Argent tufted armed unguled and winged Or. Supporters: On either side a Goat Argent tufted armed unguled and winged Or. Motto: *Aides Dieu* [Help, O God].

Chute

Arms: Gules three Swords fesswise in pale points to the dexter Argent hilts pommels and quillons Or. Crest: On a Wreath of the Colours (Argent and Gules) A Hand in a Gauntlet proper grasping a broken Sword Argent hilt, pommel and quillons Or. Motto: *Fortune de Guerre* [The fortune of war].

Sir William Sandys, KG (*c.*1470-1540) of The Vyne was created

Lord Sandys in 1523. The arms first appear in mid-fifteenth-century rolls of arms. There is no record in the College of Arms of a grant of the crest, badge or supporters. The 4th Lord Sandys died without issue in 1629. His heir was his half-sister Elizabeth, wife of Sir Edwin Sandys of Latimer, Buckinghamshire. Her grandson, William Sandys (*c.*1626-1668), successfully claimed the barony in 1660 and sat in the House of Lords as 6th Lord Sandys, being succeeded by his younger brothers as 7th and 8th Lords Sandys.

Chaloner Chute, who purchased The Vyne from the 6th Lord Sandys in 1653, appears on a pedigree recorded by his father at the 1634 Visitation of London. The arms were then stated to be *Gules three Swords fesswise in pale Argent in an orle of Mullets Or*. These with a canton are the arms of his great-grandfather's brother, Philip Chute or Chowte (d.1567) of Appledore, Kent, whose arms were supposedly augmented by a *Canton per fess Argent and Vert charged with a Lion passant guardant Or* – a lion of England on the Tudor livery colours – for his valour as standard bearer to the men-at-arms of the King's band at the Siege of Boulogne in 1544. There is, however, no evidence that the arms existed prior to the grant of the canton as the entry for Philip Chute, Captain of the Castle of Camber, in the 1531 Visitation of Kent shows the canton. Either the augmentation was not for valour in 1544 but for some deed in or before 1531; or – more likely – the arms were added to the Visitation record at a later date; or the copy of the Visitation dates from 1544 or later. The final simplification of the family arms came on a pedigree registered by John Chute (d.1776) in 1750 when no mullets are shown. The crest and motto both appear on the 1531 Visitation entry, and in 1750 the arms are quartered with those of Keck *Sable a Bend Ermine cotised flory on the outer edge Or*.

On the death of John Chute in 1776 The Vyne passed to his cousin, Thomas Lobb (1721-1790), who assumed the additional name of Chute. He took no formal steps to assume the arms. Thomas Lobb Chute married Anne Rachel Wiggett, and in 1827 a member of her family, William Lyde Wiggett, succeeded to The Vyne. He took the additional name of Chute by Royal Licence and as William Lyde Wiggett-Chute was granted quarterly arms in 1827 of (1&4) Chute with for difference *A Canton Ermine*; (2&3) Wiggett *Ermine three Mullets 2&1 Azure pierced Gules on a Chief wavy Sable a Dove reguardant proper*. The arms of Wiggett had been granted to his father the Rev. James Wiggett the day before. Two crests are shown (1) for Chute: *On a Wreath of the Colours (Argent and Gules) A dexter cubit Arm in armour the hand in a gauntlet grasping a broken Sword in bend sinister proper pommel and hilt Or and for difference the Arm encircled by a Wreath of Laurel Vert* (2) for Wiggett: *On a Wreath of the Colours (Argent and Azure) A Griffin's Head couped Sable holding in the beak an Ear of Wheat proper between two Wings Argent each charged with a Mullet Gules.*

WALLINGTON

BLACKETT, Baronets

ARMS: Argent on a Chevron between three Mullets Sable three Escallops Argent. CREST: On a Wreath of the Colours (Argent and Sable) A Falcon's Head erased proper. MOTTO: *Nous Travaillerons en Esperance* [We will labour in hope].

BLACKETT formerly CALVERLEY, Baronets

ARMS: Sable an Inescutcheon in an orle of Owls Argent. CRESTS: (1) On a Wreath of the Colours (Argent and Sable) A Horned Owl Argent; (2) Issuing from a Crest Coronet Or a Calf's Head erect Sable.

TREVELYAN, Baronets

ARMS: Gules a demi Horse Argent issuing from Water barry wavy Argent and Azure. CREST: On a Wreath of the Colours (Argent and Gules) Two Arms embowed habited Azure cuffed Argent the hands proper holding a Bezant. MOTTO: *Tyme Tryeth Troth*.

The arms were granted by Norroy to Thomas Blackett of Woodcroft, Co. Durham when he entered a pedigree at the 1575 Visitation of Durham. There is no record of a crest and no crest is shown on the 1615 entry. The arms next appear, again without a crest, in 1674 on the pedigree of Sir William Blackett, 1st Baronet (d.1680). Sir William Blackett's younger son William became the 1st Baronet of Wallington.

Although the family claimed descent from the Blacketts of Woodcroft in the parish of Stanhope, the established pedigree in the College of Arms does not go back beyond William Blackett of Hoppyland in the parish of Hamsterley in Durham, said to have been aged forty in 1628, whose probable father was Edward Blackett of Hamsterley. There is no evidence to justify allowing the arms in 1674 and the crest is also an unofficial assumption. Sir William Blackett, 2nd Baronet, died without legitimate issue in 1728. His illegitimate daughter, Elizabeth Ord, married his nephew, Walter Calverley, who, in compliance with his uncle's will, assumed the surname of Blackett. He had done this by 1730 when the arms of Blackett in a bordure Argent were granted to his wife. This replaced arms of *Azure two Salmon naiant in pale proper in chief a Mullet Argent between two Escallops Or* granted to her in June 1729.

In 1733 Walter (Calverley) Blackett obtained a private Act of Parliament to confirm his assumption of the surname of Blackett. As after his father's death in 1749 he was referred to as Sir Walter Calverley Blackett, it is interesting that the Act states that he 'shall from henceforth and at all times hereafter take upon himself and use immediately following after his said name of baptism the said sirname (sic) of Blackett only ...' The Act makes no mention of arms, and Sir Walter did not obtain a Royal Licence to bear those of Blackett. Consequently, he bore the arms of Calverley although named Blackett.

A remote ancestor of the Calverley family is said to have come from Scotland in 1100 in the train of Matilda, wife of Henry I. Early generations bore the surname Scot and John Scot married the daughter of the Lord of Calverley in Yorkshire. Subsequently they took their surname from their place of residence and although the earliest charters are sealed with a lion rampant, by the mid-fourteenth century an *Inescutcheon in an Orle of Owls* was used. There are sometimes six but usually eight owls. The owl crest also appears on a mid-fourteenth-century seal standing on a chapeau on the helmet. On later seals it is on a crest wreath. In most of the Visitations of Yorkshire, arms alone were entered for Calverley. However, at the last Visitation in 1666 the crest of *Issuing from a crest Coronet Or a Calf's Head erect Sable* was recorded. It is tempting to regard this as an error as it is a slight variation of the crest of an unrelated Cheshire family of Calveley, who took their surname from the parish of Calveley in Cheshire. No motto appears for the family in the College of Arms.

Sir Walter Calverley Blackett was succeeded by his nephew, Sir John Trevelyan, 4th Baronet. The arms of Trevelyan first appear in late fifteenth-century sources. Although the demi horse is sometimes blazoned as with a gold mane and hooves, early sources show it as all Argent. Supporters of two dolphins were used without any official sanction until granted in 1969 as *On either side a Dolphin Azure crowned with a Baron's Coronet proper* to Humphrey, Baron Trevelyan, a great-nephew of Sir Charles Edward Trevelyan (d.1886) of Wallington.

WIMPOLE HALL

HARLEY, Earls of Oxford

ARMS: Or a Bend cotised Sable. CREST: On a Wreath of the Colours (Or and Sable) A Castle triple towered Argent issuing from behind the central tower a demi Lion rampant Gules. SUPPORTERS: On either side an Angel proper the habit and wings displayed Or. MOTTO: *Virtute et Fide* [By Valour and Faith].

YORKE, Earls of Hardwicke

ARMS: Argent on a Saltire Azure a Bezant. CREST: On a Wreath of the Colours (Argent and Azure) A Lion's Head erased proper collared Gules the collar charged with a Bezant. SUPPORTERS: (Dexter) A Lion guardant Or collared Gules the collar charged with a Bezant; (Sinister) A Stag proper attired and unguled Or collared Gules the collar charged with a Bezant. MOTTO: *Nec Cupias Nec Metuas* [Neither desire nor fear].

The arms of Harley are of medieval origin and appear on fourteenth-century seals. The crest was granted to Sir Robert Harley in 1643. The blazon describes a two-dimensional representation of the crest; if it were carved in three dimensions, four towers would probably be shown on the castle. The supporters were granted in 1711 to Sir Robert's grandson, Robert (Harley), 1st Earl of Oxford, Lord High Treasurer of Great Britain.

Lord Hardwicke's supporters were granted by Garter in December 1733. The grantee, Sir Philip Yorke, Lord Chief Justice of the King's Bench, and subsequently Lord Chancellor, had been elevated to the peerage as a baron with the title of Lord Hardwicke in November 1733. The patent also purports, by way of augmentation, to alter his arms with the addition of a bezant and to grant a new crest. The arms *Argent on a Saltire Azure* were those of Sir Richard Yorke (1430–1498), ancestor of the Yorke family of Bewerley and Halton Place in Yorkshire but from whom Lord Hardwicke was not descended.

Gazetteer

Anglesey Abbey

CAMBRIDGESHIRE

Broughton, Baron Fairhaven

ARMS: Argent two Bars and in the dexter chief point a Saltire couped Gules

CREST: On a Wreath of the Colours (Argent and Gules) In front of a Bull's Head erased Sable armed collared and chained Or three Fleurs de lys Gold

BADGE: A Bull's Head erased Sable gorged with a Baron's Coronet and charged on the neck with three Escallops fessewise Or

SUPPORTERS: On either side a winged Bull Sable each armed and gorged with a chain Or pendent therefrom an escocheon charged with the arms of Broughton

MOTTO: *Si Je Puis* [If I can]

The arms, crest and badge were granted in 1923 to Urban Hanlon Broughton by Garter and Clarenceux. The arms and crest were modified by Garter in March 1929 in a patent granting supporters to his son Urban Huttleston Rogers Broughton, Baron Fairhaven, and the crest was altered again in July 1929. Lord Fairhaven's arms with supporters and a baron's coronet are carved in stone over the front porch. Inside the Hall, the arms can be seen framed in a Bavarian seventeenth-century giltwood cartouche supported by plump cherubs, and they appear again complete with coronet and supporters, woven into the border of the tapestry picture of Anglesey Abbey, at the foot of the Spiral Stairs. The Fairhaven arms are inlaid in marble in the tops of a series of side tables made for the house, and embossed in cast iron on the firebacks of the Living Room and Library chimneypieces, while the Broughton bull's head crest is engraved on much of the silver. Also of interest at Anglesey is all the heterogeneous heraldic detail to be found in Lord Fairhaven's collection, such as the banner with the Altieri arms in Claude's *Landing of Aeneas*, painted in 1675 for Prince Altieri.

Antony House

CORNWALL

Carew, Pole-Carew and Carew Pole

ARMS: Or three Lions passant in pale Sable

CREST: On a Wreath of the Colours (Or and Sable) Issuant from the round top of a Mainmast between six Spears Or their heads Argent a demi Lion rampant Sable

MOTTO: *Nil Conscire Sibi* [To have a conscience free from guilt]

The arms of Carew first appear on seals in the fourteenth century and the crest appears in its present form by 1620. Despite its owners' medieval ancestry, the exterior of Antony exudes early Georgian restraint, and armorial display is limited to the Carew arms impaling Coventry for Sir William Carew 5th Bt (d.1744) and his wife, Lady Anne, embossed on the rainwater heads, with the three-dimensional Carew crest sticking up above them. Inside, the hall chairs display the crest in the conventional manner, and the arms of Coventry can be seen in eighteenth-century shellwork in the Library.

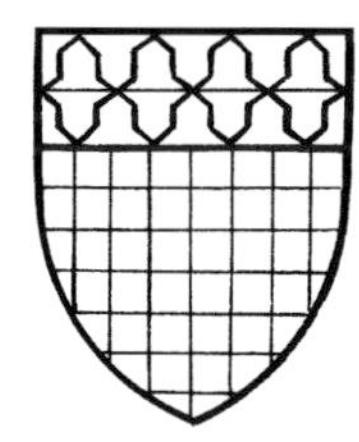

Arlington Court

DEVON

Chichester, sometime Baronets

ARMS: Checky Or and Gules a Chief Vair

CREST: On a Wreath of the Colours (Or and Gules) A Heron rising with an Eel in its beak proper

MOTTO: *Firm en Foi* [Firm in faith]

The family is a cadet branch of Chichester of Raleigh in Devon. The arms first appear attributed to Chichester in the mid-fifteenth century, but there are fourteenth-century references to the coat being that of Raleigh. A nineteenth-century pedigree on display at Arlington suggests that the arms were adopted in 1385 following the marriage of Sir John Chichester and Thomazin, heiress of Sir John Raleigh.

Inside the plain Neo-classical architecture of the house, several rooms redecorated in the late 1830s by John Crace show the nineteenth-century fashion for heraldry. The Staircase Hall windows are richly embellished with coloured shields of arms, tracing the family's descent, marriages and connections through the centuries. In the Boudoir is a late eighteenth-century armorial tea service made for Col. John Chichester (d.1823). The heron crest can be seen on the clock turret of the Stables, and again in the Courtyard, carved in the central niche.

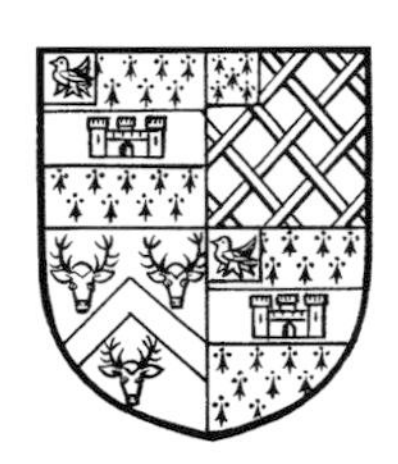

Attingham Park
SHROPSHIRE

Hill, subsequently Noel-Hill, Barons Berwick

ARMS: Quarterly (1&4 Hill) Ermine on a Fess Sable a Castle of three towers Argent on a Canton Gules a Martlet Or
(2 Noel) Or fretty Gules a Canton Ermine
(3 Harwood) Or a Chevron between three Stags' Heads caboshed Gules

CREST: (1 Noel) On a Wreath of the Colours (Or and Gules) A Stag Statant Argent
(2 Hill) On a Wreath of the Colours (Argent and Sable) The upper half of a Tower Argent statant thereon a Fawn Argent plain gorged a Chain attached thereto and reflexed over the back Or
(3 Harwood) On a Wreath of the Colours (Or and Gules) A Stag's head caboshed Sable holding in the mouth a sprig of Oak fructed proper

SUPPORTERS: (Dexter) A winged Horse Argent plain collared Sable and thereon a Martlet Or; (Sinister) A Stag Argent attired Or plain gorged Sable the Collar charged with a Leopard's face Or a Chain attached to the Collar and reflexed over the back Or

MOTTO: *Qui Uti Scit Ei Bona* [Let wealth be his who knows how to use it]

The arms in this form with the three crests date from 1824 when William and Richard Hill, brothers of the 2nd Lord Berwick, obtained a Royal Licence to bear the additional surname of Noel. They are a simplified version of an earlier quartered coat assigned to Noel Hill, the creator of Attingham Park, when he became Lord Berwick in 1784. The architectural use of heraldry at Attingham is restrained: the supporters appear in roundels on the park side of the entrance gate and the Victorian downpipes on the house have a baron's coronet with the date 1861. A magnificent set of Regency silver-gilt ambassadorial plate is engraved with the Berwick arms and the royal arms, and the family's three crests are displayed on the hall chairs. A less stereotyped display can be found on some election jugs.

Barrington Court
SOMERSET

Strode

ARMS: Ermine on a Canton Sable a Crescent Argent

CREST: On a Wreath of the Colours (Argent and Sable) A demi Lion rampant Or

William Strode (d.1666) the Shepton Mallet clothier, presbyterian elder and subsequently a Colonel in the Parliamentary army, purchased Barrington in 1625. His descendants owned it until 1745 and he occurs on an extensive pedigree of the family recorded at the 1623 Heralds' Visitation of Dorset and Somerset. He married Joanna Barnard, the heiress of Downside and their impaled arms are carved in stone over the Library door and are painted on a chimneypiece in an upstairs room.

Basildon Park
BERKSHIRE

Sykes

ARMS: Argent an Eagle rising between two Sykes or Fountains proper on a Canton Gules a Caduceus Or wings Argent

CREST: On a Wreath of the Colours (Argent and Azure) A demi Lady of Bengal in the complete dress of that Kingdom holding in the dexter hand proper a Rose Gules

MOTTO: *Sapiens Qui Assiduus* [He is wise who is industrious]

The arms and crest were granted on 1 March 1763 to Francis Sykes (d.1804) 'of Ackworth Park in the County of York, Esquire, late Chief or Governor of Cossimbuzar a factory belonging to the Honorable East India Company in the Kingdom of Bengal in the East Indies' who was created a baronet in 1781. The grant was made to him and the other descendants of his father, Francis Sykes of Thornhill near

Wakefield. No motto is shown on the Patent. A fine Chinese export dinner service made in the 1760s for the future 1st Baronet shows his arms and crest, and is a good example of eighteenth-century armorial porcelain. There is, however, no surviving architectural heraldry at Basildon.

Benthall Hall

SHROPSHIRE

Benthall

Arms: Or a Lion rampant queue fourchy Azure crowned Gules
Crest: On a Coronet Or a Leopard statant Argent spotted Sable
Motto: *Pro Rege Patria et Deo* [For King, Country and God]

The arms are recorded in the 1584 Visitation, and with the crest in 1620 and 1663. Most of the heraldry in the house commemorates the seventeenth-century marriage of the Royalist Colonel Lawrence Benthall (d.1652) to Katherine Cassey: the overmantels in the Dining Room and Drawing Room show their impaled arms. The Hall overmantel shows the heraldically remarkable and incorrect sight of the arms of Benthall not only impaling Cassey, but also impaling those of his mother-in-law, whose illustrious descent from one of the Conqueror's inner circle was presumably too great to resist. The finest and most unusual heraldic feature of the house is the early seventeenth-century staircase which contains panels of both the Benthall arms and crest.

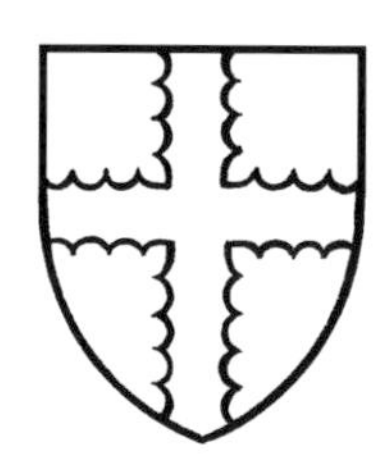

Bodiam Castle

SUSSEX

Dallingridge

Arms: Argent a Cross engrailed Gules
Crest: On a Wreath A Unicorn's Head [tinctures unknown]

The arms appear in early medieval rolls for de la Lynde, and were adopted by John Dallingridge (d.1335) on his marriage to Joan de la Lynde. Their grandson, Edward (d.1393), was a mercenary soldier in France during the Hundred Years War, and built the castle to proclaim his enhanced status thanks to the spoils of war and a series of lucrative family marriages. The heraldry on the Gatehouse is an intrinsic part of this proclamation: Edward Dallingridge's own arms and unicorn crest are flanked by the arms of Wardieu, for his wife, an heiress who brought him the Bodiam estate, and Radingden, for his mother's family. On the Postern Tower is the achievement of Sir Robert Knollys, a military leader in France during the 1360s.

Buscot Park

BERKSHIRE

Henderson, Baron Faringdon

Arms: Or three Piles issuant from the sinister Vert on a Chief Ermine three Torteaux
Crest: On a Wreath of the Colours (Or and Vert) A Hand holding a Torteaux charged with a Mullet of six points Argent
Supporters: (Dexter) A Chevalier armed at all points holding in his dexter hand a Lance with his Lordship's Pennon bearing the motto Sursum Corda all proper; (Sinister) A Centaur drawing his bow proper
Motto: *Sola Virtus Nobilitat* [Virtue alone enobles]

The blazon is a copy of the original which comes from the Scottish heraldic authority, the Court of the Lord Lyon in Edinburgh. The arms and crest date from 1902 when the baronetcy was created, and the supporters from 1916 when Sir Alexander Henderson became a peer. The crest appears in the pediment, and the front entrance steps are flanked by a pair of bronze copies of the antique Capitoline Centaurs – a subtle allusion to the sinister supporter. The eighteenth-century Chinese export porcelain bears the arms of Laurence Sulivan, chairman of the East India Company and an ancestor of the 2nd Lord Faringdon's mother.

Calke Abbey

DERBYSHIRE

Harpur, Crewe and Harpur Crewe, Baronets

Arms: (1&4 Crewe) Azure a Lion rampant Argent
(2&3 Harpur) Argent a Lion rampant within a Bordure engrailed Sable

Crests: (1 Crewe) Out of a Ducal Coronet Or a Lion's Gamb erect Argent
(2 Harpur) On a Wreath of the Colours (Argent and Sable) A Boar passant Or ducally gorged and bristled Gules

Motto: *Degeneranti genus Opprobrium* [To a degenerate man, his family is a disgrace]

The arms of Harpur were confirmed and a crest granted to Richard Harpur in January 1565/6. The baronetcy was created in 1626; the arms of the 1st Baronet, Sir Henry Harpur, appear on an elaborately carved Jacobean chimneypiece. His great grandson the 4th Baronet, who rebuilt the house, adorning the rainwater heads with his boar's head crest, married Catherine Crewe in the early eighteenth century, but it was not until 1808 that the 7th Baronet Henry Harpur obtained a Royal Licence to bear the quartered arms and crests of both families. Both crests appear on the hall chairs and carriages at Calke, and the boar's head alone appears on the rainwater heads while quartered arms are carved on a Jacobean chimneypiece.

Canons Ashby

NORTHAMPTONSHIRE

Dryden, Baronets

Arms: Azure a Lion rampant and in chief an Armillary Sphere between two Estoiles Or

Crest: On a Wreath of the Colours (Or and Azure) A demi Lion holding in his dexter paw an Armillary Sphere on a Staff Or

The date of the grant of the arms and crest by Hervy, Clarenceux, to John Dryden, the builder of Canons Ashby, is unrecorded, but may have been made at the 1564 Visitation of Northamptonshire. His son, Erasmus (d.1632) was created a baronet in 1619. The Dryden family came originally from Cumberland and in the papers of Augustine Vincent, Windsor Herald (d.1626) there is a note: 'The first Dryden that came into this shire was a schoolmaster'. Most of the heraldic art in the house is Elizabethan and Jacobean. The original decoration of 1590, with arabesques and coats of arms was recently uncovered in the Winter Parlour. The Drawing Room has a magnificent chimneypiece and a domed plaster ceiling dominated by a moulded and coloured achievement of the impaled and quartered Dryden arms relating to the 2nd Baronet's third marriage in 1632, and in the eighteenth century the Hall was filled with arms and armour and heraldic cartouches to create the look of a medieval hall. The Church is hung with Dryden hatchments and the funerary achievements of Sir Robert Dryden, 3rd Baronet (d.1708).

Compton Castle

DEVON

Gilbert

Arms: Ermine on a Chevron Sable three Roses Argent barbed and seeded proper

Crest: On a Wreath of the Colours (Argent and Sable) A Squirrel sejant erect Gules

Motto: *Mallem Mori Quam Mutari* [I would rather die than be changed]

The arms were recorded at the 1620 Heralds' Visitation of Devon. The castle was acquired by the Gilberts in the early fourteenth century but fell into decay and was sold in 1775. But in 1930 it was bought back and restored by Commander Walter Raleigh Gilbert. The earliest parts still date from the fourteenth century, and the north-east tower has a window head decorated with carved roses, derived from the arms, and their squirrel crest. Modern painted shields depicting family connections hang round the top of the wall in the Great Hall.

Croft Castle

HEREFORDSHIRE

Croft, Baronets and Barons

Arms: Quarterly per fess indented Azure and Argent in the first quarter a Lion passant guardant Or

Crests: (1) On a Wreath of the Colours (Argent and Azure) A Lion passant guardant Argent;
(2) On a Wreath of the Colours (Argent and Azure) A Wyvern sejant wings addorsed Sable vulned on the breast Gules; Badge: Grass Vert enclosed by a Fence Or [i.e. a Croft]

Supporters: (Dexter) A Lion quarterly per fess indented Azure and Argent; (Sinister) A Wyvern Sable vulned in the side Gules

Motto: *Esse Quam Videri* [To be rather than seem to be]

The arms are of medieval origin; both crests occur in early sixteenth-century records of the family and they also appear as badges with the badge of a croft on the standard of Sir Richard Croft (d.1509) who used the motto *In Good Hope*. The castle was sold in 1746 and although re-acquired in 1923, it missed the nineteenth-century heraldic revival. A modern stained glass panel in the Hall shows the Croft shield.

Dyrham Park

GLOUCESTERSHIRE

Blathwayt

ARMS: Per pale Or and Sable two Bendlets engrailed counterchanged

CREST: On a Wreath of the Colours (Or and Sable) Upon a Rock proper an Eagle rising Sable winged and charged on the body with two Bendlets engrailed Or

MOTTO: *Virtute et Veritate* [By virtue and truth]

Though long used by the family in a simpler form, the arms and crest were only formally granted in 1910 to Charles George Blathwayt (d.1916) and to the other descendants of his father and uncle. The eagle crest appears proudly and prominently in the seventeenth-century architecture in the centre of the balustrade with the motto. It reappears again in the sconces of the Drawing Room and in the seventeenth-century ceiling of the West Hall, which also has a black marble chimneypiece showing the quartered arms of Blathwayt. Nine Blathwayt hatchments are in the adjoining Parish Church.

Farnborough Hall

WARWICKSHIRE

Holbech

ARMS: Vert six Escallops three, two and one Argent

CREST: On a Wreath of the Colours (Argent and Vert) A Maunch Vert semy of Escallops Argent

MOTTO: *Deo Duce Signo Cruce* [With God as my guide and with the Cross as a sign]

The arms were first recorded at the 1619 Visitation of Warwickshire, when another branch of the family recorded *Vert five Escallops Argent*. The story goes that the arms of Thomas Holbech, who was living in 1483, were originally of five escallops, and that his grandson, William, who had six sons, was allowed to add a sixth escallop in the sixteenth century as a reward for his prowess in war. The heraldic evidence does not support this as a coat of six escallops is attributed to Holbech on Portington's roll of arms, which dates from the mid-fifteenth century, as well as in early sixteenth-century sources. The arms and crest, which was entered at the 1683 Visitation, may be seen embossed on the late seventeenth-century rainwater heads on the west front, and the family shells also appear on the forecourt gatepiers. Inside the house the initials and impaled arms of William Holbech and his wife Elizabeth Alington may be seen in the late seventeenth-century plasterwork staircase ceiling.

Gunby Hall

LINCOLNSHIRE

Massingberd, sometime Baronets

ARMS: Azure three Quatrefoils (2&1) and in chief a Boar passant Or charged with a Cross formy Gules

CREST: On a Wreath Or and Sable A Lion's Head erased Azure charged with two Arrows in saltire points downwards between four Gouttes Argent

BADGE: Two Arrows in saltire points downwards between four Gouttes all Argent

MOTTO: *Est Meruisse Satis* [It is sufficient to have deserved]

The crest was granted to Thomas Massingberd of Gunby (d.1552) by Garter and Clarenceux in 1513. There is no record of the grant of arms, which do not appear in medieval sources, or of the badge, which appears on Sir Thomas Massingberd's standard. The family rose to prominence during the sixteenth century and Sir Henry Massingberd was created a Baronet by Oliver Cromwell in 1658. This was 'overlooked' at the Restoration, and Charles II recreated the Baronetcy in 1660. Gunby Hall was built for the 2nd Baronet in 1700. A baroque cartouche of the Massingberd arms appears over the front door and there is a rare early eighteenth-century painted panel on wood with the arms in the arched entrance to the Stable Yard.

Hailes Abbey

GLOUCESTERSHIRE

ARMS: Argent a Crozier in bend Sable head Gules over all a Lion rampant Gules in a Bordure Sable charged with Roundels Or

The arms are derived from the founder, Richard, Earl of Cornwall (d.1272), younger son of King John, who bore *Argent a Lion rampant Gules crowned Or within a Bordure Sable charged with Roundels Or*. Hailes is noted for its thirteenth-century encaustic tiles, an early example of the decorative use of heraldry. The pavement has tiles showing the arms of Richard, Earl of Cornwall as Count of Poitou and as King of the Romans; the arms of de Clare, Provence and von Falkenburg for Richard's three wives; the royal arms, and the arms of other medieval families, including the vairy coat of Ferrers (q.v. Baddesley Clinton).

Ham House

SURREY

Murray, subsequently Tollemache, Earls of Dysart

MURRAY

ARMS: Azure an Imperial Crown Or between three Mullets Argent within a double tressure flory counterflory Or

CREST: On a Wreath of the Colours (Or and Azure) A Mermaid holding a Mirror in her right hand and in her left a Comb all proper

SUPPORTERS: On either side a Lion Gules collared Azure each Collar charged with three Mullets Argent

MOTTO: *Tout Prest* [Quite ready]

TOLLEMACHE

ARMS: Argent a Fret Sable

CREST: On a Wreath of the Colours (Argent and Sable) A Horse's Head erased Gules maned Or between two Wings Or semy of roundels Sable

SUPPORTERS: On either side an Antelope proper attired and unguled Or

MOTTO: *Confido Conquiesco* [I trust and am contented]

The full achievement of the arms of Murray, Earls of Dysart is entered in a Lyon Office manuscript *Arms of Scottish Peers* by Henry Frazer, Ross Herald (1687-1724). The arms of Tollemache appear on some of the earliest rolls of arms of the late thirteenth century. The crest is typical of the mid-sixteenth century and entered at the 1561 Visitation, but no record of a grant survives in the College of Arms. Lionel Tollemache was created a Baronet in 1611. The 3rd Baronet married Elizabeth Murray, Countess of Dysart, and their son succeeded as 3rd Earl of Dysart after the death in 1697 of his mother, who had married as her second husband the Duke of Lauderdale. The quartered arms of (1&4) Tollemache and (2&3) Murray over the entrance at Ham are probably his. But Elizabeth, Duchess of Lauderdale was principally responsible for the wonderfully rich State Rooms. Her ducal coronet and cypher appears in the marquetry and scagliola decorations of the Queen's Closet. The Tollemache crest appears in the hall chairs and some mirror and picture frames. More Tollemache heraldry can be seen in the spandrels of the front door and in the garden gates.

Horton Court

GLOUCESTERSHIRE

Knight, Bishop of Bath and Wells (1541-7)

ARMS: Per fess Or and Gules in chief an Eagle displayed with two heads Sable both crowned Or charged on the breast with a Rose Gules barbed and seeded proper dimidiated and conjoined in base to a Sun in Splendour Or also dimidiated

The arms were granted by Emperor Maximillian I in 1514 to William Knight (d.1547) Prothonotary to the apostolic seat and ambassador from Henry VIII to the Emperor, and later Bishop of Bath and Wells. The Porch has Knight's arms beneath a Prothonotary's hat incorporated in Renaissance arabesque ornament, an early example of the combination of the medieval concept of heraldry with Italian inspired classicism in England. Inside the house is a Tudor chimneypiece with the arms, a renaissance frieze, fluted classical pilasters and the inscription 'Wilhelmus Knight Prothonotarius Ano 1521'.

Kingston Lacy

DORSET

Bankes

ARMS: Sable a Cross engrailed Ermine between four Fleur de Lys Or

CREST: On a Wreath of the Colours (Argent and Sable) A Moor's Head affronty proper wearing a Chapeau Gules turned up Ermine thereon a Fleur de Lys Or

MOTTO: *Velle Quod Vult Deus* [Desire what God wishes]

The arms were confirmed and the crest granted by Garter in a patent of 1613 to the twenty-four-year-old John Bankes (d.1644). He was subsequently knighted and bought Corfe Castle (also in Dorset) and Kingston Lacy. The heraldic interest of Kingston Lacy is concentrated in the embellishments of William John Bankes (d.1855), who spent the later part of his life in enforced exile in Italy. In buying Italian works of art for the house he was also partly inspired by the family heraldry: the oak doors between the Saloon and the Drawing Room were allegedly from the Vatican. They display a single fleur de lys from the Farnese family arms of Pope Paul III (d.1549) which was, as Bankes said, 'the same as ours'. The Venetian bronze knockers in the Entrance Hall include several commissioned by Bankes with the moor's head crest. A large carved stone chimneypiece in the Inner Hall has the fleur de lys in the keystone, the Bankes arms quartered with Wynne and Brune (in the wrong order), and the motto, and arms also appear on the bronze radiator covers on the staircase.

Little Moreton Hall

CHESHIRE

Moreton

ARMS, Quarterly: (1&4 Moreton) Argent a Greyhound courant Sable plain Collared Argent with a Ring attached thereto Or (2&3 Macclesfield) Gules a Cross engrailed Ermine

CREST: On a Wreath of the Colours (Argent and Sable) A Wolf's Head couped Argent gorged with a Torse Vert

MOTTO: *Nisi Cum Re* [Not without substance]

The arms of Moreton share an origin with those of the Cheshire family of Holford. In 1216 Sir Gralam de Lostock married Lettice de Moreton. The descendants of their eldest son Richard assumed the surname Holford from their place of residence and bore *Argent a Greyhound passant Sable*. Their younger son, Geoffrey, assumed the name de Moreton and differenced the arms by adding a collar and a ring to the greyhound, which is usually shown as running. Geoffrey de Moreton's great grandson married Margaret de Macclesfield and at the 1580 and 1663 Visitations of Cheshire their quartered arms are shown. The wolf's head may be found carved on some of the woodwork, in the painted frieze in the Parlour and in the heraldic glass in the Withdrawing Room. The quartered arms and crest are on the carved wooden overmantel in the upper Porch Room, and the stained glass in the Drawing Room depicts the Moreton arms and crest, the wolf's head and a tun, or barrel, for the rebus on the family name: Maw–tun.

Moseley Old Hall

STAFFORDSHIRE

Whitgreave

ARMS: Azure on a Cross quarter pierced Or four Chevrons Gules in dexter chief a Trefoil Argent

CREST: Issuing from a Crest Coronet Gules a demi heraldic Antelope Or charged on the shoulder with a Trefoil untinctured

MOTTO: *Regem Defendere Victum* [To defend the conquered King]

The arms and crest without the trefoil are a rare example of a private grant. They were granted to Robert Whitgreave in 1422 by Humphrey, Duke of Buckingham (d.1460) when Earl of Stafford, and are derived from the Stafford supporters. Robert Whitgreave's descendant, Thomas, sheltered Charles II at Moseley after the battle of Worcester in 1651. In 1838 his great great grandson, George Thomas Whitgreave received an augmentation to the arms to commemerate the devotion of his ancestor. The augmented arms are embroidered on a cushion in the Parlour and the unaugmented arms are found impaled with Clifford on the back of a chair in the Dressing Room.

Penrhyn Castle

GWYNEDD

Pennant, Baron Penrhyn, subsequently Dawkins-Pennant and finally Douglas-Pennant, Barons Penrhyn

Arms: Per bend sinister Ermine and Ermines a Lion rampant Or

Crest: Out of a ducal Coronet an Antelope's Head Argent maned and tufted Or

Motto: *Aequo Animo* [With equanimity]

The Pennant family was of Welsh descent and bore the arms attributed since the late fifteenth century to Tudor Trevor, a chieftain said to have lived *c.*900 and described in nineteenth century pedigrees as founder of the Tribe of the Marches. Richard Pennant, Lord Penrhyn (d.1808) was succeeded by his cousin, George Hay Dawkins (d.1840), who in 1808 assumed the name and arms of Pennant in addition to his paternal arms *Gules a Lion passant guardant Or between two Roses in pale Argent two Flaunches Or each charged with a Lion rampant Sable* and crest *On a Wreath of the Colours (Or and Gules) A dexter Arm couped at the shoulder holding a Battle Axe bendwise sinister proper thereon a Rose Gules.* The crests of the Dawkins and Pennant families appear above the entrance door and on the clock tower of the Stable block; the Library ceiling has a series of shields showing the connections of the Pennants and heraldic glass showing the fifteen noble and five royal tribes of Wales in the top of the windows.

Shugborough

STAFFORDSHIRE

Anson, Baron and Viscounts Anson, subsequently Earls of Lichfield

Arms: Argent three Bends engrailed and in sinister chief a Crescent Gules

Crest: On a Wreath of the Colours (Argent and Gules) A Spear Argent issuing out of a Ducal Coronet Or

Supporters (1747): (Dexter) A Sea Horse; (Sinister) A Sea Lion both proper and charged on the neck with two Bars gemel Or

Motto: *Nil Desperandum* [Never despair]

Arms (1806), Quarterly: (1 Anson) Argent three Bendlets engrailed and in sinister chief a Crescent Gules
(2 Adams) Ermine three Cats-a-Mountain passant guardant in pale Sable
(3 Sambrooke) Azure three Salmon naiant in pale per pale Or and Argent
(4 Carrier) Sable a Bend Or between three Spear Heads Argent

Crests (1806): (1 Anson) On a Wreath of the Colours (Argent and Gules) A Spear Purpure the head proper issuing out of a Ducal Coronet Or
(2 Adams) On a Wreath of the Colours (Argent and Sable) A Greyhound's Head erased Ermines gorged with a Collar double gemel Or

Supporters: (Dexter) A Sea Horse; (Sinister) A Lion guardant proper each gorged with a Collar double gemel Or

Motto: *Nil Desperandum* [Never despair]

A pedigree was recorded by William Anson of Shugborough at the 1663 Visitation of Staffordshire without arms or a crest. His grandson, Admiral George Anson, the circumnavigator and 1st Lord of the Admiralty 1747-62 was created Lord Anson in 1747, when supporters were granted and the arms confirmed. The proceeds of the Admiral's exploits enabled his elder brother, Thomas Anson, to expand the park and reconstruct the house at Shugborough. Both the Admiral and Thomas Anson died without issue and the property passed to their nephew, George Adams, who took the name and arms of Anson in 1773. His son was created Viscount Anson in 1806 and was granted supporters. In a separate patent, quarterings were established for Adams, Sambrook and Carrier and a second crest granted for Adams. In 1831 the 2nd Viscount was created Earl of Lichfield. The spear head crest may be seen on the Lichfield Lodges, and in the metopes of the Doric frieze in the Entrance Hall, designed by Samuel Wyatt. Admiral Anson's arms are on the silver salvers by Paul de Lamerie in the Dining Room and on the *famille verte* dinner service. The arms of the 2nd Earl of Lichfield appear on the nineteenth-century Dining Room pelmet and curtains, in ormolu.

Sudbury Hall

DERBYSHIRE

Vernon, Barons Vernon

Arms: Argent a Fret Sable

Crest: On a Wreath of the Colours (Argent and Sable) A Boar's Head erased Sable ducally gorged Or

SUPPORTERS: (Dexter) A Lion Gules gorged with a Collar and Chain affixed thereto passing between his forelegs and reflexed over his back Or; (Sinister) A Boar Sable gorged with a Ducal Coronet and a like Chain Or

MOTTO: *Vernon Semper Viret* [Vernon always flourishes]

The arms are of medieval origin and the supporters were granted in 1762 to George Venables Vernon on his elevation to the peerage. Sudbury is renowned for the richness of the craftsmanship in wood and plaster which embellishes the interior, much of it the work of leading London artificers of the day: Edward Pierce, Grinling Gibbons, Robert Bradbury, James Pettifer and Louis Laguerre. But with the exception of the Drawing Room ceiling, which contains two shields of the Vernon fret, none of this decoration made use of the family heraldry. The door handles in the Saloon have the boar's head crest and the lock guards are decorated with the fret.

TRERICE

CORNWALL

Arundell, Barons Arundell

ARMS: Sable six Swallows 3,2 & 1 close Argent

CREST: On a Cap of Maintenance Sable turned up Ermine a Swallow close statant Argent

SUPPORTERS: On either side a Panther Or spotted Sable with flames of fire issuing out of each of their mouths and ears

Trerice was acquired through the fourteenth-century marriage of Ralph Arundell and Jane, daughter and heiress of Michael Trerice of Trerice and remained in the family for four hundred years. The arms are canting heraldry, the French for swallow being *hirondelle* – hence Arundell. The sixteenth-century plasterwork in the Hall and Great Chamber was executed for Sir John Arundell IV (d.1580). The Hall ceiling is decorated with oak leaves, which may refer to the Fitzalan oakleaf, commemorating the Arundells' most distinguished marital connection at the time the house was rebuilt in the 1570s. The relationship is also celebrated in the Great Chamber, with the achievement of Henry Fitzalan, 12th Earl of Arundel, encircled by the Garter in the tympanum of the west wall. The plaster overmantel shows the quartered Arundell arms flanked by shields of Sir John's two wives, and the two swallows perched on the strapwork refer to the family heraldry.

WEST WYCOMBE PARK

BUCKINGHAMSHIRE

Dashwood, Baronets

ARMS: Argent on a Fess double cotised Gules three Griffin's Heads erased Or

CREST: On a Wreath of the Colours (Argent and Gules) A Griffin's Head Erminois beaked and erased Gules

MOTTO: *Pro Magna Charta* [For Magna Carta]

The arms and crest were granted in 1662 to Francis Dashwood, described in the patent as 'late an Alderman of London'. His son, Sir Francis Dashwood of West Wycombe was created a baronet in 1707, and his son, also Sir Francis, 2nd Baronet (d.1781) became a co-heir to the Barony of Le Despencer on the death of his uncle, 7th Earl of Westmorland, in 1762. Lord Westmorland's bust with his arms on the plinth is above the door in the Saloon. This Sir Francis was Chancellor of the Exchequer and a founder member of the Society of Dilettanti. West Wycombe is the realisation of many of the ideals of the Dilettanti Society with its classical porticoes and mythological frescoes, and the heraldry is restricted to the contents. The *verre églomisé* mirror in the Study has the initials M.J.D. for Mary Jennings Dashwood, the 1st Baronet's first wife, and the Dashwood crest. In the Dining Room the quartered arms appear in the portrait of Sir Francis Dashwood by George Knapton. The Tapestry Room has a watercolour of the arms with the red hand of Ulster, the badge of the baronetage, and a replica of the seventeenth-century Saddler's Company cup which has the arms of both the Company and the Dashwoods, the original having been presented to the Company by the Dashwoods.

English Kings of Arms

Garter Kings of Arms

1415–50	William Bruges
1450–78	John Smert
1478–1504	John Wrythe
1505–34	Sir Thomas Wrythe, alias Wriothesley (son of John Wrythe)
1534–6	Thomas Wall (son of Thomas Wall, Norroy)
1536–50	Sir Christopher Barker
1550–84	Sir Gilbert Dethick
1584–6	vacancy (Robert Cooke, Clarenceux appointed Acting Garter)
1586–1606	Sir William Dethick (son of Sir Gilbert Dethick)
1607–33	Sir William Segar
1633–43	Sir John Borough
1643–4	Sir Henry St George (son of Sir Richard St George, Clarenceux)
1645–77	Sir Edward Walker
1643–60	Sir Edward Bysshe, intruded *c.*1643, confirmed by Parliament 20 Oct. 1646, deposed at Restoration 1660 (subsequently Clarenceux)
1677–86	Sir William Dugdale
1686–1703	Sir Thomas St George (eldest son of Sir Henry St George)
1703–15	Sir Henry St George (second surviving son of Sir Henry St George)
1715–18	vacancy (disputed Gartership)
1718–44	John Anstis
1744–54	John Anstis (son of above and joint Garter with his father 1727–44)
1754–73	Stephen Martin Leake
1773–4	Sir Charles Townley
1774–80	Thomas Browne
1780–4	Ralph Bigland
1784–1822	Sir Isaac Heard
1822–31	Sir George Nayler
1831–8	Sir Ralph Bigland (nephew of Ralph Bigland)
1838–42	Sir William Woods
1842–69	Sir Charles George Young
1869–1904	Sir Albert William Woods (son of Sir William Woods)
1904–18	Sir Alfred Scott Scott-Gatty
1918–30	Sir Henry Farnham Burke
1930–44	Sir Gerald Woods Wollaston (subsequently Norroy and Ulster)
1944–50	Sir Algar Henry Stafford Howard
1950–61	The Hon. Sir George Rothe Bellew
1961–78	Sir Anthony Richard Wagner (subsequently Clarenceux)
1978–92	Sir Alexander Colin Cole
1992–95	Sir Conrad Marshall John Fisher Swan
1995–	Peter Llewellyn Gwynn-Jones

Clarenceux King of Arms

*c.*1334	Andrew —
*c.*1383	Richard Spenser
*c.*1419	William Horsley
*c.*1425	John Cosoun
1435–60	Roger Legh or Lygh
1461–76	William Hawkeslowe
1476–85	Sir Thomas Holme
1485–7	vacancy (possibly filled by John More as Normandy King of Arms)
1487–93	Sir Thomas Holme (reappointed)
1493–1510	Roger Machado
1510–11	Christopher Carlill
1511–34	Thomas Benolt
1534–6	Thomas Tonge
1536–57	Thomas Hawley
1557–67	William Hervy
1567–93	Robert Cooke
1594–7	Richard Lee or Leigh
1597–1623	William Camden
1623–35	Sir Richard St George
1635–46	Sir William Le Neve
1646–50	Arthur Squibb, appointed by vote of Parliament, 20 Oct 1646
1650–5	Edward Bysshe, appointed by Parliament 12 June 1650 (as well as Garter)
1658–61	William Ryley, intruded c. Sept 1658
1661–79	Sir Edward Bysshe (previously intruded Garter)
1680–1703	Sir Henry St George (subsequently Garter)
1704–26	Sir John Vanbrugh
1726–41	Knox Ward
1741–54	Stephen Martin Leake (subsequently Garter)
1755–73	Charles Townley (subsequently Garter)
1773–4	Thomas Browne (subsequently Garter)
1774–80	Ralph Bigland (subsequently Garter)
1780–4	Isaac Heard (subsequently Garter)
1784–1803	Thomas Lock
1803–20	George Harrison
1820–2	Sir George Nayler (subsequently Garter)
1822–31	Ralph Bigland (subsequently Garter)
1831–8	William Woods (subsequently Garter)
1838–9	Edmund Lodge
1839–46	Joseph Hawker
1846–8	Francis Martin
1848–59	James Pulman
1859–82	Robert Laurie
1882–94	Walter Aston Blount
1894–1911	George Edward Cokayne

1911–19	Sir William Henry Weldon
1919–22	Charles Harold Athill
1922–6	William Alexander Lindsay
1926–7	Gordon Ambrose de Lisle Lee
1927–54	Sir Arthur William Steuart Cochrane
1954–5	Archibald George Blomefield Russell
1955–67	Sir John Dunamace Heaton-Armstrong
1968–78	John Riddell Bromhead Walker
1978–95	Sir Anthony Richard Wagner (formerly Garter)
1995–7	John Philip Brooke Brooke-Little
1997–	David Hubert Boothby Chesshyre

Norroy Kings of Arms

*c.*1276	Peter (?de Horbury)
*c.*1323	William de Morlee
*c.*1338	Andrew —
*c.*1386	John Lake or Othelake, alias March
temp. Ric.II	?Roger Durroit
*c.*1399	Richard Bruges or Del Brugge
*c.*1426	John Ashwell
1436	William Boys
*c.*1450	William Tyndale or Tendale
*c.*1462	William Grimsby
1464–76	Thomas Holme (subsequently Clarenceux)
1477–8	John Wrythe (subsequently Garter)
1478–85	John More
1485–93	Roger Machado (subsequently Clarenceux)
1494–1510	Christopher Carlill (subsequently Clarenceux)
1510–11	Thomas Benolt (subsequently Clarenceux)
1511–16	John Yonge or Young
1516–22	Thomas Wall
1522	John Joyner
1522–34	Thomas Tonge (subsequently Clarenceux)
1534–6	Thomas Hawley or Halley (subsequently Clarenceux)
1536	Christopher Barker (subsequently Garter)
1536–47	William Fellow
1547–50	Gilbert Dethick (subsequently Garter)
1550–7	William Hervy (subsequently Clarenceux)
1557–61	Laurence Dalton
1562–88	William Flower
1588–92	vacancy
1592–3	Edmund Knight
1593–7	vacancy
1597–1604	William Segar (subsequently Garter)
1604–23	Richard St George (subsequently Clarenceux)
1623–33	John Borough (subsequently Garter)
1633–5	William Le Neve (subsequently Clarenceux)
1635–43	Sir Henry St George (subsequently Garter)
1643–5	Edward Walker (subsequently Garter)
1646–58	William Ryley (intruded 20 Aug and confirmed by Parliament 20 Oct. 1646)
1658–60	George Owen (intruded *c.*Sept. 1658)
1660–77	William Dugdale (subsequently Garter)
1677–80	Sir Henry St George (subsequently Clarenceux and Garter)
1680–86	Sir Thomas St George (subsequently Garter)
1686–1700	Sir John Dugdale
1700–4	Robert Devenish
1704–29	Peter Le Neve
1729–41	Stephen Martin Leake (subsequently Clarenceux and Garter)
1741–51	John Cheale
1751–5	Charles Townley (subsequently Clarenceux and Garter)
1755–61	William Oldys
1761–73	Thomas Browne (subsequently Clarenceux and Garter)
1773–4	Ralph Bigland (subsequently Clarenceux and Garter)
1774–80	Isaac Heard (subsequently Clarenceux and Garter)
1780–1	Peter Dore
1781–4	Thomas Lock (subsequently Clarenceux)
1784–1803	George Harrison (subsequently Clarenceux)
1803–22	Ralph Bigland (subsequently Clarenceux and Garter)
1822–38	Edmund Lodge (subsequently Clarenceux)
1838–9	Joseph Hawker (subsequently Clarenceux)
1839–46	Francis Martin (subsequently Clarenceux)
1846–8	James Pulman (subsequently Clarenceux)
1848–9	Edward Howard Gibbon, afterwards Howard-Gibbon
1849–59	Robert Laurie (subsequently Clarenceux)
1859–82	Walter Aston Blount (subsequently Clarenceux)
1882–94	George Edward Cokayne (subsequently Clarenceux)
1894–1911	William Henry Weldon (subsequently Clarenceux)
1911–19	Henry Farnham Burke (subsequently Garter)
1919	Charles Harold Athill (subsequently Clarenceux)
1919–22	William Alexander Lindsay (subsequently Clarenceux)
1922–6	Gordon Ambrose De Lisle Lee (subsequently Clarenceux)
1926–8	Arthur William Steuart Cochrane (subsequently Clarenceux)
1928–30	Gerald Woods Wollaston (subsequently Garter and later Norroy and Ulster)
1930–43	Algar Henry Stafford Howard (subsequently Garter)

Norroy and Ulster King of Arms

1943–4	Algar Henry Stafford Howard
1944–57	Sir Gerald Woods Wollaston (formerly Garter)
1957–66	Aubrey John Toppin
1966–71	Richard Preston Graham-Vivian
1971–80	Walter John George Verco
1980–95	John Philip Brooke Brooke-Little (subsequently Clarenceux)
1995–7	David Hubert Boothby Chesshyre (subsequently Clarenceux)
1997–	Thomas Woodcock

Glossary

Many terms of blazon have more than one accepted spelling. Fess/fesse, caboshed/cabossed and luce/lucy are examples. This in part reflects the French origin of some words and their subsequent Anglicization as in semé and its alternative, semy.

Accolled: Having a collar, synonymous with gorged [crest of Meller of Erddig]; also of two shields placed side by side by French Heralds as an alternative to impalement.

Addorsed: Back to back, frequently used of wings which are elevated [crest of Herbert of Powis Castle].

Affronty: Facing the spectator.

Annulet: A ring [Heathcoat-Amory of Knightshayes Court].

Antelope, Heraldic: A monster with the body of an antelope, two horns, a mane and long tail.

Appaumé or Appaumy: With the palm of the hand facing the spectator.

Argent: Heraldic term for silver or white.

Armed: As a term of blazon refers to a creature's offensive and defensive weapons; in the case of birds, beaks and talons, but not legs, although as a term of falconry it includes the scaly part of legs [crest of Hobart of Blickling Hall].

Armillary Sphere: A skeleton celestial globe [Dryden of Canons Ashby].

Attired: With antlers, blazoned if of a different tincture from the head [supporters of Hobart of Blickling Hall].

Azure: Heraldic term for blue.

Bar: A horizontal stripe on the shield; a diminutive of the fess [Broughton of Anglesey Abbey].

Bar gemel: Two thin bars borne together, visually identical to a voided bar [Throckmorton of Coughton Court].

Barbed: With roses this refers to the leaves enclosing the bud which appear between the petals of an open rose, and if blazoned 'proper', Vert is shown [Hardwick of Hardwick Hall]. Alternatively, the point of a sharp weapon.

Barry: Said of a field or charge divided horizontally into an even number of stripes [Selby of Ightham Mote].

Barry wavy: Equal number of wavy horizontal divisions resembling water [Trevelyan of Wallington].

Baston or Baton: A couped bend.

Bend: The fourth Honourable Ordinary; a diagonal stripe drawn across the shield from the dexter chief to the sinister base [Curzon of Kedleston Hall].

Bendlet: Diminutive of the bend [Kay-Shuttleworth of Gawthorpe Hall].

Bendways or Bendwise: Said of charges when shown at the same angle as a bend [Hesketh of Rufford Old Hall]. This is to be contrasted with 'in bend', where the charges are arranged across the shield diagonally but the angle at which they stand is not specified.

Bewits: The straps or cords attaching bells to the legs of birds of prey [supporters of Onslow of Clandon Park].

Bezant: A gold roundel [Yorke of Wimpole Hall].

Bezanty: Field or charge powdered with bezants [Hobart of Blickling Hall].

Billetty: A pattern of billets or rectangles derived from the vulgar Latin *bilia* – a tree trunk [crest of Lucy of Charlecote].

Border or Bordure: A border round the edge of the shield [Jones of Chastleton].

Bouget or Water Bouget: Two leather pouches suspended from a yoke used to carry water [Bourchier of Beningbrough Hall].

Caboshed or Cabossed: Animal's head, often a stag's affronty, without a neck [Parker of Saltram].

Caduceus: Rod of Mercury [Sykes of Basildon Park].

Canting arms: Arms containing charges which allude punningly to the name of the bearer, as in the shuttles of Shuttleworth of Gawthorpe Hall.

Canton: A square division, the same depth as a chief, in one of the upper corners of the shield, usually in dexter chief. Often charged and used as an augmentation [Ferrers of Baddesley Clinton].

Chaplet: Synonymous with floral wreath, e.g. chaplet of roses [Edgcumbe of Cotehele].

Charge: A bearing or figure represented on the shield.

Chequy, Checquy or Checky: A term applied to a field or charge divided into three or more rows of small squares of alternate tinctures like a chess board. See also gobony [Chichester of Arlington Court].

Chevron: The seventh Honourable Ordinary derived from a similar French word meaning a triangular-shaped wooden lathe round which roofing tiles are placed, and resembling an upturned 'V' [Windham of Felbrigg].

Chief: The second Honourable Ordinary created by drawing a horizontal line across the shield and occupying at most the upper third of the shield [Henderson of Buscot Park].

Cinquefoil: Charge similar to a five-leafed clover.

Clarion: An organ rest [Grenville of Buckland Abbey].

Close: With wings against the body [crest of Arundel of Trerice].

Cockatrice: A two-legged dragon or wyvern, with a cock's head [the badge of Curzon of Kedleston Hall].

Colours: The principal colours are blue (Azure), red (Gules), black (Sable), green (Vert) and purple (Purpure). See also tinctures.

Compony or Gobony: Composed of a single row of squares of two alternate tinctures; said of a bordure, bend etc. See also chequy and countercompony.

Conjoined: Joined together [Ferrers of Baddesley Clinton].

Cordon: A knotted cord [Hobart of Blickling].

Cornucopia: Horn of Plenty [held by supporter of Curzon of Kedleston].

Cotise: A diminutive of the bend, one quarter of its width, and only borne in pairs on either side of it [Edgcumbe of Cotehele].

Counterchanged. When the field is divided between a metal and a colour, and those charges or parts of charges which fall upon the metal are of the colour and vice versa, the charges are said to be counterchanged [Watt of Speke Hall].

Countercompony or Countergobony: A double row of squares of alternating tinctures. See also company and chequy [crest of Wyndham of Petworth].

Couped: With the end cut off straight (see also erased). When used of an Honourable Ordinary it means the ends do not touch the sides of the shield [Broughton of Anglesey Abbey].

Courant or Current: Running [Moreton of Little Moreton Hall].
Crescent: Can be either a charge [Strode of Barrington] or a cadency mark [Jones of Chastleton].
Crined: Haired [crest of Vernon of Hanbury Hall].
Cross: The first Honourable Ordinary. Many variations exist such as Cross paty [Sharington of Lacock Abbey], Cross raguly [Sandys of The Vyne] and Cross quarter pierced [Whitgreave of Moseley Old Hall].
Cross Crosslet: A cross with the limbs crossed, often occurs 'fitchy' or pointed at the foot [Vernon of Hanbury].
Crozier: An ecclesiastical crook or staff [Hailes Abbey].
Cubit: Arm cut off below the elbow, usually shown palewise [crest of Kay-Shuttleworth of Gawthorpe].
Dancetty: A zigzag line of partition as in the arms of West sometimes quartered with Sackville of Knole. This developed to be similar to, but larger in size, than indented.
Demi or Demy: The upper half of a beast, bird, etc. [crest of Whitmore-Jones of Chastleton].
Dexter: Right, as opposed to left (sinister), when describing charges on the shield. All blazon assumes one is standing behind the shield; the dexter half of the shield is consequently the left-hand side to the spectator.
Diapering: An optional patterning with scrollwork or flourishes on uncharged parts of a shield executed in the same tincture to relieve the surface, especially in stained glass.
Difference: To make an addition or alteration to arms and crest, usually to mark a distinction between the coats of arms of closely related persons whose shields would otherwise be the same.
Displayed: Used of birds, usually eagles, with outstretched wings [Bedingfeld of Oxburgh Hall].
Doubled: Used of the lining of mantling usually Or or Argent.
Dragon: The four-legged monster of mythology.
Eagle: The bird which occurs with greatest frequency in early heraldry and usually shown displayed [Winn of Nostell Priory] and sometimes with two heads [Hoare of Stourhead].
Elevated: Raised (of wings) [badge of Curzon of Kedleston].
Embattled: Crenellated [supporters of Temple of Stowe].
Embowed: Bent at the elbow [Armstrong of Cragside].
Embrued: With blood on its point.
Engrailed: Indented in a series of curves with the points outward to make a concave pattern [Dallingridge of Bodiam Castle].
Erased: Cut off with a jagged base line, as compared to 'couped', which is straight cut [Windham of Felbrigg Hall].
Erect: Upright [Booth of Dunham Massey].
Ermine: One of the furs with black Ermine tails on white; variants include *Ermines* – white tails on black [Pennant of Penrhyn Castle], *Erminois* – black tails on gold, and *Pean* – gold tails on black.
Escallop: The shell [Strickland of Sizergh Castle].
Escroll: A scroll or strip of parchment on which the motto is written [crest of Drake of Buckland Abbey].
Escutcheon: Shield. When used as a charge, synonymous with inescutcheon.
Estoile: A star usually with six wavy limbs [Hobart of Blickling Hall].
Fess: The fifth Honourable Ordinary is a band taking up the centre third of the shield and formed by two horizontal lines drawn across the shield [Onslow of Clandon Park].
Fessways or Fesswise: Lying horizontally [crest of Tresham of Lyveden New Bield].
Field: The background colour, fur or metal of the shield, always mentioned first in a blazon. It can be of more than one tincture if patterned.
Fitchy: Pointed, terminating in a point. Usually used with forms of cross.
Flaunch: A convex segmental Ordinary on either side of the shield [Hobart of Blickling Hall].
Fleur de lys: Stylised flower based on lily or iris, seen in the French Royal Arms and borne in those of England till 1801 [Bankes of Kingston Lacy].
Floretty or cross fleuretty: A type of cross with fleurs de lys emerging from the ends of the limbs. Compare cross flory, where the limbs terminate in fleurs de lys.
Flory counterflory: Denoting that the flowers with which an Ordinary (usually a tressure) is adorned have their heads placed inward and outward alternately [Murray of Ham House].
Foil: Generic term for group of flower-like charges, including trefoil, quatrefoil, cinquefoil.
Formy: A type of cross with splayed limbs and wide ends. See also cross paty [Massingberd of Gunby Hall].
Fourché or Fourchy: Forked; normally occurs as queue fourché, a forked tail [Benthall of Benthall Hall].
Fountain: A roundel barry wavy Argent and Azure [Cust of Belton House].
Fret: A mascle interlaced by a saltire [Tollemache of Ham House].
Fretty: A pattern of frets [Noel-Hill of Attingham Park].
Fructed: With fruit [crest of Strickland of Sizergh].
Fur: The principal furs are Ermine and Vair (see also tincture).
Furnished: The decoration of a movable or working part [Shuttleworth of Gawthorpe Hall].
Fusil: A thin elongated lozenge [Percy of Petworth].
Gamb: A paw, usually a lion's or a bear's [Harpur Crewe of Calke Abbey].
Garb: A sheaf, often of wheat [Hesketh of Rufford Old Hall].
Gobony or Compony: A single row of squares of alternate tinctures [crest of Cust of Belton].
Gorged: Collared [supporters of Brownlow of Belton].
Goutte: A drop, for instance of water (d'eau) or blood (de sang); different terms are used depending on the tincture [crest and badge of Massingberd of Gunby Hall].
Griffin: Winged monster with foreparts of an eagle and hindparts of a lion with a beard and ears. A male griffin has no wings and spikes emerge from the body.
Guardant: Used of a beast looking out at the spectator rather than seen in profile [Croft of Croft Castle].
Gules: Heraldic term for red.
Gutty: Powdered with gouttes, or drops [crest of Lucy of Charlecote].
Gyronny: Said of a field that is divided into triangular parts or gyrons, created by halving quarters diagonally.
Habited: Clothed [crest of Bourchier of Beningbrough Hall].
Haurient: A fish shown vertically [Lucy of Charlecote].
Indented: A line of partition resembling the blade of a saw [Paston-Bedingfeld of Oxburgh Hall].
Inescutcheon: A shield when borne as a charge on another shield [Brownlow of Belton].

Invected: The reverse of engrailed, indented with a series of curves pointing inward.
Irradiated: With rays of light emerging.
Issuant: Used of beasts or monsters, unless they are winged, when rising or emerging from another charge [Trevelyan of Wallington].
Label: A horizontal bar, usually couped, and normally with three or five dependent points. A label of three points now normally denotes an eldest son in the lifetime of his father.
Lambeaux: Another word for a label.
Langued: Tongued.
Leopard: Term used in medieval heraldry for lion passant guardant.
Leopard's Face: Term used for leopard's head caboshed [Brydges quartered by Temple of Stowe].
Lined: With a line similar to a leash, usually attached to a collar.
Lion: Most frequently found beast in heraldry.
Lozenge: A diamond shape used both as a charge and instead of a shield to display the arms of spinsters, widows and peeresses in their own right.
Luce or Lucy: A pike (fish) [Lucy of Charlecote].
Mantled: Refers to the outside rather than the lining (doubled) of mantling.
Marshal: To combine coats of arms on a single shield by quartering or other means.
Martlet: A legless bird, sometimes said to represent the swift or swallow [Luttrell of Dunster] also cadency mark [Brownlow of Belton].
Mascle: A hollow diamond-shaped device or voided lozenge [Ferrers of Baddesley Clinton].
Maunch: A device representing a medieval sleeve [Fleming quartered by Wade of Snowshill Manor].
Metal: Two metals are used, gold (Or) and silver (Argent).
Mullet: A star with straight limbs usually of five points [Jones of Chastleton].
Naiant: Swimming, usually for fish which are fesswise [Sambrook quartered by Anson of Shugborough].
Nebuly: A form of wavy line, now like a row of jigsaw tongues [Watt of Speke Hall]. No distinction was made between this and wavy in medieval heraldry.
Nowed: Knotted [crest of Cavendish of Hardwick Hall].
Or: Heraldic term for yellow or gold.
Orle: A voided escutcheon a bordure's width from the edge of the shield. Charges placed in orle follow the line of the orle [Brownlow of Belton].
Ounce: Synonymous with the post-medieval leopard [Hervey of Ickworth].
Pale: The third Honourable Ordinary. A vertical stripe in the middle of the shield occupying at most one third of the shield [Sharrington of Lacock Abbey]. A per pale division divides a shield or charge vertically [Herbert of Powis Castle].
Paleways or Palewise: Said of charges when vertical. It does not relate to the relationship between charges which might be 'palewise in bend' if arranged diagonally across the shield, although pointing upwards. When charges are one above another the term 'in pale' is used [Carew of Antony].
Pallet: A narrow vertical stripe on the shield, half the width of a pale [1806 crest of Legh of Lyme Park].
Paly: Divided into an even number of vertical stripes of equal width in alternating tinctures [supporters of Cust of Belton].
Panache: An arrangement of feathers on the helmet one of the precursors of the crest and in some cases retained as a crest [Luttrell of Dunster].
Panther: The beast which is depicted heraldically with flames issuing from its ears and mouth and with its body powdered with multi-coloured spots. [Dexter supporter of Herbert of Powis Castle].
Passant: Four-legged beast or monster depicted with the dexter foreleg raised as if walking [Drewe of Castle Drogo].
Patonce: Type of cross with splayed limbs, each ending in three points like a simple crown.
Paty: Type of cross now usually called cross formy.
Pellet: A black roundel .
Pheon: An arrowhead [Egerton of Tatton].
Phoenix: Usually shown as a demi eagle emerging from flames [Seymour of Petworth].
Pierced: Refers to a circular hole in a charge through which the field shows unless another tincture is specified. See also voided.
Pile: A triangular sub-Ordinary [Chandos quartered by Temple of Stowe].
Plain: Plain is used as a contrast to both patterned and modified. A shield could have a plain or patterned field and an Ordinary such as a cross could be plain, patterned (e.g. Ermine) or modified (e.g. engrailed).
Poix: Oil, as in *gutty de poix*, a pattern of black gouttes [supporters of Edgcumbe of Cotehele].
Pomme: A green roundel [Heathcoat-Amory of Knightshayes Court].
Pommel: The spherical end of a sword [Fuller-Eliott-Drake of Buckland Abbey].
Popinjay: A parrot [Curzon of Kedleston Hall].
Proper: Heraldic term for in natural colours.
Purpure: Heraldic term for purple.
Quarter: To divide the shield into four or more compartments of equal sizes.
Quatrefoil: Charge similar to four-leafed clover [Massingberd of Gunby Hall].
Queue: Tail of a beast [Benthall of Benthall Hall].
Quillons: Cross-piece of a sword between the hilt and blade [Chute of The Vyne].
Raguly: Designating a charge or Ordinary jagged or notched like the trunk or limbs of a tree lopped of its branches. Also a line of partition [Sandys of The Vyne].
Rampant: Beast or monster standing on one hind leg [Jones of Chastleton].
Reflexed: Curved backwards, as in a line or chain over the back of a beast [supporters of Hobart of Blickling].
Reguardant: Applied to any beast, bird or monster looking back over its shoulder [supporters of Brownlow of Belton].
Remora: A sucking fish resembling a snake [held by a supporter of Curzon of Kedleston].
Rising: Used of birds when rising, but not for beasts or monsters (see issuant) [crest of Child of Osterley].
Roundel: A circle. Can be called a bezant when Or, plate when Argent, hurt when Azure, torteau when Gules, pellet when Sable and pomme when Vert.
Sable: Heraldic term for black.
Salient: A beast springing, jumping or leaping.
Saltire: The eighth Honourable Ordinary depicted in the form of a St Andrew's cross [Hardwick of Hardwick Hall]. Per saltire divides the shield as if by a saltire [Disraeli of Hughenden Manor].
Saltireways or Saltirewise: In the shape of a St Andrew's cross, i.e. the letter 'X' [crest of Watt of Speke Hall].

Sang: Blood, as in *gutty de sang*, a pattern of red gouttes [sinister supporter of Wyndham of Petworth].
Scymitar: Curved eastern sword [crest of Eliott of Buckland].
Seeded: Centre seeds of a flower, especially of a rose [Knight of Horton Court].
Segreant: Rampant when used of griffins.
Sejant: Beasts and monsters seated erect as in the Sackville leopards at Knole.
Semy or semé: Scattered or powdered as in semy de lys (strewn with fleurs de lys) [Lucy of Charlecote].
Sinister: Left as opposed to right (dexter) when describing charges on the shield. All blazon assumes one is standing behind the shield. The sinister half of the shield is therefore the right-hand side to the spectator.
Slipped: With a stalk; the term is used with flowers and foils [Tresham of Lyveden New Bield].
Statant: Standing with all feet on the ground [crest of Hobart of Blickling Hall].
Talbot: Medieval hunting dog [crest of Amory of Knightshayes Court].
Tenné: Heraldic term for orange.
Tincture: The collective noun for colours, metals and furs.
Torse: Synonymous with the crest wreath and normally of six visible twists of cloth wound round the helmet. Often shown under the crest without a helmet [crest of Selby of Ightham Mote].
Torteau: A red roundel [Henderson of Buscot].
Trefoil: A stylised leaf resembling a three-leafed clover usually shown with a stalk when termed slipped [Hervey of Ickworth].
Tressure: A diminutive of the orle appearing as a narrow band near the edge of a coat of arms. A Double Tressure has two narrow bands, it is often ornamented with fleurs de lys on the outer and inner edges when it is blazoned flory counterflory [Murray of Ham House].
Trick: System of indicating tincture in uncoloured records by abbreviated tincture, e.g. G or Gu for Gules and Arg for Argent, used largely in uncoloured records of Heralds' Visitations.
Unguled: Hooved, of beasts or monsters [Crest and supporters of Grey of Dunham Massey].
Unicorn: Monster shown as a horse with a twisted horn, lion's tail and hooves.
Vair: A fur depicted in various stylised patterns of blue and white [Chichester of Arlington Court].
Vairy: Used for Vair in tinctures other than blue and white.
Vert: Heraldic term for green.
Vested: Clothed, synonymous with habited [crest of Selby of Ightham Mote].
Voided: With a hole in the centre of the same shape as the charge. See also pierced. [Sharrington of Lacock Abbey].
Vol: Two wings conjoined with tips upwards; a demi-vol is a single wing with the tip upwards [crest of Graham of Nunnington].
Volant: Heraldic term for flying.
Vulned: Wounded [crest of Croft of Croft Castle].
Wavy or undy: Applied to Ordinaries or lines of division which curve and re-curve like waves.
Wyvern: A two-legged dragon, a precursor of supporters on medieval heraldic seals [crest of Herbert of Powis Castle].

Bibliography

The principal bibliography of British heraldry is Thomas Moule's *Bibliotheca Heraldica* (1822) which chronologically lists printed books on heraldry down to 1821. The following list is a selection of books published since 1821. Those who want a full bibliography should refer to Moule; there is at present no equivalent source for books published after 1821. In particular, printed editions of many of the Heralds' Visitations of the Counties of England and Wales exist published by The Harleian Society and others, but have not been included here.

Ailes, A., *The Origins of the Royal Arms of England*, Graduate Centre for Medieval Studies, Reading University, 1982

Barrington, A., *Introduction to Heraldry*, H.G. Bohn, London, 1848

Barron, Oswald: Article on 'Heraldry' in 11th edition *Encyclopaedia Brittanica*, 1910

Bedford, W.K.R, *The Blazon of Episcopacy*, Oxford, 1897

Bedingfeld, H. and Gwynn-Jones, P., *Heraldry*, Magna Books, Leicester, 1993

Berry, William, *Encyclopaedia Heraldica* (3 vols), Sherwood, Gilbert & Piper, London, 1828

Birch, W. de G., *Catalogue of Seals in the Department of Manuscripts in the British Museum, London* (6 vols), Printed by Order of the Trustees, London, 1887-1900

Boumphrey, R.S. and Hudleston, C.R., *An Armorial for Westmorland and Lonsdale*, Lake District Museum Trust and Cumberland & Westmorland Antiquarian & Archaeological Society, 1975

Boutell, Charles, *Boutell's Heraldry* (first published as *The Manual of Heraldry*, 1863) revised edition by J.P. Brooke-Little, Warne, London, 1983

Brault, Gerard J., *Early Blazon*, Clarendon Press, Oxford, 1972

– *Eight thirteenth century Rolls of Arms in French and Anglo-Norman Blazon*, Pennsylvania State University Press, 1973

– *Rolls of Arms, Edward I (1272-1307)* published as *Aspilogia III* (2 vols), Society of Antiquaries, London, 1997

Briggs, Geoffrey, *Civic and Corporate Heraldry*, Heraldry Today, London, 1971

Brooke-Little, J.P. (editor), *The Coat of Arms* (an heraldic quarterly magazine), The Heraldry Society, 1950-

– *An Heraldic Alphabet*, Macdonald & Co., 1973 revised 1975; Robson Books Ltd, London, 1985 and 1996

Brown, T.H., *Coats of Arms in Cleveland*, Teeside Museums & Art Galleries Service, 1973

Burke, Bernard, *The General Armory of England, Scotland and Wales*, Harrison, London, 1884

Cherry, J. and others, *Mythical Beasts*, British Museum Press, London, 1995

Chesshyre, D.H.B. and Woodcock, T. (editors), *Dictionary of British Arms – Medieval Ordinary* (Vol. I), Society of Antiquaries, London, 1992

Child, Heather, *Heraldic Design*, G. Bell & Sons Ltd., London, 1965

Clark, Hugh, *Introduction to Heraldry*, 14th edition, H. Washbourne, London, 1845

Corder, J, *A Dictionary of Suffolk Arms*, Vol: VII, Suffolk Records Society, 1965

– *A Dictionary of Suffolk Crests*, Vol: XL, Suffolk Records Society, 1998

Craven, M., *A Derbyshire Armory*, Derbyshire Record Society, 1991

Cussans, J.E., *Handbook of Heraldry*, 3rd edition, Chatto & Windus, London, 1893

Denholm-Young, Noel, *History and Heraldry 1254-1310: A Study of the Historical Value of the Rolls of Arms*, Clarendon Press, Oxford, 1965

Dennys, Rodney, *The Heraldic Imagination*, Barrie & Jenkins, London, 1975

– *Heraldry and The Heralds*, Jonathan Cape, London, 1982

Dorling, E.E., *Leopards of England and Other Papers*, Constable, London, 1912

Eames, Elizabeth, *Medieval Craftsmen, English Tilers*, British Museum Press, London, 1992

Ellis, Roger H. (editor), *Catalogue of Seals in the Public Record Office: Personal Seals*, Vols: I & II, H.M.S.O., London, 1978 & 1981

– *Monastic Seals*, Vol: I, H.M.S.O., London, 1986

Ellis, William Smith, *The Antiquities of Heraldry*, London, 1869

Elvin, Charles Norton, *Dictionary of Heraldry*, W.H. Brown, London, 1889

Evans, Sloane, *Grammar of Heraldry*, London, 1847

Eve, George W., *Heraldry as Art: An account of its development and practice, chiefly in England*, Batsford, London, 1907

– *Decorative Heraldry: A handbook of its description and treatment*, Bell, London, 1908

Fairbairn, James, *Book of Crests of the Families of Great Britain*, (2 vols) 4th edition, Jack, London, 1904

Farrer, Rev. E., *Church Heraldry of Norfolk* (3 vols) A.H. Goose & Co., Norwich, 1887

Foster, Joseph (editor), *Two Tudor Books of Arms: being Harleian Mss: 2179 and 6163*, privately printed, de Walden Library, 1904

Fox-Davies, A.C., *A Complete Guide to Heraldry*, (first published 1909), revised by J.P. Brooke-Little, Orbis, London, 1985

Franklin, Charles A.H., *The Bearing of Coat Armour by Ladies*, John Murray, London, 1923

Franklyn, J., *Shield and Crest*, 3rd edition, Macgibbon & Key, London, 1967

Friar, Stephen (editor), *A New Dictionary of Heraldry*, A.&C. Black, London, 1987

– *Heraldry for the Local Historian and Genealogist*, Alan Sutton Publishing Ltd, Stroud, 1992

Galbreath, D.L., *Papal Heraldry*, 2nd edition revised by G. Briggs, Heraldry Today, London, 1970

Grant, F.J., *The Manual of Heraldry*, John Grant, Edinburgh, 1924

Grazebrook, H.S., *The Heraldry of Worcestershire* (2 vols), John Russell Smith, London, 1873

Heralds' Commemorative Exhibition, 1484-1934, enlarged and illustrated catalogue, London, 1936; reprinted Tabard Press, London, 1970

Heraldic Exhibition Edinburgh 1891, Memorial catalogue printed for the Committee, Constable, Edinburgh, 1892
Hope, W.H. St John, *Heraldry for Craftsmen and Designers*, J. Hogg, London, 1913
– *A Grammar of English Heraldry*, 2nd edition by A.R. Wagner, Cambridge University Press, 1953
– *The Stall Plates of the Knights of the Order of the Garter 1348-1485*, A. Constable & Co. Ltd, London, 1901
Howard, D.S., *Chinese Armorial Porcelain*, Faber and Faber, London, 1974
Howard De Walden, Thomas Evelyn (Scott-Ellis), Lord, *Some Feudal Lords and Their Seals, 1301* with an Introduction by Lord Howard de Walden, privately printed, de Walden Library, 1904
– *Banners, Standards and Badges from a Tudor Manuscript in the College of Arms* with an Introduction by Lord Howard de Walden, privately printed, de Walden Library, 1904
Hudleston, C.R. and Boumphrey, R.S., *Cumberland Families and Heraldry*, The Cumberland & Westmorland Antiquarian & Archaeological Society, 1978
Humphery-Smith, Cecil R, *Anglo-Norman Armory*, Family History, Canterbury, 1973
– *Anglo-Norman Armory Two*, Institute of Heraldic and Genealogical Studies, Canterbury, 1984
– *Armigerous Ancestors*, Family History Books, Canterbury, 1997
Huxford, J.F., *Arms of Sussex Families*, Phillimore & Co., 1982
Innes of Learney, Thomas, *Scots Heraldry*, 2nd edition, Oliver & Boyd, Edinburgh, 1956
Jones, E.J., *Medieval Heraldry*, William Lewis, Cardiff, 1943
Jones, P. Gwynn, *The Art of Heraldry*, Parkgate Books Ltd., London, 1998
Lawrance, H., *Heraldry from Military Monuments before 1350 in England and Wales* (Vol 96), Harleian Society, London, 1946
Leaf, W. and Purcell, S., *Heraldic Symbols, Islamic Insignia & Western Heraldry*, Victoria and Albert Museum, London, 1986
London, H.S., *Royal Beasts*, The Heraldry Society, 1956
London Survey Committee, *The College of Arms*, H.M.S.O., London, 1963
Louda, J. and Maclagan, M., *Lines of Succession*, Orbis, London, 1981
Lower, M.A., *Curiosities of Heraldry*, R. Smith, London, 1845
Marks, R. and Payne, A., *British Heraldry from its origins to c.1800*, British Museum Publications Ltd., London, 1978
Moncreiffe, I. and Pottinger, D., *Simple Heraldry*, Thomas Nelson, Edinburgh, 1953
Moule, T., *Bibliotheca Heraldica*, London, 1822 reprinted by Heraldry Today, 1966
– *Heraldry of Fish*, John Van Voorst, London,1842
Neubecker, O., *Heraldry, Sources, Symbols and Meaning*, Macdonald and Jane's, London, 1976
Palliser, Mrs Bury, *Historic Devices Badges and War-Cries*, Sampson Low, London, 1870
Papworth, J.W. and Morant, A.W., *An Ordinary of British Armorials*, T. Richards, London, 1874
Parker, J., *Glossary of the Terms used in Heraldry*, new edition, Oxford, 1894
Pastoureau, M., *Heraldry, Its Origins and Meaning*, English translation, Thames and Hudson, London, 1997
Pinches, J.H. and R.V., *The Royal Heraldry of England*, Heraldry Today, London, 1974
Pine, L.G., *A Dictionary of Mottoes*, Routledge & Kegan Paul, London, 1983
Planché, J.R., *The Pursuivant of Arms*, Hardwicke, London, 1859
Platts, B., *Origins of Heraldry*, Proctor Press, London, 1980
Robson, T., *British Herald* (2 vols), Sunderland, 1830
Round, J.H., *Family Origins and other Studies*, Constable, London, 1930
Scott-Giles, C.W., *The Romance of Heraldry*, J.M. Dent, London, 1965
Seton, G., *The Law and Practice of Heraldry in Scotland*, Edmonston & Douglas, Edinburgh, 1863
Siddons, M.P., *The Development of Welsh Heraldry* (3 vols), The National Library of Wales, 1991-3
Squibb. G.D., *The Law of Arms in England*, revised edition, Heraldry Society, London, 1967
– *Reports of Heraldic Cases in the Court of Chivalry 1623-1732*, (Vol 107), Harleian Society, London, 1956
– *Visitation Pedigrees and the Genealogist*, Phillimore, London, 1964
– *The High Court of Chivalry: a study of the Civil Law in England*, Clarendon Press, Oxford, 1959
Stenton, F.M. (editor), *The Bayeux Tapestry: A Comprehensive Survey*, Phaidon Press, London, 1957
Summers, P. (editor), *Hatchments in Britian, London & Chichester* (6 vols), Phillimore, 1974-1985
Summers, P. and Titterton, J.E. (editors), *Hatchments in Britain*, vols 7-10; Phillimore 1988-1994
Tyas, R., *Flowers and Heraldry*, London, 1851
Wade, W.C., *The Symbolism of Heraldry*, George Redway, London, 1898
Wagner, A.R., *Heralds of England: A History of the Office and College of Arms London*, H.M.S.O., London, 1967
– *Heralds and Heraldry in the Middle Ages*, Oxford University Press, London, 1939; 2nd edition, 1956
– *Historic Heraldry in Britain*, Oxford University Press, London, 1939
– *A Catalogue of English Medieval Rolls of Arms, Aspilogia Vol. I*, Oxford University Press for The Society of Antiquaries, London, 1950
– (General Editor) *Rolls of Arms, Henry III, Aspilogia Vol II*, Oxford University Press for The Society of Antiquaries, London, 1967
– *The Records and Collections of the College of Arms*, Burke's Peerage Ltd., London, 1952
– *Heralds and Ancestors*, Colonnade Books, London, 1978
– *Heraldry in England*, King Penguin Books, London, 1946
Willement, T., *Regal Heraldry*, London, 1821
Woodcock, T. and Robinson, J.M., *The Oxford Guide to Heraldry*, Oxford University Press, 1988
Woodcock, T., Grant, Hon. J. and Graham, I., *Dictionary of British Arms – Medieval Ordinary* Vol. II, Society of Antiquaries, London, 1996
Zieber, E., *Heraldry in America*, 2nd edition, Bailey, Banks & Biddle, Philadelphia, 1909

List of Plates

Please note that figures in bold refer to page numbers.

NTPL – National Trust Photographic Library

NT – National Trust Regional Libraries and Archives

Index

Page numbers in *italic* refer to the captions of illustrations.